W9-ABK-867

JOSEPH CONRAD, *Heart of Darkness*

A Case Study in Contemporary Criticism

JOSEPH CONRAD
Heart of Darkness

A Case Study in Contemporary Criticism

EDITED BY
Ross C Murfin
University of Miami

A Bedford Book

St. Martin's Press · NEW YORK

For Bedford Books:
Publisher: Charles H. Christensen
Associate Publisher: Joan E. Feinberg
Managing Editor: Elizabeth M. Schaaf
Developmental Editor: Stephen A. Scipione
Production Editor: Mary Lou Wilshaw
Copyeditor: Daniel Otis
Text Design: Sandra Rigney, The Book Department
Cover Design: Sally Carson, Carson Design

Library of Congress Catalog Card Number: 88–70425
Copyright © 1989 by St. Martin's Press, Inc.

Manufactured in the United States of America.

3 2 1 0 9
f   e   d   c   b   a

For information, write: St. Martin's Press, Inc.
175 Fifth Avenue, New York, NY 10010
Editorial Offices: Bedford Books *of* St. Martin's Press
29 Winchester Street, Boston, MA 02116

ISBN: 0–312–00761–2   (paperback)
ISBN: 0–312–03026–6   (hardcover)

Acknowledgments

Cover Art: Untitled photograph, 1962, 12⅝ x 9⅛ inches. From *Chiarenza: Landscapes of the Mind* by Carl Chiarenza. Copyright © 1988 by Carl Chiarenza. Reprinted by permission of David R. Godine, Publisher.

"Introduction to the *Danse Macabre:* Conrad's *Heart of Darkness*" by Frederick R. Karl is a newly revised version of the essay that appeared in *Modern Fiction Studies,* Copyright © 1968 by Purdue Research Foundation, West Lafayette, Indiana 47907. Reprinted with permission.

"Heart of Darkness Revisited" is a newly revised version of a previously published essay (Copyright © 1983) by J. Hillis Miller.

Preface

If asked to describe the way in which the study of literature is changing, most of us willing to venture an answer would say that it is becoming more *theoretical*. Undergraduate and graduate courses in critical theory have proliferated in recent years, as have the critical approaches or schools they introduce or describe. Numerous reasons could be given for the explosion of interest in critical theory, but one simple one stands out: an awareness of theoretical issues and questions makes us more sophisticated readers, interpreters, and critics.

Without some kind of theoretical underpinning, literary criticism runs the risk of being impressionistic, even illogical. Good criticism is informed by a set of consistent, rationally related assumptions about the psyche, reading, language, gender, and culture. Theory helps readers come up with coherent interpretive strategies by getting them to discover and examine the assumptions that underlie their interpretive habits. Theory also encourages readers, at least implicitly, to compare their assumptions with others that might lead to different kinds of critical conclusions.

Theory thus accomplishes several worthy goals. It forces us to test the logic that lies behind our own readings, and it reminds us that other logical readings could be developed from different points of view. To put this another way: theory lends credibility to our arguments even as it makes us more aware — and tolerant — of well-developed interpretations quite different from our own. Each new critical approach we are exposed to adds incrementally to our understanding and appreciation, not only of individual works but also of literature in general. Each has the potential to help us write our own literary criticism, using a model and vocabulary that others have collectively shared, developed, and defended.

This new edition of Conrad's *Heart of Darkness* exposes beginning students of literature to several of these current critical approaches. It presents the complete text of a great work of fiction[1] along with five analyses prepared especially for this volume for an audience of students rather than colleagues. The five analyses — by Frederick R. Karl, J. Hillis Miller, Adena Rosmarin, Johanna M. Smith, and Brook Thomas — examine the work from five influential theoretical perspectives: the psychoanalytic, reader-response, feminist, deconstructive, and new historicist. Each of the five analyses is preceded by an introduction that briefly presents the history and principles of the theoretical perspective and is followed by a bibliography that promotes further exploration in that perspective.

The five perspectives were chosen from among a host of other possibilities for three reasons. First, a knowledge of their principles is fundamental to an understanding of current theory and criticism. Second, they are particularly appropriate to the needs, interests, and capabilities of newcomers to critical theory. Novices should recognize many of the basic tenets underlying the psychoanalytic and feminist critical traditions, and they are likely to be as sympathetic to the premises of reader-response theory as they are challenged by those of deconstruction and the new historicism. Third and perhaps most important, the five perspectives seemed somehow *right* for *Heart of Darkness*. A Chinese box of narratives constructed from language as enigmatic as it is exquisite, Conrad's most famous tale is understandably fascinating to psychoanalytic critics, to critics interested in how readers respond to literary works, to deconstructors who unravel texts in order to reveal contradictions within them, and to feminist and new historicist critics, who analyze the relations of power — sexual, racial, economic, political — in literature and life.

The authoritative text and the five critical analyses with their introductions and bibliographies are complemented by additional editorial material on *Heart of Darkness* and contemporary criticism. In Part

---

[1] The text is from the 1921 Heinemann edition of the *Collected Works*, the last version Conrad approved.

One, the text of the novel is preceded by a general introduction that provides biographical and historical information, citing excerpts from letters and diaries that reveal some of the striking parallels between *Heart of Darkness* and Conrad's life and times. Part Two's case study in contemporary criticism opens with a history of reception that traces important critical responses to Conrad's tale from its publication in 1899 to the 1980s. This interpretive history shows not only how critics read *Heart of Darkness*, but also how they read each other, and suggests the theoretical implications of these intertexts for modern readings of the novel. Finally, a glossary includes succinct definitions and discussions of key terms that recur in this edition and in the literature of contemporary theory and criticism.

I am indebted to all the critics represented in this volume but especially to Johanna M. Smith and Adena Rosmarin, without whose help both the introductions to feminist and reader-response criticism and the bibliographies suggesting further readings in those areas would have been less comprehensive. I would like to thank Steven Mailloux, David Richter, Michael Meyer, and William Sheidley for their comments on the manuscript, and the people at Bedford Books, especially Charles Christensen, Joan Feinberg, Stephen Scipione, and Mary Lou Wilshaw. I am also grateful to Elaine Koch for the able assistance she afforded me during my sabbatical leave from the University of Miami. Her precise memory and unequalled organizational skills allowed me to complete this book in London, far away from the library and the word-processing center where I began it.

Finally, I wish to thank Bill and Penny Obenshain, Conrad Ellenby, Eric and Lavinia Brown, and Jenny Stein for making London a more hospitable place during its dark midwinter hours.

Contents

JOSEPH CONRAD, *Heart of Darkness*

A Case Study in Contemporary Criticism

PART ONE

Heart of Darkness:
The Complete Text

Introduction:
The Biographical and
Historical Background

Polish, not English, was the language Joseph Conrad grew up speaking. English wasn't even his second language: French was. The fact that Conrad achieved fame in his third language is testimony to his genius — genius that could be contained neither by linguistic barriers nor by national boundaries. Early political persecution and exile failed to stifle it; even the loss of family and deep personal unhappiness could only restrain it temporarily.

Conrad was christened Josef Konrad Nalecz Korzeniowski. Both his mother, Ewa, and his father, Apollo, were descended from wealthy Polish families. Born in 1857 — "in the 85th year of Muscovite Oppression," as his father put it — Josef found himself, from childhood on, a person without a country. In 1772 Poland had been divided up between Russia, Prussia, and Austria, only to be redivided in 1793 and 1795.

Thus, although Conrad was born into the landed gentry of Polish culture (in what had become a western Russian province), his childhood years were full of uncertainty. His headstrong, talented father, a poet and translator of French and English literature, was dedicated to the cause of Polish independence from Russia. Just before a Polish uprising was quelled in 1863, Apollo was arrested and exiled to the village of Vologda, hundreds of miles north of Moscow.

The trip to Vologda nearly killed young Josef, and the brutal

3

winters there hastened the demise of both his parents. Ewa died of tuberculosis in 1865, her despairing husband shortly thereafter, in 1869. Josef, who was but twelve years old, was adopted by his mother's uncle, an at once firm but indulgent gentleman named Tadeusz Bobrowski.

Uncle Tadeusz cared well for his orphaned nephew, sending him first to school in Krakow, later to Geneva with a tutor. But the young Conrad could adjust neither to the rigors of school life nor to the personal attentions of his private teacher, who continually tried to reform his pupil's romantic views on life and the world. Finally, the exasperated Josef persuaded his Uncle Tadeusz to let him join the French merchant navy.

The four years following were more adventure-filled, but apparently no more satisfying, than the earlier, teenage years. Conrad sailed to the West Indies and Venezuela, squandered a small fortune, lost in love, got involved in a gun-running venture for the Carlists (who were seeking to seize the throne of Spain for Carlos de Bourbon), and attempted suicide in 1878. That same year, French immigration authorities prevented him from continuing as a sailor on merchant marine vessels.

This last turn of events seems in the long run to have been a fortunate one, since Conrad was to sail for the next sixteen years on British ships and to become a British subject in 1887. Conrad's metamorphosis from a French sailor to an English one caused him to master the language in which he would ultimately choose to write his novels. The greatest of these — including *Heart of Darkness, Lord Jim, Nostromo, The Secret Agent,* and *Victory* — have been, almost since their publication, ranked with the most powerful and poetic novels ever written in English.

Like other geniuses, Conrad had a way of turning disadvantage into advantage. He made unconventional, poetic use of a language he was forced to master by circumstance. A lesser talent would have been blunted by twenty trying years of life on deck; Conrad transformed his experiences into art.

From his years in the East and West Indies, he gained the atmosphere as well as the insights into human nature that he was to draw upon while writing works from *Almayer's Folly* (published in 1895, when Conrad was in his thirties) to *The Rescue* (published in 1920, four years before Conrad's death).

But it was not only in the East and West Indies that Conrad came by the store of experiences that were later to be metamorphosed into art. Indeed, the voyage that seems to have had the greatest impact on

Conrad's life and art was not by sea at all — or at least the most memorable part of the trip was not. That was the expedition that saw Conrad far up the Congo River on a rusty steamboat with a shrill whistle.

Conrad had begun writing *Almayer's Folly,* his first novel, in 1889, just before commencing the trip up to Stanley (now Boyoma) Falls in 1890. In spite of the near-torturous nature of the journey, he managed to make continual progress on the book while en route. The trip from Boma to Stanley Falls and back was one of the last Conrad ever made as a sailor. It marked, in a sense, the beginning of a brief but crucial period of his life, a period that came to an end in 1894, the year his beloved Uncle Tadeusz died. For it was then that Conrad decided to devote himself to writing full time. Shortly after making that decision, he was to marry Jessie George. The troubled Pole without a clear-cut family, nationality, language, love, or even calling in life was now Joseph Conrad, a British subject, husband, and writer.

Present-day Zaire, one of the largest nations in Africa, was known as the Belgian Congo from 1908 until 1960, when it gained its independence. The Congo visited by Conrad and by the narrator of *Heart of Darkness* was officially called "L'État Independent du Congo" (customarily if roughly translated into English as "the Congo Free State"). But Belgian the Congo was, from 1885 on, thanks to a conference called in Berlin in 1884 by Otto von Bismarck, first chancellor of the newly formed German Empire.

Not that Belgium had opened up the Congo to European exploration, exploitation, and development. The celebrated Scot, Dr. David Livingstone, had gone there in 1856, to be "found" by the Americanized Welshman, Henry Morton Stanley, in 1871. Livingstone and Stanley, moreover, had been preceded by Portuguese, Dutch, and French pioneers. In fact, until 1876, King Leopold II of Belgium had merely sat back and watched with interest. In that year, though, this ambitious and notoriously immoral monarch of a nation less than fifty years old made his first move. He organized a meeting in Brussels to discuss a plan "to open to civilization the only part of our globe where Christianity has not yet penetrated and to pierce the darkness which envelops the entire population."[1]

Bismarck, who had gradually come to realize that no nation would win anything if all were drawn into a territorial, theological, or trade

---

[1]Quoted by Maurice Hennessy in *Congo: A Brief History and Appraisal* (London: Pall Mall Press, 1961), p. 13.

war, eventually called his own conference in Berlin. To the surprise of astute political forecasters throughout the Western world, Bismarck's 1884 convention resulted in a decision to make the Congo the personal property of Leopold II. All the king had to do was guarantee that all nations would be permitted to trade freely there, that taxes and tariffs would not be collected, and that nations would not be granted monopolies on particular items of trade. Leopold, who ended up shirking most of his commitments, controlled the Congo until he died in 1908. In a will written in 1889, he bequeathed the territory to Belgium in exchange for a government loan of 150 million francs.

Thus, the Congo had been all but Belgian since long before 1908. And it had been ruled by a tyrant whose promise to bring civilization to Africa had turned out to be little more than a cruel joke. Leopold had divided the country into sixteen districts, each governed by a commissioner who rendered the local chiefs impotent. Some of these officials went on to build personal fortunes by collecting taxes from the natives, and since few of the natives had anything to give but their labor, the commissioners were, in effect, slaveholders, and the Congolese were slaves in all but name. Leopold, in turn, received a portion of all profits made by his administrators, so it was in his interest to make sure that when Africans rebelled against the sentries who guarded them while they worked out their taxes, they be taught a swift and brutal lesson.

Reports of atrocities were drifting back to Europe within a few years after Leopold had been granted proprietorship. Baptist missionaries duped by the king's stated goal of Christianizing the Congo were among the first to cry foul. But the Congo was far from Europe, and the damning reports from scattered missionaries were relatively few and far between. And anyway, people wondered in Europe, wasn't it inevitable that the lives of some Africans would be lost? When natives rebelled, weren't the sentries merely protecting themselves, or at worst doing their duty? King Leopold assured his people that their "agents" were "profoundly reluctant to use force." However, he explained, unfortunate incidents were bound to happen, since many of the sentries were "wretched negroes" with "sanguinary habits" recruited from the local population, natives who were, in other words, prone to turn viciously on their own people.[2]

Many of the station managers and traders that Leopold refers to as his agents were drawn from the ranks of the Belgian army,

---

[2]Quoted by Guy Burrows in *The Land of the Pigmies* (London: C. A. Pearson, 1898), p. 286.

and by 1890 they had, with Leopold's blessing, given the lie to their king's promise that the Congo would be a free-trade territory. Ivory, the most valuable commodity, had become a Belgian monopoly; non-Belgian traders caught carrying it could be summarily shot, either by Leopold's army-trained representatives or by their sentries. Among these sentries were natives "freed" from their black slaveowners and offered "protection" by the white invaders. They had to work seven years for their new master, wherever he chose to send them, for whatever wages he sought to bestow, and in whatever conditions he saw fit to provide.

Why did Conrad go to such a place? Since the mid-1870s, he had been sailing the high seas, mainly on English ships. Why would he want to ride a leaky Belgian steamboat upriver into the troubled heart of Africa when the open seas led to a whole world of places whose names surely conjured up more images of romance and adventure?

Part of the answer can perhaps be found in Conrad's late essay, "Geography and Some Explorers," in which he recalls that, as an adolescent, he had been particularly fascinated by stories of polar explorers. Of Leopold McClintock's book, *The Voyage of the "Fox" in the Arctic Seas* (1859), Conrad writes: "There could hardly have been imagined a better book for letting in the breath of the stern romance of polar exploration. . . . The great spirit of the realities of the story sent me off on the romantic explorations of my inner self."[3]

Another, complementary explanation of why Conrad wanted to visit King Leopold's troubled Congo may lie in the same essay, in the paragraphs that tell of a lifelong fascination with maps. By age thirteen, he recalls, he was "addicted" to "map-gazing," much as other people become hooked on star-gazing. "And it was Africa," Conrad writes, "the Continent out of which the Romans used to say some new thing was always coming," that seemed particularly fascinating. So much of that continent was unknown and unexplored that maps of whole regions of it would be covered by "exciting spaces of white paper." Thus, owing to its "regions unknown," the "heart of Africa" as represented by maps was "white and big."[4]

At about the age of sixteen, Conrad made a public commitment to travel someday to unknown Africa. "One day," he recalls, "putting

---

[3]Joseph Conrad, "Geography and Some Explorers," in *Last Essays,* ed. Richard Curle (London: J. M. Dent and Sons, 1926), pp. 16–17.
[4]Ibid., pp. 19–20.

my finger on a spot in the very middle of the then white heart of Africa,
I declared that some day I would go there."[5] Long before he was sixteen
and even before he read *The Voyage of the "Fox" in the Arctic Seas*, though,
Conrad had expressed his intention to do what he finally did in 1890
on the steamer *Roi des Belges*. In his late, autobiographical retrospective
entitled *Some Reminiscences*, Conrad claims that the decision was made
during childhood:

> It was 1868, when I was nine years old or thereabouts,
> that while looking at a map of Africa of the time and putting my
> finger on the blank space then representing the unsolved mystery
> of the continent, I said to myself with absolute assurance and
> an amazing audacity which are no longer in my character now:
> "When I grow up I shall go there."[6]

Conrad then says that he gave that proclamation no further thought
until, more than twenty years later, the opportunity to travel up the
Congo River to Stanley Falls actually presented itself. For Stanley Falls
was the very spot on the map he had pointed at in 1868: "the blankest
of blank spaces on the earth's figured surface."[7]

These various personal records suggest that Conrad decided to
go to the Congo for several closely related reasons. In part because
the interior of Africa had been represented by cartographers as a mysterious white blankness, and in part because tales of polar exploration
had equated white blankness with the unknown and explorers of the
white wilderness with true heroism, Conrad associated the Congo with
the unknown and equated a voyage there with the most important, heroic kind of voyage. Tales of seamen wandering the South Pacific were
tales of the "acquisitive spirit," of those urged on by "the desire of trade
. . . or loot," whereas the "aims" of the polar explorers were "as pure as
the air of those high latitudes."[8] If mere stories of such men sent Conrad
"off on . . . explorations of [his] inner self," how much more he was
likely to learn about his own nature and human nature in general by
traveling into the great expanse of white that lay beyond the colored,
mapped areas of Africa.

There is an obvious irony in Conrad's implicit association of the
unknown Congo, hot and humid home of a dark race, with whiteness
and the arctic. Another irony emerges as we read Conrad's novel set

---

[5]Ibid., p. 24.
[6]Joseph Conrad, *Some Reminiscences* (London: Eveleigh Nash, 1912), p. 41.
[7]Ibid.
[8]Conrad, "Geography and Some Explorers," p. 14.

in the Congo: the aims of several white "explorers" portrayed in it were morally black as pitch — not at all like the "pure" aims of arctic wayfarers in search of the Northwest Passage. So obvious are these ironies that they were, obviously, intended.

Still, we must remember that the Conrad who wrote not *Heart of Whiteness* but, rather, *Heart of Darkness* — the Conrad who still later penned *Some Reminiscences* and the essay on maps and explorers — was an older and wiser Conrad than the young man who set sail from France on the sixth of May, 1890, for the Congolese coast. Conrad could not have known until he actually experienced the Congo just how much its "explorers" were prompted by the desire for "loot." The Congo was supposed to be a relatively free, peaceable state, open to all traders and therefore free not only of the murderous violence but also of the slavery found in so many other areas of the world.

Conrad had to discover, personally, just how false that supposition was. In seeing how easily Europeans who set forth in ships to enlighten and civilize can corrupt and destroy, Conrad came to a profound realization about human nature: whiteness and light may turn out to be blackness and darkness, and blackness and darkness may be relatively pure. In learning that hard lesson, Conrad also discovered something profound about himself: that it was as a writer, not as a merchant sailor, that he wanted to explore the world — especially the inner world of "civilized" humanity.[9] Thus, even though Conrad could not have been prepared to find what he found in the Congo by white spaces on a map, tales of polar exploration, or accounts of the Congo Free State that amounted to a king's whitewash, he did, in a sense, find in the Congo exactly what, as a schoolboy, he had somehow sensed he would find: the mysterious unknown, self-knowledge, and even, it seems fair to say, his destiny.

There were, of course, practical reasons why Conrad decided to go to the Congo. Fated though it seems he was by the promise he had made in childhood to go there, drawn as he was to the idea of discovering something about himself while voyaging into uncharted territory, Conrad was also attracted to the Congo because it promised a much-needed source of financial support (Conrad had used up his

[9]Frederick Karl develops this idea in *Joseph Conrad: The Three Lives* (New York: Farrar, Straus and Giroux, 1979). I am indebted to Karl not only for this idea but also for bringing together illuminating excerpts from Conrad's letters and diary, some of which are quoted below.

inheritance by the age of twenty-one) and because there, it seemed, he would be not just a sailor but a captain. He had briefly served as master of an Australian vessel, but it was not until 1886 that he had passed the examination qualifying him for a commission certified by the British Board of Trade.

In 1889 Conrad approached Albert Thys, managing director of the Société Anonyme Belge pour le Commerce du Haut-Congo, in the hope that Thys could procure him a position commanding a steamer plying the Congo River. But Conrad also looked into other positions that, had they materialized, would have sent him back to the West Indies as a captain. Neither destination beckoned immediately; Thys had nothing to offer, perhaps because Conrad wanted a long-term commitment. "A short visit would not be worth the trouble and expense of leaving [Europe] for," he remarked to Thys in a letter dated December 27, 1889.[10]

With no immediate prospects, Conrad decided to visit Uncle Tadeusz in the Ukraine, then to return to England by way of Brussels, where he hoped not only to reassert his interest in a Congo command but also to visit with his "Aunt" Marguerite and "Uncle" Aleksander Poradowska. (Uncle Aleksander was actually Conrad's cousin; Aunt Marguerite, a writer of novels and short stories, was only related to Conrad by marriage.) Hearing that Aleksander was ill and failing fast, Conrad changed his plans and went to Brussels first. He arrived on February 5, 1890; two days later his cousin died. Although Conrad was soon to enter a close relationship and correspondence with Marguerite, he left her before her husband was buried, traveling to Warsaw, then to Lublin, and finally to Kazimierowka, where he stayed with Uncle Tadeusz for two months.

In spite of Tadeusz's attempt to discourage him from his interest in a Congo command, Conrad returned to Brussels on April 26, 1890. There he learned that a steamer captain named Freiesleben had died in the Congo and that a command was available. Actually, Conrad's turn in luck was due to far more than the death of the ship's captain; Aunt Marguerite had, with Conrad's permission, used her considerable influence on several important men involved in the colonization effort, including Thys. After signing with Thys, Conrad headed for a French port, from which he shipped for Boma, the main port of entry to the Congo.

---

[10]Translated in Karl, *Joseph Conrad: The Three Lives*, p. 276; text of letter, in French, in *The Collected Letters of Joseph Conrad*, ed. Frederick Karl and Laurence Davies (Cambridge: Cambridge University Press, 1983), 1:28.

Conrad wrote letters back to Marguerite Poradowska, so we have a fair idea of what his journey to the heart of the "Haut-Congo" was like — or at least the first, easiest part of his journey. He was working at *Almayer's Folly* and thinking constantly of his "aunt," who seems to have been not only a mother figure but also a woman whose image raised romantic possibilities in his mind. ("You have endowed my life with new interest, new affection," he tells her in a letter mailed from Libreville.[11]) Conrad arrived at his destination on June 12, after an interminable-seeming sea voyage down the African coast. The trip, from Bordeaux to Boma on the *Ville de Maceio*, had taken more than a month.

Forty miles from Boma, in Matadi, Conrad met Roger Casement, who had come to the Congo Free State thinking that he would abolish the slave trade carried on by Arabs in the area and establish a railway that would link the coastal region with Stanley (now Malebo) Pool, where the Congo River becomes navigable and stays navigable all the way inland to Stanley (Boyoma) Falls. When he met Conrad in the spring of 1890, Casement was beginning the railway project, as yet unaware (like Conrad) that many of King Leopold's men were using the natives as slave labor. Conrad shared a room with Casement for almost a month, at the end of which he began the overland journey made arduous by the lack of a railway and fresh water, and by the presence of what turned out to be three virtual plagues: heat, mosquitoes, and one of Leopold's agents, Prosper Harou.

The trip to Stanley Pool had to be made by foot: "Not an ass here," Conrad joked in a letter to Marguerite, "except your very humble servant."[12] But there were other things to see along the way, not beasts of burden but evidence that men and women were being treated worse than animals. Conrad kept a diary in which he recorded these sights and sounds: "Saw at a camp place the dead body of a Backongo. Shot? Horrid smell" [July 3]. "Saw another dead body lying by the path in an attitude of meditative repose. . . . At night when the moon rose heard shouts and drumming in distant villages. Passed a bad night" [July 4].

Agent Harou, apparently, passed a worse one: "H. lame and not in very good form," Conrad wrote on July 25. "Passed a skeleton tied

[11]Translated in Karl, *Joseph Conrad: The Three Lives*, p. 285; text of letter, in French, in Karl and Davies, *The Collected Letters*, 1:53.

[12]Translated in Karl, *Joseph Conrad: The Three Lives*, p. 289; text of letter, in French, in Karl and Davies, *The Collected Letters*, 1:56.

up to a post," Conrad was to write some days later; "put [Harou] in hammock."[13]

Harou's crippling lameness made the trip more difficult for everyone, but it was far from the most disappointing development to try Conrad's spirits during the thirty-six-day trip that ended on August second. On July 29, Conrad met a man named Louette who was transporting another sick agent back in the direction of Boma. From Louette Conrad learned that the steamer he had been hired to command now lay sunk on the bottom of the river. Having come all the way from Belgium to captain *The Florida,* Conrad suddenly learned that he would be shipping upriver not as a captain but as a sailor on the *Roi des Belges.*

Rather miraculously, Conrad had continually been writing *Almayer's Folly* while making the torturous overland trek. Although work had proceeded fitfully, something definite had been accomplished. The loss of a command was a serious blow to Conrad and may have made him prefer the slow progress of writing to the unpredictable vagaries besetting a would-be captain. Certainly, the period commencing just before Conrad's arrival at Kinshasa marked the beginning of a period of disillusionment — with Africa, with life on deck, with colonial trade, and with white European agents running trading stations throughout the Congo. Conrad seems to have particularly disliked Camille Delcommune, the manager of the station at Kinshasa, whom he later called "a common ivory dealer with base instincts."[14] To Conrad's dismay, Delcommune decided to make the trip on the *Roi des Belges* all the way to the Inner Station at Stanley Falls, where an agent named Klein lay desperately ill. That four-week trip and the return downriver to Kinshasa with the corpse of Klein seem not only to have cured Conrad's weakness for life aboard ship but also to have very nearly robbed him of all taste for life in general. "Everything here is repellent to me," he wrote to Marguerite once the round trip had been completed. "Men and things, but above all men."[15]

Conrad, who wished to leave Africa as quickly as possible, got out of his contract with the Société Anonyme Belge pour le Commerce du Haut-Congo. A terrible case of dysentery that he had picked

[13]Passages from Conrad's diary quoted in Karl, *Joseph Conrad: The Three Lives,* pp. 290–92.

[14]Translated in Karl, *Joseph Conrad: The Three Lives,* p. 294; text of letter, in French, in Karl and Davies, *The Collected Letters,* 1:59.

[15]Ibid.

up on his journey turned out to be an adequate excuse. Perhaps fearing that it wouldn't be adequate, Conrad had written Brussels to ask Marguerite to inform Albert Thys that the Société had failed to live up to its terms: a command had been promised, whereas in fact Conrad had served only as mate, except for a brief period during the return trip, when Captain L. R. Koch was even sicker than Conrad was.

What Conrad couldn't wriggle out of was his Congo experience; it seems to permeate *Heart of Darkness,* even though the novel wasn't begun for almost a decade following its author's departure from Africa. Some of the parallels between *Heart of Darkenss* and Conrad's Congo adventure are so obvious that it may be tempting to think of the novel as thinly veiled autobiography.

It may be tempting, but it may also be treacherous, for reasons that have perhaps been best articulated by formalist critics. A work of art, formalists would argue, is not undigested experience; rather, it is characterized by *form.* That characteristic form is to be discovered by finding the patterns and relationships that exist within the work itself, not the connections that may seem to exist between the work and its author's life story.

Still, even formalists would not have us be unaware of those connections. For one thing, we have to know that connections exist before we can affirm or deny their ultimate significance. For another, knowing the biographical background of a text helps us to better appreciate the text's *difference;* that is, the shape it has been given by the artist's imagination. And there is still another reason to become aware of the parallels between Conrad's Congo experience and Marlow's. With such an awareness comes the possibility of deciding that the formalist view is too narrow, too limiting.

To summarize the parallels briefly: Marlow, the novel's protagonist and narrator, tells his listeners about his childhood passion for maps and about his declared intention to go, someday, to the blank heart of Africa. He describes how, years later, he signed up for a Congo command in the office of a "great man" — "pale plumpness in a frock-coat" — after receiving some behind-the-scenes help from "an aunt, a dear enthusiastic soul." Whereas Conrad got his command due to the death of a captain named Freiesleben, Marlow is signed on shortly after the demise of the unlucky Captain Fresleven.

Marlow's description of his sea voyage down the African coast ("Every day looked the same") reads like Conrad's diary, and his description of an overland journey from a company station not far from the African coast to the "Central Station" repeats many of Conrad's experiences in traveling from Matadi to Kinshasa, by Stanley Pool. Heat and mosquitoes and the lack of water are mentioned, as is "a white companion" who becomes so sick with fever that he has to be "carried in a hammock slung under a pole." A corpse like the one Conrad was shocked to see while on his overland trek turns up in *Heart of Darkness*: "Can't say I saw any road or any upkeep," Marlow recalls, "unless the body of a middle-aged negro, with a bullet hole in the forehead, upon which I absolutely stumbled . . . may be considered as a permanent improvement."

Marlow, like Conrad, learns that an accident has befallen the steamer that he was to have commanded; like Conrad he journeys upriver to retrieve a sick agent who dies on board shortly after being rescued. And Marlow is accompanied on his travels by a man who must have been modeled on Camille Delcommune, the station manager at Kinshasa whom Conrad referred to as "a common ivory dealer with base instincts." (Marlow calls the manager of the Central Station, who accompanies him upriver to the Inner Station, "a common trader" with "no learning and no intelligence.")

But the differences between Conrad's experiences and those of Charlie Marlow are as striking as the similarities. To begin with, there is the matter of Marlow himself, a thoroughly English Everyman — not a Polish intellectual who happens to be a sailor, too. Marlow is a recognizable kind of guy, one perfectly capable of joking that a corpse may be a road improvement, and one made more than a little uncomfortable by the efforts made in his behalf by his aunt: "Would you believe it?" he asks the other men listening to his story, "I, Charlie Marlow, set the women to work — to get a job."

Other differences abound. The "great man" who hires Marlow is not named Thys — in fact, no names are given for Marlow's aunt, the station manager modeled on Delcommune, or the "white companion" who becomes sick and has to be carried much as Prosper Harou became lame and unable to walk. The ship Marlow travels upriver on is left similarly unnamed, as is the "Company" that Conrad knew as the Société Anonyme Belge pour le Commerce du Haut-Congo. No character in the novel bears more than a passing resemblance to Roger Casement, whom Conrad stayed with in Matadi. Whereas Conrad didn't get to captain a ship, thanks to the damage done to his intended vessel, Marlow waits months for rivets and repairs that eventually allow him to command his steamboat. Marlow retrieves Kurtz only to have him die on his ship; Anton Klein was the name of the agent who died on

Conrad's ship. But whereas all we know about Klein is that he had fallen ill near Stanley Falls, Kurtz is a marvelously mysterious imaginative creation, a kind of Everyman, like Marlow ("All Europe contributed to the making of Kurtz," Marlow says, when the matter of his lineage comes up), but a mythological demon figure as well. Critics have often compared him to Faust and to Satan.

Kurtz is, then, someone who exceeds the dimensions of anyone Conrad met in the Congo, just as the Africa in *Heart of Darkness* is far more than a continent — it has universal dimensions. There are minor characters, too, who testify to Conrad's ability not just to transcribe reality but to invent a world full of powerful significances. In the area that corresponds to the place where Conrad met Casement, Marlow meets a wonderfully sleazy accountant whom he describes as a "hairdresser's dummy." There is a station manager modeled after Delcommune, but his agent, characterized as a "papier-mâché Mephistopheles," seems to be pure invention. Even more fascinating is the Russian mindlessly loyal to the murderous Kurtz, a harlequin figure "covered with patches all over, with bright patches, blue, red, and yellow — patches on the back, patches on the front, patches on elbows, on knees; coloured binding around his jacket, scarlet edging at the bottom of his trousers." These characters are not part of any diary or historical record; rather, they are masterful touches in a great work of novelistic art.

Not all of the artfulness of *Heart of Darkness* is to be found in its characters. Part of the creative complexity of the work lies in the form Conrad's narrative takes; that is to say, in the way the story is told. After all, we are not told the tale of a trip to Africa by an omniscient, authorial narrator. Instead, we find ourselves reading a story within a story. We must learn about Kurtz and the harlequin, the hairdresser's dummy and the Eldorado Explorers, from a nameless, anonymous source, a man who repeats the tale he says Charlie Marlow told him and four other men one night sitting on a cruising yawl anchored in the Thames River.

Thus, part of the meaning of the story is the way we learn about "reality" through other people's accounts of it, many of which are, themselves, twice-told tales. Part of the meaning of the novel, too, is the possibly unreliable nature of our teachers; Marlow is the source of our story, but he is also a character within the story we read, and a flawed one at that. Marlow's macho comments about women and his insensitive reaction to the "dead negro" with a "bullet hole in his forehead" cause us to refocus our critical attention, to shift it from the story being retold, to the storyteller whose supposedly autobiographical yarn is being repeated.

Because we occasionally judge Marlow negatively, we find ourselves having to take certain passages ironically, and the ironic distance that we experience between ourselves and our narrator is another important difference between a novel like *Heart of Darkness* and a diary or a history book. Irony, after all, makes possible a complex form of humor in which we find ourselves laughing at as well as with the chronicler. It is irony, too, that causes us to apprehend something profound about the human self; namely, its capacity to understand or "see through" others while remaining self-destructively ignorant about its own identity. We see what Marlow shows us, but we also see Marlow, and one of the things about him we can see is his blindness to his own nature.

Marlow interrupts the story he tells to the Lawyer, the Accountant, the Chief of Companies, and the person who retells his story to put it this way: "Of course in this you fellows see more than I could then. You see me, whom you know. . . ." What he fails to mention is that his listeners "see" different things, for the Marlow known to each of them is surely different from the one known to all the others. We, as readers, enjoy the same privilege — and suffer the same predicament — as Marlow's auditors. What we "see in" the story depends on the nature and extent of our knowledge. Knowledge of Conrad's life may lead us to "see" Marlow's story as Conrad's own. Further knowledge — of formalist theory, for instance — may cause us to decide that Marlow is, after all, an artificial construct: a narrator, and an unreliable one at that. But there is still more to know about Conrad and his times — for example, the kind of knowledge that psychoanalytic, feminist, and new historicist critics would bring to bear. And there is more, too, to see in literary art than formalist theorists have seen in it. Deconstructors, for instance, would make us aware not of the definite form of a text but, rather, of its surprisingly contradictory elements. Reader-response critics might argue that a work of art is what we make of it. Each of these ways of knowing (which are explored in Part Two of this edition) causes us to see more in Marlow's story than the Lawyer, the Accountant, or the Chief of Companies did — perhaps even more than Conrad did. But one thing is sure: each of these ways of knowing brings a different kind of light and color to *Heart of Darkness*.

Heart of Darkness

I

The *Nellie,* a cruising yawl, swung to her anchor without a flutter of the sails, and was at rest. The flood had made, the wind was nearly calm, and being bound down the river, the only thing for it was to come to and wait for the turn of the tide.

The sea-reach of the Thames stretched before us like the beginning of an interminable waterway. In the offing the sea and the sky were welded together without a joint, and in the luminous space the tanned sails of the barges drifting up with the tide seemed to stand still in red clusters of canvas sharply peaked, with gleams of varnished sprits. A haze rested on the low shores that ran out to sea in vanishing flatness. The air was dark above Gravesend, and farther back still seemed condensed into a mournful gloom, brooding motionless over the biggest, and the greatest, town on earth.

The Director of Companies was our captain and our host. We four affectionately watched his back as he stood in the bows looking to seaward. On the whole river there was nothing that looked half so nautical. He resembled a pilot, which to a seaman is trustworthiness personified. It was difficult to realise his work was not out there in the luminous estuary, but behind him, within the brooding gloom.

Between us there was, as I have already said somewhere, the bond of the sea. Besides holding our hearts together through long periods of separation, it had the effect of making us tolerant of each other's yarns — and even convictions. The Lawyer — the best of old fellows — had, because of his many years and many virtues, the only cushion on deck, and was lying on the only rug. The Accountant had brought out already a box of dominoes, and was toying architecturally with the bones. Marlow sat cross-legged right aft, leaning against the mizzenmast. He had sunken cheeks, a yellow complexion, a straight back, an ascetic aspect, and, with his arms dropped, the palms of hands outwards, resembled an idol. The Director, satisfied the anchor had good hold, made his way aft and sat down amongst us. We exchanged a few words lazily. Afterwards there was silence on board the yacht. For some reason or other we did not begin that game of dominoes. We felt meditative, and fit for nothing but placid staring. The day was ending in a serenity of still and exquisite brilliance. The water shone pacifically; the sky, without a speck, was a benign immensity of unstained light; the very mist on the Essex marshes was like a gauzy and radiant fabric, hung from the wooded rises inland, and draping the low shores in diaphanous folds. Only the gloom to the west, brooding over the upper reaches, became more sombre every minute, as if angered by the approach of the sun.

And at last, in its curved and imperceptible fall, the sun sank low, and from glowing white changed to a dull red without rays and without heat, as if about to go out suddenly, stricken to death by the touch of that gloom brooding over a crowd of men.

Forthwith a change came over the waters, and the serenity became less brilliant but more profound. The old river in its broad reach rested unruffled at the decline of day, after ages of good service done to the race that peopled its banks, spread out in the tranquil dignity of a waterway leading to the uttermost ends of the earth. We looked at the venerable stream not in the vivid flush of a short day that comes and departs for ever, but in the august light of abiding memories. And indeed nothing is easier for a man who has, as the phrase goes, "followed the sea" with reverence and affection, than to evoke the great spirit of the past upon the lower reaches of the Thames. The tidal current runs to and fro in its unceasing service, crowded with memories of men and ships it has borne to the rest of home or to the battles of the sea. It had known and served all the men of whom the nation is proud, from Sir Francis Drake to Sir John Franklin, knights all, titled and untitled — the great knights-errant of the sea. It had borne all the ships whose names are like jewels flashing in the night of time, from the *Golden Hind* returning with her round flanks full of treasure, to be visited by the Queen's Highness and thus pass out of the gigantic tale, to the *Erebus* and *Terror,* bound on other conquests — and that never returned. It had known the ships and the men. They had sailed from Deptford, from Greenwich, from Erith — the adventurers and the settlers; kings' ships and the ships of men on 'Change; captains, admirals, the dark "interlopers" of the Eastern trade, and the commissioned "generals" of East India fleets. Hunters for gold or pursuers of fame, they all had gone out on that stream, bearing the sword, and often the torch, messengers of the might within the land, bearers of a spark from the sacred fire. What greatness had not floated on the ebb of that river into the mystery of an unknown earth! . . . The dreams of men, the seed of commonwealths, the germs of empires.

The sun set; the dusk fell on the stream, and lights began to appear along the shore. The Chapman lighthouse, a three-legged thing erect on a mud-flat, shone strongly. Lights of ships moved in the fairway — a great stir of lights going up and going down. And farther west on the upper reaches the place of the monstrous town was still marked ominously on the sky, a brooding gloom in sunshine, a lurid glare under the stars.

"And this also," said Marlow suddenly, "has been one of the dark places of the earth."

He was the only man of us who still "followed the sea." The worst that could be said of him was that he did not represent his class. He was a seaman, but he was a wanderer too, while most seamen lead, if one may so express it, a sedentary life. Their minds are of the stay-at-home order, and their home is always with them — the ship; and so is their country — the sea. One ship is very much like another, and the sea is always the same. In the immutability of their surroundings the foreign shores, the foreign faces, the changing immensity of life, glide past, veiled not by a sense of mystery but by a slightly disdainful ignorance; for there is nothing mysterious to a seaman unless it be the sea itself, which is the mistress of his existence and as inscrutable as Destiny. For the rest, after his hours of work, a casual stroll or a casual spree on shore suffices to unfold for him the secret of a whole continent, and generally he finds the secret not worth knowing. The yarns of seamen have a direct simplicity, the whole meaning of which lies within the shell of a cracked nut. But Marlow was not typical (if his propensity to spin yarns be excepted), and to him the meaning of an episode was not inside like a kernel but outside, enveloping the tale which brought it out only as a glow brings out a haze, in the likeness of one of these misty halos that sometimes are made visible by the spectral illumination of moonshine.

His remark did not seem at all surprising. It was just like Marlow. It was accepted in silence. No one took the trouble to grunt even; and presently he said, very slow:

"I was thinking of very old times, when the Romans first came here, nineteen hundred years ago — the other day. . . . Light came out of this river since — you say Knights? Yes; but it is like a running blaze on a plain, like a flash of lightning in the clouds. We live in the flicker — may it last as long as the old earth keeps rolling! But darkness was here yesterday. Imagine the feelings of a commander of a fine — what d'ye call 'em? — trireme in the Mediterranean, ordered suddenly to the north; run overland across the Gauls in a hurry; put in charge of one of these craft the legionaries — a wonderful lot of handy men they must have been too — used to build, apparently by the hundred, in a month or two, if we may believe what we read. Imagine him here — the very end of the world, a sea the colour of lead, a sky the colour of smoke, a kind of ship about as rigid as a concertina — and going up this river with stores, or orders, or what you like. Sandbanks, marshes, forests, savages — precious little to eat fit for a civilised man, nothing but Thames water to drink. No Falernian wine here, no going ashore. Here and there a military camp lost in a wilderness, like a needle in a bundle of hay — cold, fog, tempests, disease, exile, and death — death skulking in the air, in the water, in the bush. They must have been dying like flies here. Oh yes — he did it. Did it very well, too, no doubt, and without thinking much about it either, except afterwards to brag of what he had gone through in his time, perhaps. They were men enough to face the darkness. And perhaps he was cheered by keeping his eye on a chance of promotion to the fleet at Ravenna by and by, if he had good friends in Rome and survived the awful climate. Or think of a decent young citizen in a toga — perhaps too much dice, you know — coming out here in the train of some prefect, or tax-gatherer, or trader, even, to mend his fortunes. Land in a swamp, march through the woods, and in some inland post feel the savagery, the utter savagery, had closed round him — all that mysterious life of the wilderness that stirs in the forest, in the jungles, in the hearts of wild men. There's no initiation either into such mysteries. He has to live in the midst of the incomprehensible, which is also detestable. And it has a fascination, too, that goes to work upon him. The fascination of the abomination — you know. Imagine the growing regrets, the longing to escape, the powerless disgust, the surrender, the hate."

He paused.

"Mind," he began again, lifting one arm from the elbow, the palm of the hand outwards, so that, with his legs folded before him, he had the pose of a Buddha preaching in European clothes and without a lotus-flower — "Mind, none of us would feel exactly like this. What saves us is efficiency — the devotion to efficiency. But these chaps were not much account, really. They were no colonists; their administration was merely a squeeze, and nothing more, I suspect. They were conquerors, and for that you want only brute force — nothing to boast of, when you have it, since your strength is just an accident arising from the weakness of others. They grabbed what they could get for the sake of what was to be got. It was just robbery with violence, aggravated murder on a great scale, and men going at it blind — as is very proper for those who tackle a darkness. The conquest of the earth, which mostly means the taking it away from those who have a different complexion or slightly flatter noses than ourselves, is not a pretty thing when you look into it too much. What redeems it is the idea only. An idea at the back of it; not a sentimental pretence but an idea; and an unselfish belief in the idea — something you can set up, and bow down before, and offer a sacrifice to. . . ."

He broke off. Flames glided in the river, small green flames, red flames, white flames, pursuing, overtaking, joining, crossing each other — then separating slowly or hastily. The traffic of the great city went on in the deepening night upon the sleepless river. We looked on, waiting patiently — there was nothing else to do till the end of the flood; but it was only after a long silence, when he said, in a hesitating voice, "I suppose you fellows remember I did once turn fresh-water sailor for a bit," that we knew we were fated, before the ebb began to run, to hear about one of Marlow's inconclusive experiences.

"I don't want to bother you much with what happened to me personally," he began, showing in this remark the weakness of many tellers of tales who seem so often unaware of what their audience would best like to hear; "yet to understand the effect of it on me you ought to know how I got out there, what I saw, how I went up that river to the place where I first met the poor chap. It was the farthest point of navigation and the culminating point of my experience. It seemed somehow to throw a kind of light on everything about me — and into my thoughts. It was sombre enough too — and pitiful — not extraordinary in any way — not very clear either. No, not very clear. And yet it seemed to throw a kind of light.

"I had then, as you remember, just returned to London after a lot of Indian Ocean, Pacific, China Seas — a regular dose of the East — six years or so, and I was loafing about, hindering you fellows in your work and invading your homes, just as though I had got a heavenly mission to civilise you. It was very fine for a time, but after a bit I did get tired of resting. Then I began to look for a ship — I should think the hardest work on earth. But the ships wouldn't even look at me. And I got tired of that game too.

"Now when I was a little chap I had a passion for maps. I would look for hours at South America, or Africa, or Australia, and lose myself in all the glories of exploration. At that time there were many blank spaces on the earth, and when I saw one that looked particularly inviting on a map (but they all look that) I would put my finger on it and say, When I grow up I will go there. The North Pole was one of these places, I remember. Well, I haven't been there yet, and shall not try now. The glamour's off. Other places were scattered about the Equator, and in every sort of latitude all over the two hemispheres. I have been in some of them, and . . . well, we won't talk about that. But there was one yet — the biggest, the most blank, so to speak — that I had a hankering after.

"True, by this time it was not a blank space any more. It had got filled since my boyhood with rivers and lakes and names. It had ceased to be a blank space of delightful mystery — a white patch for a boy to dream gloriously over. It had become a place of darkness. But there was in it one river especially, a mighty big river, that you could see on the map, resembling an immense snake uncoiled, with its head in the sea, its body at rest curving afar over a vast country, and its tail lost in the depths of the land. And as I looked at the map of it in a shop-window, it fascinated me as a snake would a bird — a silly little bird. Then I remembered there was a big concern, a Company for trade on that river. Dash it all! I thought to myself, they can't trade without using some kind of craft on that lot of fresh water — steamboats! Why shouldn't I try to get charge of one? I went on along Fleet Street, but could not shake off the idea. The snake had charmed me.

"You understand it was a Continental concern, that Trading Society; but I have a lot of relations living on the Continent, because it's cheap and not so nasty as it looks, they say.

"I am sorry to own I began to worry them. This was already a fresh departure for me. I was not used to get things that way, you know. I always went my own road and on my own legs where I had a mind to go. I wouldn't have believed it of myself; but, then — you see — I felt somehow I must get there by hook or by crook. So I worried them. The men said, 'My dear fellow,' and did nothing. Then — would you believe it? — I tried the women. I, Charlie Marlow, set the women to work — to get a job. Heavens! Well, you see, the notion drove me. I had an aunt, a dear enthusiastic soul. She wrote: 'It will be delightful. I am ready to do anything, anything for you. It is a glorious idea. I know the wife of a very high personage in the Administration, and also a man who has lots of influence with,' etc. etc. She was determined to make no end of fuss to get me appointed skipper of a river steamboat, if such was my fancy.

"I got my appointment — of course; and I got it very quick. It appears the Company had received news that one of their captains had been killed in a scuffle with the natives. This was my chance, and it made me the more anxious to go. It was only months and months afterwards, when I made the attempt to recover what was left of the body, that I heard the original quarrel arose from a misunderstanding about some hens. Yes, two black hens. Fresleven — that was the fellow's name, a Dane — thought himself wronged somehow in the bargain, so he went ashore and started to hammer the chief of the village with a stick. Oh, it didn't surprise me in the least to hear this, and at the same time to be told that Fresleven was the gentlest, quietest creature that ever walked on two legs. No doubt he was; but he had been a couple of years already out there engaged in the noble cause, you know, and he probably felt the need at last of asserting his self-respect in some way. Therefore he whacked the old nigger mercilessly, while a big crowd of his people watched him, thunderstruck, till some man — I was told the chief's son — in desperation at hearing the old chap yell, made a tentative jab with a spear at the white man — and of course it went quite easy between the shoulder-blades. Then the whole population cleared into the forest, expecting all kinds of calamities to happen, while, on the other hand, the steamer Fresleven commanded left also in a bad panic, in charge of the engineer, I believe. Afterwards nobody seemed to trouble much about Fresleven's remains, till I got out and stepped into his shoes. I couldn't let it rest, though; but when an opportunity offered at last to meet my predecessor, the grass growing through his ribs was tall enough to hide his bones. They were all there. The supernatural being had not been touched after he fell. And the village was deserted, the huts gaped black, rotting, all askew within the fallen enclosures. A calamity had come to it, sure enough. The people had vanished. Mad terror had scattered them, men, women, and children, through the bush, and they had never returned. What became of the hens I don't know either. I should think the cause of progress got them, anyhow. However, through this glorious affair I got my appointment, before I had fairly begun to hope for it.

"I flew around like mad to get ready, and before forty-eight hours I was crossing the Channel to show myself to my employers, and sign the contract. In a very few hours I arrived in a city that always makes me think of a whited sepulchre. Prejudice no doubt. I had no difficulty in finding the Company's offices. It was the biggest thing in the town, and everybody I met was full of it. They were going to run an oversea empire, and make no end of coin by trade.

"A narrow and deserted street in deep shadow, high houses, innumerable windows with venetian blinds, a dead silence, grass sprouting between the stones, imposing carriage archways right and left, immense double doors standing ponderously ajar. I slipped through one of these cracks, went up a swept and ungarnished staircase, as arid as a desert, and opened the first door I came to. Two women, one fat and the other slim, sat on straw-bottomed chairs, knitting black wool. The slim one got up and walked straight at me — still knitting with downcast eyes — and only just as I began to think of getting out of her way, as you would for a somnambulist, stood still, and looked up. Her dress was as plain as an umbrella-cover, and she turned round without a word and preceded me into a waiting-room. I gave my name, and looked about. Deal table in the middle, plain chairs all round the walls, on one end a large shining map, marked with all the colours of a rainbow. There was a vast amount of red — good to see at any time, because one knows that some real work is done in there, a deuce of a lot of blue, a little green, smears of orange, and, on the East Coast, a purple patch, to show where the jolly pioneers of progress drink the jolly lager-beer. However, I wasn't going into any of these. I was going into the yellow. Dead in the centre. And the river was there — fascinating — deadly — like a snake. Ough! A door opened, a white-haired secretarial head, but wearing a compassionate expression, appeared, and a skinny forefinger beckoned me into the sanctuary. Its light was dim, and a heavy writing-desk squatted in the middle. From behind that structure came out an impression of pale plumpness in a frock-coat. The great man himself. He was five feet six, I should judge, and had his grip on the handle-end of ever so many millions. He shook hands, I fancy, murmured vaguely, was satisfied with my French. *Bon voyage*.

"In about forty-five seconds I found myself again in the waiting-room with the compassionate secretary, who, full of desolation and sympathy, made me sign some document. I believe I undertook amongst other things not to disclose any trade secrets. Well, I am not going to.

"I began to feel slightly uneasy. You know I am not used to such ceremonies, and there was something ominous in the atmosphere. It was just as though I had been let into some conspiracy — I don't know — something not quite right; and I was glad to get out. In the outer room the two women knitted black wool feverishly. People were arriving, and the younger one was walking back and forth introducing them. The old one sat on her chair. Her flat cloth slippers were propped up on a foot-warmer, and a cat reposed on her lap. She wore a starched white affair on her head, had a wart on one cheek, and silver-rimmed spectacles hung on the tip of her nose. She glanced at me above the glasses. The swift and indifferent placidity of that look troubled me. Two youths with foolish and cheery countenances were being piloted over, and she threw at them the same quick glance of unconcerned wisdom. She seemed to know all about them and about me too. An eerie feeling came over me. She seemed uncanny and fateful. Often far away there I thought of these two, guarding the door of Darkness, knitting black wool as for a warm pall, one introducing, introducing continuously to the unknown, the other scrutinising the cheery and foolish faces with unconcerned old eyes. *Ave!* Old knitter of black wool. *Morituri te salutant.* Not many of those she looked at ever saw her again — not half, by a long way.

"There was yet a visit to the doctor. 'A simple formality,' assured me the secretary, with an air of taking an immense part in all my sorrows. Accordingly a young chap wearing his hat over the left eyebrow, some clerk I suppose — there must have been clerks in the business, though the house was as still as a house in a city of the dead — came from somewhere upstairs, and led me forth. He was shabby and careless, with ink-stains on the sleeves of his jacket, and his cravat was large and billowy, under a chin shaped like the toe of an old boot. It was a little too early for the doctor, so I proposed a drink, and thereupon he developed a vein of joviality. As we sat over our vermuths he glorified the Company's business, and by and by I expressed casually my surprise at him not going out there. He became very cool and collected all at once. 'I am not such a fool as I look, quoth Plato to his disciples,' he said sententiously, emptied his glass with great resolution, and we rose.

"The old doctor felt my pulse, evidently thinking of something else the while. 'Good, good for there,' he mumbled, and then with a certain eagerness asked me whether I would let him measure my head. Rather surprised, I said Yes, when he produced a thing like callipers and got the dimensions back and front and every way, taking notes carefully. He was an unshaven little man in a threadbare coat like a gaberdine, with his feet in slippers, and I thought him a harmless fool. 'I always ask leave, in the interests of science, to measure the crania of those going out there,' he said. 'And when they come back too?' I asked. 'Oh, I never see them,' he remarked; 'and, moreover, the changes take place inside, you know.' He smiled, as if at some quiet joke. 'So you are going out there. Famous. Interesting too.' He gave me a searching glance, and made another note. 'Ever any madness in your family?' he asked, in a matter-of-fact tone. I felt very annoyed. 'Is that question in the interests of science too?' 'It would be,' he said, without taking notice of my irritation, 'interesting for science to watch the mental changes of individuals, on the spot, but . . .' 'Are you an alienist?' I interrupted. 'Every doctor should be — a little,' answered that original imperturbably. 'I have a little theory which you Messieurs who go out there must help me to prove. This is my share in the advantages my country shall reap from the possession of such a magnificent dependency. The mere wealth I leave to others. Pardon my questions, but you are the first Englishman coming under my observation . . .' I hastened to assure him I was not in the least typical. 'If I were,' said I, 'I wouldn't be talking like this with you.' 'What you say is rather profound, and probably erroneous,' he said, with a laugh. 'Avoid irritation more than exposure to the sun. Adieu. How do you English say, eh? Good-bye. Ah! Good-bye. Adieu. In the tropics one must before everything keep calm.' . . . He lifted a warning forefinger. . . . *Du calme, du calme. Adieu.*'

"One thing more remained to do — say goodbye to my excellent aunt. I found her triumphant. I had a cup of tea — the last decent cup of tea for many days — and in a room that most soothingly looked just as you would expect a lady's drawing-room to look, we had a long quiet chat by the fireside. In the course of these confidences it became quite plain to me I had been represented to the wife of the high dignitary, and goodness knows to how many more people besides, as an exceptional and gifted creature — a piece of good fortune for the Company — a man you don't get hold of every day. Good Heavens! and I was going to take charge of a two-penny-halfpenny river-steamboat with a penny whistle attached! It appeared, however, I was also one of the Workers, with a capital — you know. Something like an emissary of light, something like a lower sort of apostle. There had been a lot of such rot let loose in print and talk just about that time, and the excellent woman, living right in the rush of all that humbug, got carried off her feet. She talked about 'weaning those ignorant millions from their horrid ways,' till, upon my word, she made me quite uncomfortable. I ventured to hint that the Company was run for profit.

" 'You forget, dear Charlie, that the labourer is worthy of his hire,' she said brightly. It's queer how out of touch with truth women are. They live in a world of their own, and there had never been anything like it, and never can be. It is too beautiful altogether, and if they were to set it up it would go to pieces before the first sunset. Some confounded fact we men have been living contentedly with ever since the day of creation would start up and knock the whole thing over.

"After this I got embraced, told to wear flannel, be sure to write often, and so on — and I left. In the street — I don't know why — a queer feeling came to me that I was an impostor. Odd thing that I, who used to clear out for any part of the world at twenty-four hours' notice, with less thought than most men give to the crossing of a street, had a moment — I won't say of hesitation, but of startled pause, before this commonplace affair. The best way I can explain it to you is by saying that, for a second or two, I felt as though, instead of going to the centre of a continent, I were about to set off for the centre of the earth.

"I left in a French steamer, and she called in every blamed port they have out there, for, as far as I could see, the sole purpose of landing soldiers and custom-house officers. I watched the coast. Watching a coast as it slips by the ship is like thinking about an enigma. There it is before you — smiling, frowning, inviting, grand, mean, insipid, or savage, and always mute with an air of whispering, Come and find out. This one was almost featureless, as if still in the making, with an aspect of monotonous grimness. The edge of a colossal jungle, so dark green as to be almost black, fringed with white surf, ran straight, like a ruled line, far, far away along a blue sea whose glitter was blurred by a creeping mist. The sun was fierce, the land seemed to glisten and drip with steam. Here and there greyish-whitish specks showed up clustered inside the white surf, with a flag flying above them perhaps — settlements some centuries old, and still no bigger than pinheads on the untouched expanse of their background. We pounded along, stopped, landed soldiers; went on, landed custom-house clerks to levy toll in what looked like a God-forsaken wilderness, with a tin shed and a flag-pole lost in it; landed more soldiers — to take care of the custom-house clerks presumably. Some, I heard, got drowned in the surf; but whether they did or not, nobody seemed particularly to care. They were just flung out there, and on we went. Every day the coast looked the same, as though we had not moved; but we passed various places — trading places — with names like Gran' Bassam, Little Popo; names that seemed to belong to some sordid farce acted in front of a sinister back-cloth. The idleness of a passenger, my isolation amongst all these men with whom I had no point of contact, the oily and languid sea, the uniform sombreness of the coast, seemed to keep me away from the truth of things, within the toil of a mournful and senseless delusion. The voice of the surf heard now and then was a positive pleasure, like the speech of a brother. It was something natural, that had its reason, that had a meaning. Now and then a boat from the shore gave one a momentary contact with reality. It was paddled by black fellows. You could see from afar the white of their eyeballs glistening. They shouted, sang; their bodies streamed with perspiration; they had faces like grotesque masks — these chaps; but they had bone, muscle, a wild vitality, an intense energy of movement, that was as natural and true as the surf along their coast. They wanted no excuse for being there. They were a great comfort to look at. For a time I would feel I belonged still to a world of straightforward facts; but the feeling would not last long. Something would turn up to scare it away. Once, I remember, we came upon a man-of-war anchored off the coast. There wasn't even a shed there, and she was shelling the bush. It appears the French had one of their wars going on thereabouts. Her ensign dropped limp like a rag; the muzzles of the long six-inch guns stuck out all over the low hull; the greasy, slimy swell swung her up lazily and let her down, swaying her thin masts. In the empty immensity of earth, sky, and water, there she was, incomprehensible, firing into a continent. Pop, would go one of the six-inch guns; a small flame would dart and vanish, a little white smoke would disappear, a tiny projectile would give a feeble screech — and nothing happened. Nothing could happen. There was a touch of insanity in the proceeding, a sense of lugubrious drollery in the sight; and it was not dissipated by somebody on board assuring me earnestly there was a camp of natives — he called them enemies! — hidden out of sight somewhere.

"We gave her her letters (I heard the men in that lonely ship were dying of fever at the rate of three a day) and went on. We called at some more places with farcical names, where the merry dance of death and trade goes on in a still and earthy atmosphere as of an overheated catacomb; all along the formless coast bordered by dangerous surf, as if Nature herself had tried to ward off intruders; in and out of rivers, streams of death in life, whose banks were rotting into mud, whose waters, thickened into slime, invaded the contorted mangroves, that seemed to writhe at us in the extremity of an impotent despair.

Nowhere did we stop long enough to get a particularised impression, but the general sense of vague and oppressive wonder grew upon me. It was like a weary pilgrimage amongst hints for nightmares.

"It was upward of thirty days before I saw the mouth of the big river. We anchored off the seat of the government. But my work would not begin till some two hundred miles farther on. So as soon as I could I made a start for a place thirty miles higher up.

"I had my passage on a little sea-going steamer. Her captain was a Swede, and knowing me for a seaman, invited me on the bridge. He was a young man, lean, fair, and morose, with lanky hair and a shuffling gait. As we left the miserable little wharf, he tossed his head contemptuously at the shore. 'Been living there?' he asked. I said, 'Yes.' 'Fine lot these government chaps — are they not?' he went on, speaking English with great precision and considerable bitterness. 'It is funny what some people will do for a few francs a month. I wonder what becomes of that kind when it goes up country?' I said to him I expected to see that soon. 'So-o-o!' he exclaimed. He shuffled athwart, keeping one eye ahead vigilantly. 'Don't be too sure,' he continued. 'The other day I took up a man who hanged himself on the road. He was a Swede, too.' 'Hanged himself! Why, in God's name?' I cried. He kept on looking out watchfully. 'Who knows? The sun too much for him, or the country perhaps.'

"At last we opened a reach. A rocky cliff appeared, mounds of turned-up earth by the shore, houses on a hill, others with iron roofs, amongst a waste of excavations, or hanging to the declivity. A continuous noise of the rapids above hovered over this scene of inhabited devastation. A lot of people, mostly black and naked, moved about like ants. A jetty projected into the river. A blinding sunlight drowned all this at times in a sudden recrudescence of glare. 'There's your Company's station,' said the Swede, pointing to three wooden barrack-like structures on the rocky slope. 'I will send your things up. Four boxes did you say? So. Farewell.'

"I came upon a boiler wallowing in the grass, then found a path leading up the hill. It turned aside for the boulders, and also for an undersized railway truck lying there on its back with its wheels in the air. One was off. The thing looked as dead as the carcass of some animal. I came upon more pieces of decaying machinery, a stack of rusty rails. To the left a clump of trees made a shady spot, where dark things seemed to stir feebly. I blinked, the path was steep. A horn tooted to the right, and I saw the black people run. A heavy and dull detonation shook the ground, a puff of smoke came out of the cliff, and that was all. No change appeared on the face of the rock. They were building a railway. The cliff was not in the way or anything; but this objectless blasting was all the work going on.

"A slight clinking behind me made me turn my head. Six black men advanced in a file, toiling up the path. They walked erect and slow, balancing small baskets full of earth on their heads, and the clink kept time with their footsteps. Black rags were wound round their loins, and the short ends behind waggled to and fro like tails. I could see every rib, the joints of their limbs were like knots in a rope; each had an iron collar on his neck, and all were connected together with a chain whose bights swung between them, rhythmically clinking. Another report from the cliff made me think suddenly of that ship of war I had seen firing into a continent. It was the same kind of ominous voice; but these men could by no stretch of imagination be called enemies. They were called criminals, and the outraged law, like the bursting shells, had come to them, an insoluble mystery from the sea. All their meagre breasts panted together, the violently dilated nostrils quivered, the eyes stared stonily uphill. They passed me within six inches, without a glance, with that complete, deathlike indifference of unhappy savages. Behind this raw matter one of the reclaimed, the product of the new forces at work, strolled despondently, carrying a rifle by its middle. He had a uniform jacket with one button off, and seeing a white man on the path, hoisted his weapon to his shoulder with alacrity. This was simple prudence, white men being so much alike at a distance that he could not tell who I might be. He was speedily reassured, and with a large, white, rascally grin, and a glance at his charge, seemed to take me into partnership in his exalted trust. After all, I also was a part of the great cause of these high and just proceedings.

"Instead of going up, I turned and descended to the left. My idea was to let that chain-gang get out of sight before I climbed the hill. You know I am not particularly tender; I've had to strike and to fend off. I've had to resist and to attack sometimes — that's only one way of resisting — without counting the exact cost, according to the demands of such sort of life as I had blundered into. I've seen the devil of violence, and the devil of greed, and the devil of hot desire; but, by all the stars! these were strong, lusty, red-eyed devils, that swayed and drove men — men, I tell you. But as I stood on this hillside, I foresaw that in the blinding sunshine of that land I would become acquainted with a flabby, pretending, weak-eyed devil of a rapacious and pitiless folly. How insidious he could be, too, I was only to find out several months later and a thousand miles farther. For a moment I stood appalled, as though by a warning. Finally I descended the hill, obliquely, towards the trees I had seen.

"I avoided a vast artificial hole somebody had been digging on the slope, the purpose of which I found it impossible to divine. It wasn't a quarry or a sandpit, anyhow. It was just a hole. It might have been connected with the philanthropic desire of giving the criminals something to do. I don't know. Then I nearly fell into a very narrow ravine, almost no more than a scar in the hillside. I discovered that a lot of imported drainage-pipes for the settlement had been tumbled in there. There wasn't one that was not broken. It was a wanton smash-up. At last I got under the trees. My purpose was to stroll into the shade for a moment; but no sooner within than it seemed to me I had stepped into the gloomy circle of some Inferno. The rapids were near, and an uninterrupted, uniform, headlong, rushing noise filled the mournful stillness of the grove, where not a breath stirred, not a leaf moved, with a mysterious sound — as though the tearing pace of the launched earth had suddenly become audible.

"Black shapes crouched, lay, sat between the trees, leaning against the trunks, clinging to the earth, half coming out, half effaced within the dim light, in all the attitudes of pain, abandonment, and despair. Another mine on the cliff went off, followed by a slight shudder of the soil under my feet. The work was going on. The work! And this was the place where some of the helpers had withdrawn to die.

"They were dying slowly — it was very clear. They were not enemies, they were not criminals, they were nothing earthly now — nothing but black shadows of disease and starvation, lying confusedly in the greenish gloom. Brought from all the recesses of the coast in all the legality of time contracts, lost in uncongenial surroundings, fed on unfamiliar food, they sickened, became inefficient, and were then allowed to crawl away and rest. These moribund shapes were free as air — and nearly as thin. I began to distinguish the gleam of the eyes under the trees. Then, glancing down, I saw a face near my hand. The black bones reclined at full length with one shoulder against the tree, and slowly the eyelids rose and the sunken eyes looked up at me, enormous and vacant, a kind of blind, white flicker in the depths of the orbs, which died out slowly. The man seemed young — almost a boy — but you know with them it's hard to tell. I found nothing else to do but to offer him one of my good Swede's ship's biscuits I had in my pocket. The fingers closed slowly on it and held — there was no other movement and no other glance. He had tied a bit of white worsted

round his neck — Why? Where did he get it? Was it a badge — an
ornament — a charm — a propitiatory act? Was there any idea at all
connected with it? It looked startling round his black neck, this bit of
white thread from beyond the seas.

"Near the same tree two more bundles of acute angles sat with
their legs drawn up. One, with his chin propped on his knees, stared at
nothing, in an intolerable and appalling manner: his brother phantom
rested its forehead, as if overcome with a great weariness; and all about
others were scattered in every pose of contorted collapse, as in some
picture of a massacre or a pestilence. While I stood horror-struck, one
of these creatures rose to his hands and knees, and went off on all-fours
towards the river to drink. He lapped out of his hand, then sat up in
the sunlight, crossing his shins in front of him, and after a time let his
woolly head fall on his breastbone.

"I didn't want any more loitering in the shade, and I made haste
towards the station. When near the buildings I met a white man, in such
an unexpected elegance of get-up that in the first moment I took him for
a sort of vision. I saw a high starched collar, white cuffs, a light alpaca
jacket, snowy trousers, a clean necktie, and varnished boots. No hat.
Hair parted, brushed, oiled, under a green-lined parasol held in a big
white hand. He was amazing, and had a pen-holder behind his ear.

"I shook hands with this miracle, and I learned he was the Company's chief accountant, and that all the book-keeping was done at this
station. He had come out for a moment, he said, 'to get a breath of
fresh air.' The expression sounded wonderfully odd, with its suggestion of sedentary desk-life. I wouldn't have mentioned the fellow to
you at all, only it was from his lips that I first heard the name of the
man who is so indissolubly connected with the memories of that time.
Moreover, I respected the fellow. Yes; I respected his collars, his vast
cuffs, his brushed hair. His appearance was certainly that of a hairdresser's dummy; but in the great demoralisation of the land he kept
up his appearance. That's backbone. His starched collars and got-up
shirt-fronts were achievements of character. He had been out nearly
three years; and, later, I could not help asking him how he managed
to sport such linen. He had just the faintest blush, and said modestly,
'I've been teaching one of the native women about the station. It was
difficult. She had a distaste for the work.' Thus this man had verily accomplished something. And he was devoted to his books, which were
in apple-pie order.

"Everything else in the station was in a muddle, — heads, things,
buildings. Strings of dusty niggers with splay feet arrived and departed;

a stream of manufactured goods, rubbishy cottons, beads, and brass-wire set into the depths of darkness, and in return came a precious trickle of ivory.

"I had to wait in the station for ten days — an eternity. I lived in a hut in the yard, but to be out of the chaos I would sometimes get into the accountant's office. It was built of horizontal planks, and so badly put together that, as he bent over his high desk, he was barred from neck to heels with narrow strips of sunlight. There was no need to open the big shutter to see. It was hot there too; big flies buzzed fiendishly, and did not sting, but stabbed. I sat generally on the floor, while, of faultless appearance (and even slightly scented), perching on a high stool, he wrote, he wrote. Sometimes he stood up for exercise. When a truckle-bed with a sick man (some invalided agent from up-country) was put in there, he exhibited a gentle annoyance. 'The groans of this sick person,' he said, 'distract my attention. And without that it is extremely difficult to guard against clerical errors in this climate.'

"One day he remarked, without lifting his head, 'In the interior you will no doubt meet Mr. Kurtz.' On my asking who Mr. Kurtz was, he said he was a first-class agent; and seeing my disappointment at this information, he added slowly, laying down his pen, 'He is a very remarkable person.' Further questions elicited from him that Mr. Kurtz was at present in charge of a trading-post, a very important one, in the true ivory-country, at 'the very bottom of there. Sends in as much ivory as all the others put together . . .' He began to write again. The sick man was too ill to groan. The flies buzzed in a great peace.

"Suddenly there was a growing murmur of voices and a great tramping of feet. A caravan had come in. A violent babble of uncouth sounds burst out on the other side of the planks. All the carriers were speaking together, and in the midst of the uproar the lamentable voice of the chief agent was heard 'giving it up' tearfully for the twentieth time that day. . . . He rose slowly. 'What a frightful row,' he said. He crossed the room gently to look at the sick man, and returning, said to me, 'He does not hear.' 'What! Dead?' I asked, startled. 'No, not yet,' he answered, with great composure. Then, alluding with a toss of the head to the tumult in the station-yard, 'When one has got to make correct entries, one comes to hate those savages — hate them to death.' He remained thoughtful for a moment. 'When you see Mr. Kurtz,' he went on, 'tell him for me that everything here' — he glanced at the desk — 'is very satisfactory. I don't like to write to him — with those messengers of ours you never know who may get hold of your letter — at that Central Station.' He stared at me for a moment with his mild, bulging eyes. 'Oh, he will go far, very far,' he began again. 'He will be a somebody in the Administration before long. They, above — the Council in Europe, you know — mean him to be.'

"He turned to his work. The noise outside had ceased, and presently in going out I stopped at the door. In the steady buzz of flies the homeward-bound agent was lying flushed and insensible; the other, bent over his books, was making correct entries of perfectly correct transactions; and fifty feet below the doorstep I could see the still tree-tops of the grove of death.

"Next day I left that station at last, with a caravan of sixty men, for a two-hundred-mile tramp.

"No use telling you much about that. Paths, paths, everywhere; a stamped-in network of paths spreading over the empty land, through long grass, through burnt grass, through thickets, down and up chilly ravines, up and down stony hills ablaze with heat; and a solitude, a solitude, nobody, not a hut. The population had cleared out a long time ago. Well, if a lot of mysterious niggers armed with all kinds of fearful weapons suddenly took to travelling on the road between Deal and Gravesend, catching the yokels right and left to carry heavy loads for them, I fancy every farm and cottage thereabouts would get empty very soon. Only here the dwellings were gone too. Still, I passed through several abandoned villages. There's something pathetically childish in the ruins of grass walls. Day after day, with the stamp and shuffle of sixty pair of bare feet behind me, each pair under a 60-lb. load. Camp, cook, sleep; strike camp, march. Now and then a carrier dead in harness, at rest in the long grass near the path, with an empty water-gourd and his long staff lying by his side. A great silence around and above. Perhaps on some quiet night the tremor of far-off drums, sinking, swelling, a tremor vast, faint; a sound weird, appealing, suggestive, and wild — and perhaps with as profound a meaning as the sound of bells in a Christian country. Once a white man in an unbuttoned uniform, camping on the path with an armed escort of lank Zanzibaris, very hospitable and festive — not to say drunk. Was looking after the upkeep of the road, he declared. Can't say I saw any road or any upkeep, unless the body of a middle-aged negro, with a bullet-hole in the forehead, upon which I absolutely stumbled three miles farther on, may be considered as a permanent improvement. I had a white companion too, not a bad chap, but rather too fleshy and with the exasperating habit of fainting on the hot hillsides, miles away from the least bit of shade and water. Annoying, you know, to hold your own coat like a parasol over a man's head while he is coming to. I couldn't help asking him once what he meant by coming there at all. 'To make money, of course. What do you think?' he said scornfully. Then he got fever, and had to be carried in a hammock slung under a pole. As he weighed sixteen stone I had no end of rows with the carriers. They jibbed, ran away, sneaked off with their loads in the night — quite a mutiny. So, one evening, I made a speech in English with gestures, not one of which was lost to the sixty pairs of eyes before me, and the next morning I started the hammock off in front all right. An hour afterwards I came upon the whole concern wrecked in a bush — man, hammock, groans, blankets, horrors. The heavy pole had skinned his poor nose. He was very anxious for me to kill somebody, but there wasn't the shadow of a carrier near. I remembered the old doctor — 'It would be interesting for science to watch the mental changes of individuals, on the spot.' I felt I was becoming scientifically interesting. However, all that is to no purpose. On the fifteenth day I came in sight of the big river again, and hobbled into the Central Station. It was on a back water surrounded by scrub and forest, with a pretty border of smelly mud on one side, and on the three others enclosed by a crazy fence of rushes. A neglected gap was all the gate it had, and the first glance at the place was enough to let you see the flabby devil was running that show. White men with long staves in their hands appeared languidly from amongst the buildings, strolling up to take a look at me, and then retired out of sight somewhere. One of them, a stout, excitable chap with black moustaches, informed me with great volubility and many digressions, as soon as I told him who I was, that my steamer was at the bottom of the river. I was thunderstruck. What, how, why? Oh, it was 'all right.' The 'manager himself' was there. All quite correct. 'Everybody had behaved splendidly! splendidly!' — 'You must,' he said in agitation, 'go and see the general manager at once. He is waiting!'

"I did not see the real significance of that wreck at once. I fancy I see it now, but I am not sure — not at all. Certainly the affair was too stupid — when I think of it — to be altogether natural. Still . . . But at the moment it presented itself simply as a confounded nuisance. The steamer was sunk. They had started two days before in a sudden hurry up the river with the manager on board, in charge of some volunteer skipper, and before they had been out three hours they tore the bottom out of her on stones, and she sank near the south bank. I asked myself what I was to do there, now my boat was lost. As a matter of fact, I had plenty to do in fishing my command out of the river. I had to set about it the very next day. That, and the repairs when I brought the pieces to the station, took some months.

"My first interview with the manager was curious. He did not ask me to sit down after my twenty-mile walk that morning. He was commonplace in complexion, in feature, in manners, and in voice. He was of middle size and of ordinary build. His eyes, of the usual blue, were perhaps remarkably cold, and he certainly could make his glance fall on one as trenchant and heavy as an axe. But even at these times the rest of his person seemed to disclaim the intention. Otherwise there was only an indefinable, faint expression of his lips, something stealthy — a smile — not a smile — I remember it, but I can't explain. It was unconscious, this smile was, though just after he had said something it got intensified for an instant. It came at the end of his speeches like a seal applied on the words to make the meaning of the commonest phrase appear absolutely inscrutable. He was a common trader, from his youth up employed in these parts — nothing more. He was obeyed, yet he inspired neither love nor fear, nor even respect. He inspired uneasiness. That was it! Uneasiness. Not a definite mistrust — just uneasiness — nothing more. You have no idea how effective such a . . . a . . . faculty can be. He had no genius for organising, for initiative, or for order even. That was evident in such things as the deplorable state of the station. He had no learning, and no intelligence. His position had come to him — why? Perhaps because he was never ill . . . He had served three terms of three years out there . . . Because triumphant health in the general rout of constitutions is a kind of power in itself. When he went home on leave he rioted on a large scale — pompously. Jack ashore — with a difference — in externals only. This one could gather from his casual talk. He originated nothing, he could keep the routine going — that's all. But he was great. He was great by this little thing that it was impossible to tell what could control such a man. He never gave that secret away. Perhaps there was nothing within him. Such a suspicion made one pause — for out there there were no external checks. Once when various tropical diseases had laid low almost every 'agent' in the station, he was heard to say, 'Men who come out here should have no entrails.' He sealed the utterance with that smile of his, as though it had been a door opening into a darkness he had in his keeping. You fancied you had seen things — but the seal was on. When annoyed at meal-times by the constant quarrels of the white men about precedence, he ordered an immense round table to be made, for which a special house had to be built. This was the station's mess-room. Where he sat was the first place — the rest were nowhere. One felt this to be his unalterable conviction. He was neither civil nor uncivil. He was quiet. He allowed his 'boy' — an overfed young negro from the coast — to treat the white men, under his very eyes, with provoking insolence.

"He began to speak as soon as he saw me. I had been very long on the road. He could not wait. Had to start without me. The up-river stations had to be relieved. There had been so many delays already that he did not know who was dead and who was alive, and how they got on — and so on, and so on. He paid no attention to my explanations, and, playing with a stick of sealing-wax, repeated several times that the situation was 'very grave, very grave.' There were rumours that a very important station was in jeopardy, and its chief, Mr. Kurtz, was ill. Hoped it was not true. Mr. Kurtz was . . . I felt weary and irritable. Hang Kurtz, I thought. I interrupted him by saying I had heard of Mr. Kurtz on the coast. 'Ah! So they talk of him down there,' he murmured to himself. Then he began again, assuring me Mr. Kurtz was the best agent he had, an exceptional man, of the greatest importance to the Company; therefore I could understand his anxiety. He was, he said, 'very, very uneasy.' Certainly he fidgeted on his chair a good deal, exclaimed, 'Ah, Mr. Kurtz!' broke the stick of sealing-wax and seemed dumbfounded by the accident. Next thing he wanted to know 'how long it would take to' . . . I interrupted him again. Being hungry, you know, and kept on my feet too, I was getting savage. 'How can I tell?' I said. 'I haven't even seen the wreck yet — some months, no doubt.' All this talk seemed to me so futile. 'Some months,' he said. 'Well, let us say three months before we can make a start. Yes. That ought to do the affair.' I flung out of his hut (he lived all alone in a clay hut with a sort of verandah) muttering to myself my opinion of him. He was a chattering idiot. Afterwards I took it back when it was borne in upon me startlingly with what extreme nicety he had estimated the time requisite for the 'affair.'

"I went to work the next day, turning, so to speak, my back on that station. In that way only it seemed to me I could keep my hold on the redeeming facts of life. Still, one must look about sometimes; and then I saw this station, these men strolling aimlessly about in the sunshine of the yard. I asked myself sometimes what it all meant. They wandered here and there with their absurd long staves in their hands, like a lot of faithless pilgrims bewitched inside a rotten fence. The word 'ivory' rang in the air, was whispered, was sighed. You would think they were praying to it. A taint of imbecile rapacity blew through it all, like a whiff from some corpse. By Jove! I've never seen anything so unreal in my life. And outside, the silent wilderness surrounding this cleared speck on the earth struck me as something great and invincible, like evil or truth, waiting patiently for the passing away of this fantastic invasion.

"Oh, those months! Well, never mind. Various things happened. One evening a grass shed full of calico, cotton prints, beads, and I don't know what else, burst into a blaze so suddenly that you would have thought the earth had opened to let an avenging fire consume all that trash. I was smoking my pipe quietly by my dismantled steamer, and saw them all cutting capers in the light, with their arms lifted high, when the stout man with moustaches came tearing down to the river, a tin pail in his hand, assured me that everybody was 'behaving splendidly, splendidly,' dipped about a quart of water and tore back again. I noticed there was a hole in the bottom of his pail.

"I strolled up. There was no hurry. You see the thing had gone off like a box of matches. It had been hopeless from the very first. The flame had leaped high, driven everybody back, lighted up everything — and collapsed. The shed was already a heap of embers glowing fiercely. A nigger was being beaten near by. They said he had caused the fire in some way; be that as it may, he was screeching most horribly. I saw him, later, for several days, sitting in a bit of shade looking very sick and trying to recover himself: afterwards he arose and went out — and the wilderness without a sound took him into its bosom again. As I approached the glow from the dark I found myself at the back of two men, talking. I heard the name of Kurtz pronounced, then the words 'take advantage of this unfortunate accident.' One of the men was the manager. I wished him a good evening. 'Did you ever see anything like it — eh? it is incredible,' he said, and walked off. The other man remained. He was a first-class agent, young, gentlemanly, a bit reserved, with a forked little beard and a hooked nose. He was stand-offish with the other agents, and they on their side said he was the manager's spy upon them. As to me, I had hardly ever spoken to him before. We got into talk, and by and by we strolled away from the hissing ruins. Then he asked me to his room, which was in the main building of the station. He struck a match, and I perceived that this young aristocrat had not only a silver-mounted dressing-case but also a whole candle all to himself. Just at that time the manager was the only man supposed to have any right to candles. Native mats covered the clay walls; a collection of spears, assegais, shields, knives, was hung up in trophies. The business entrusted to this fellow was the making of bricks — so I had been informed; but there wasn't a fragment of a brick anywhere in the station, and he had been there more than a year — waiting. It seems he could not make bricks without something, I don't know what — straw maybe. Anyway, it could not be found there, and as it was not likely to be sent from Europe, it did not appear clear to me what he was waiting for. An act of special creation perhaps. However, they were all waiting — all the sixteen or twenty pilgrims of them — for something; and upon my word it did not seem an uncongenial occupation, from the way they took it, though the only thing that ever came to them was disease — as far as I could see. They beguiled the time by backbiting and intriguing against each other in a foolish kind of way. There was an air of plotting about that station, but nothing came of it, of course. It was as unreal as everything else — as the philanthropic pretence of the whole concern, as their talk, as their government, as their show of work. The only real feeling was a desire to get appointed to a trading-post where ivory was to be had, so that they could earn percentages. They intrigued and slandered and hated each other only on that account — but as to effectually lifting a little finger — oh no. By Heavens! there is something after all in the world allowing one man to steal a horse while another must not look at a halter. Steal a horse straight out. Very well. He has done it. Perhaps he can ride. But there is a way of looking at a halter that would provoke the most charitable of saints into a kick.

"I had no idea why he wanted to be sociable, but as we chatted in there it suddenly occurred to me the fellow was trying to get at something — in fact, pumping me. He alluded constantly to Europe, to the people I was supposed to know there — putting leading questions as to my acquaintances in the sepulchral city, and so on. His little eyes glittered like mica discs — with curiosity — though he tried to keep up a bit of superciliousness. At first I was astonished, but very soon I became awfully curious to see what he would find out from me. I couldn't possibly imagine what I had in me to make it worth his while. It was very pretty to see how he baffled himself, for in truth my body was full only of chills, and my head had nothing in it but that wretched steamboat business. It was evident he took me for a perfectly shameless prevaricator. At last he got angry, and, to conceal a movement of furious annoyance, he yawned. I rose. Then I noticed a small sketch in oils, on a panel, representing a woman, draped and blindfolded, carrying a lighted torch. The background was sombre — almost black. The movement of the woman was stately, and the effect of the torchlight on the face was sinister.

"It arrested me, and he stood by civilly, holding an empty half-pint champagne bottle (medical comforts) with the candle stuck in it. To my question he said Mr. Kurtz had painted this — in this very station more than a year ago — while waiting for means to go to his trading-post. 'Tell me, pray,' said I, 'who is this Mr. Kurtz?'

" 'The chief of the Inner Station,' he answered in a short tone, looking away. 'Much obliged,' I said, laughing. 'And you are the brick-maker of the Central Station. Every one knows that.' He was silent for a while. 'He is a prodigy,' he said at last. 'He is an emissary of pity, and science, and progress, and devil knows what else. We want,' he began to declaim suddenly, 'for the guidance of the cause entrusted to us by Europe, so to speak, higher intelligence, wide sympathies, a singleness of purpose.' 'Who says that?' I asked. 'Lots of them,' he re-plied. 'Some even write that; and so *he* comes here, a special being, as you ought to know.' 'Why ought I to know?' I interrupted, really surprised. He paid no attention. 'Yes. To-day he is chief of the best station, next year he will be assistant-manager, two years more and . . . but I daresay you know what he will be in two years' time. You are of the new gang — the gang of virtue. The same people who sent him specially also recommended you. Oh, don't say no. I've my own eyes to trust.' Light dawned upon me. My dear aunt's influential acquaint-ances were producing an unexpected effect upon that young man. I nearly burst into a laugh. 'Do you read the Company's confidential correspondence?' I asked. He hadn't a word to say. It was great fun. 'When Mr. Kurtz,' I continued severely, 'is General Manager, you won't have the opportunity.'

"He blew the candle out suddenly, and we went outside. The moon had risen. Black figures strolled about listlessly, pouring water on the glow, whence proceeded a sound of hissing; steam ascended in the moonlight; the beaten nigger groaned somewhere. 'What a row the brute makes!' said the indefatigable man with the moustaches, appear-ing near us. 'Serve him right. Transgression — punishment — bang! Pitiless, pitiless. That's the only way. This will prevent all conflagrations for the future. I was just telling the manager . . .' He noticed my com-panion, and became crestfallen all at once. 'Not in bed yet,' he said, with a kind of servile heartiness; 'it's so natural. Ha! Danger — agitation.' He vanished. I went on to the river-side, and the other followed me. I heard a scathing murmur at my ear, 'Heaps of muffs — go to.' The pilgrims could be seen in knots gesticulating, discussing. Several had still their staves in their hands. I verily believe they took these sticks to bed with them. Beyond the fence the forest stood up spectrally in the moonlight, and through the dim stir, through the faint sounds of that lamentable courtyard, the silence of the land went home to one's very heart — its mystery, its greatness, the amazing reality of its concealed life. The hurt nigger moaned feebly somewhere near by, and then fetched a deep sigh that made me mend my pace away from there. I felt a hand introducing itself under my arm. 'My dear sir,' said the fellow, 'I don't want to be misunderstood, and especially by you, who will see Mr. Kurtz long before I can have that pleasure. I wouldn't like him to get a false idea of my disposition. . . .'

"I let him run on, this papier-mâché Mephistopheles, and it seemed to me that if I tried I could poke my forefinger through him, and would find nothing inside but a little loose dirt, maybe. He, don't you see, had been planning to be assistant-manager by and by under the present man, and I could see that the coming of that Kurtz had upset them both not a little. He talked precipitately, and I did not try to stop him. I had my shoulders against the wreck of my steamer, hauled up on the slope like a carcass of some big river animal. The smell of mud, of primeval mud, by Jove! was in my nostrils, the high stillness of primeval forest was before my eyes; there were shiny patches on the black creek. The moon had spread over everything a thin layer of silver — over the rank grass, over the mud, upon the wall of matted vegetation standing higher than the wall of a temple, over the great river I could see through a sombre gap glittering, glittering, as it flowed broadly by without a murmur. All this was great, expectant, mute, while the man jabbered about himself. I wondered whether the stillness on the face of the immensity looking at us two were meant as an appeal or as a menace. What were we who had strayed in here? Could we handle that dumb thing, or would it handle us? I felt how big, how confoundedly big, was that thing that couldn't talk and perhaps was deaf as well. What was in there? I could see a little ivory coming out from there, and I had heard Mr. Kurtz was in there. I had heard enough about it too — God knows! Yet somehow it didn't bring any image with it — no more than if I had been told an angel or a fiend was in there. I believed it in the same way one of you might believe there are inhabitants in the planet Mars. I knew once a Scotch sailmaker who was certain, dead sure, there were people in Mars. If you asked him for some idea how they looked and behaved, he would get shy and mutter something about 'walking on all-fours.' If you as much as smiled, he would — though a man of sixty — offer to fight you. I would not have gone so far as to fight for Kurtz, but I went for him near enough to a lie. You know I hate, detest, and can't bear a lie, not because I am straighter than the rest of us, but simply because it appals me. There is a taint of death, a flavour of mortality in lies — which is exactly what I hate and detest in the world — what I want to forget. It makes me miserable and sick, like biting something rotten would do. Temperament, I suppose. Well, I went near enough to it by letting the young fool there believe anything he liked to imagine as to my influence in Europe. I became in an instant as much of a pretence as the rest of the bewitched pilgrims. This simply because I had a notion it somehow would be of help to that Kurtz whom at the time I did not see — you understand. He was just a word for me. I did not see the man in the name any more than you do. Do you see him? Do you see the story? Do you see anything? It seems to me I am trying to tell you a dream — making a vain attempt, because no relation of a dream can convey the dream-sensation, that commingling of absurdity, surprise, and bewilderment in a tremor of struggling revolt, that notion of being captured by the incredible which is of the very essence of dreams. . . ."

He was silent for a while.

". . . No, it is impossible; it is impossible to convey the life-sensation of any given epoch of one's existence — that which makes its truth, its meaning — its subtle and penetrating essence. It is impossible. We live, as we dream — alone. . . ."

He paused again as if reflecting, then added:

"Of course in this you fellows see more than I could then. You see me, whom you know. . . ."

It had become so pitch dark that we listeners could hardly see one another. For a long time already he, sitting apart, had been no more to us than a voice. There was not a word from anybody. The others might have been asleep, but I was awake. I listened, I listened on the watch for the sentence, for the word, that would give me the clue to the faint uneasiness inspired by this narrative that seemed to shape itself without human lips in the heavy night-air of the river.

". . . Yes — I let him run on," Marlow began again, "and think what he pleased about the powers that were behind me. I did! And there was nothing behind me! There was nothing but that wretched, old, mangled steamboat I was leaning against, while he talked fluently about 'the necessity for every man to get on.' 'And when one comes out here, you conceive, it is not to gaze at the moon.' Mr. Kurtz was a 'universal genius,' but even a genius would find it easier to work with 'adequate tools — intelligent men.' He did not make bricks — why, there was a physical impossibility in the way — as I was well aware; and if he did secretarial work for the manager, it was because 'no sensible man rejects wantonly the confidence of his superiors.' Did I see it? I saw it. What more did I want? What I really wanted was rivets, by Heaven! Rivets. To get on with the work — to stop the hole. Rivets

I wanted. There were cases of them down at the coast — cases — piled up — burst — split! You kicked a loose rivet at every second step in that station yard on the hillside. Rivets had rolled into the grove of death. You could fill your pockets with rivets for the trouble of stooping down — and there wasn't one rivet to be found where it was wanted. We had plates that would do, but nothing to fasten them with. And every week the messenger, a lone negro, letter-bag on shoulder and staff in hand, left our station for the coast. And several times a week a coast caravan came in with trade goods — ghastly glazed calico that made you shudder only to look at it, glass beads value about a penny a quart, confounded spotted cotton handkerchiefs. And no rivets. Three carriers could have brought all that was wanted to set that steamboat afloat.

"He was becoming confidential now, but I fancy my unresponsive attitude must have exasperated him at last, for he judged it necessary to inform me he feared neither God nor devil, let alone any mere man. I said I could see that very well, but what I wanted was a certain quantity of rivets — and rivets were what really Mr. Kurtz wanted, if he had only known it. Now letters went to the coast every week. . . . 'My dear sir,' he cried, 'I write from dictation.' I demanded rivets. There was a way — for an intelligent man. He changed his manner; became very cold, and suddenly began to talk about a hippopotamus; wondered whether sleeping on board the steamer (I stuck to my salvage night and day) I wasn't disturbed. There was an old hippo that had the bad habit of getting out on the bank and roaming at night over the station grounds. The pilgrims used to turn out in a body and empty every rifle they could lay hands on at him. Some even had sat up o' nights for him. All this energy was wasted, though. 'That animal has a charmed life,' he said; 'but you can say this only of brutes in this country. No man — you apprehend me? — no man here bears a charmed life.' He stood there for a moment in the moonlight with his delicate hooked nose set a little askew, and his mica eyes glittering without a wink, then, with a curt Good-night, he strode off. I could see he was disturbed and considerably puzzled, which made me feel more hopeful than I had been for days. It was a great comfort to turn from that chap to my influential friend, the battered, twisted, ruined, tin-pot steamboat. I clambered on board. She rang under my feet like an empty Huntley & Palmer biscuit-tin kicked along a gutter; she was nothing so solid in make, and rather less pretty in shape, but I had expended enough hard work on her to make me love her. No influential friend would have served me better. She had given me a chance to come out a bit — to find out what I could do. No, I don't like work. I had rather laze about and think of all the fine things that can be done. I don't like work — no man does — but I like what is in the work — the chance to find yourself. Your own reality — for yourself, not for others — what no other man can ever know. They can only see the mere show, and never can tell what it really means.

"I was not surprised to see somebody sitting aft, on the deck, with his legs dangling over the mud. You see I rather chummed with the few mechanics there were in that station, whom the other pilgrims naturally despised — on account of their imperfect manners, I suppose. This was the foreman — a boiler-maker by trade — a good worker. He was a lank, bony, yellow-faced man, with big intense eyes. His aspect was worried, and his head was as bald as the palm of my hand; but his hair in falling seemed to have stuck to his chin, and had prospered in the new locality, for his beard hung down to his waist. He was a widower with six young children (he had left them in charge of a sister of his to come out there), and the passion of his life was pigeon-flying. He was an enthusiast and a connoisseur. He would rave about pigeons. After work hours he used sometimes to come over from his hut for a talk about his children and his pigeons; at work, when he had to crawl in the mud under the bottom of the steamboat, he would tie up that beard of his in a kind of white serviette he brought for the purpose. It had loops to go over his ears. In the evening he could be seen squatted on the bank rinsing that wrapper in the creek with great care, then spreading it solemnly on a bush to dry.

"I slapped him on the back and shouted 'We shall have rivets!' He scrambled to his feet exclaiming 'No! Rivets!' as though he couldn't believe his ears. Then in a low voice, 'You . . . eh?' I don't know why we behaved like lunatics. I put my finger to the side of my nose and nodded mysteriously. 'Good for you!' he cried, snapped his fingers above his head, lifting one foot. I tried a jig. We capered on the iron deck. A frightful clatter came out of that hulk, and the virgin forest on the other bank of the creek sent it back in a thundering roll upon the sleeping station. It must have made some of the pilgrims sit up in their hovels. A dark figure obscured the lighted doorway of the manager's hut, vanished, then, a second or so after, the doorway itself vanished too. We stopped, and the silence driven away by the stamping of our feet flowed back again from the recesses of the land. The great wall of vegetation, an exuberant and entangled mass of trunks, branches, leaves, boughs, festoons, motionless in the moonlight, was like a rioting invasion of soundless life, a rolling wave of plants, piled up, crested, ready to topple over the creek, to sweep every little man of us out of his little existence. And it moved not. A deadened burst of mighty splashes and snorts reached us from afar, as though an ichthyosaurus had been taking a bath of glitter in the great river. 'After all,' said the boiler-maker in a reasonable tone, 'why shouldn't we get the rivets?' Why not, indeed! I did not know of any reason why we shouldn't. 'They'll come in three weeks,' I said confidently.

"But they didn't. Instead of rivets there came an invasion, an infliction, a visitation. It came in sections during the next three weeks, each section headed by a donkey carrying a white man in new clothes and tan shoes, bowing from that elevation right and left to the impressed pilgrims. A quarrelsome band of footsore sulky niggers trod on the heels of the donkey; a lot of tents, camp-stools, tin boxes, white cases, brown bales would be shot down in the courtyard, and the air of mystery would deepen a little over the muddle of the station. Five such instalments came, with their absurd air of disorderly flight with the loot of innumerable outfit shops and provision stores, that, one would think, they were lugging, after a raid, into the wilderness for equitable division. It was an inextricable mess of things decent in themselves but that human folly made look like the spoils of thieving.

"This devoted band called itself the Eldorado Exploring Expedition, and I believe they were sworn to secrecy. Their talk, however, was the talk of sordid buccaneers: it was reckless without hardihood, greedy without audacity, and cruel without courage; there was not an atom of foresight or of serious intention in the whole batch of them, and they did not seem aware these things are wanted for the work of the world. To tear treasure out of the bowels of the land was their desire, with no more moral purpose at the back of it than there is in burglars breaking into a safe. Who paid the expenses of the noble enterprise I don't know; but the uncle of our manager was leader of that lot.

"In exterior he resembled a butcher in a poor neighbourhood, and his eyes had a look of sleepy cunning. He carried his fat paunch with ostentation on his short legs, and during the time his gang infested the station spoke to no one but his nephew. You could see these two roaming about all day long with their heads close together in an everlasting confab.

"I had given up worrying myself about the rivets. One's capacity for that kind of folly is more limited than you would suppose. I said Hang! — and let things slide. I had plenty of time for meditation, and now and then I would give some thought to Kurtz. I wasn't very interested in him. No. Still, I was curious to see whether this man, who had come out equipped with moral ideas of some sort, would climb to the top after all, and how he would set about his work when there."

II

"One evening as I was lying flat on the deck of my steamboat, I heard voices approaching — and there were the nephew and the uncle strolling along the bank. I laid my head on my arm again, and had nearly lost myself in a doze, when somebody said in my ear, as it were: 'I am as harmless as a little child, but I don't like to be dictated to. Am I the manager — or am I not? I was ordered to send him there. It's incredible.' . . . I became aware that the two were standing on the shore alongside the forepart of the steamboat, just below my head. I did not move; it did not occur to me to move: I was sleepy. 'It *is* unpleasant,' grunted the uncle. 'He has asked the Administration to be sent there,' said the other, 'with the idea of showing what he could do; and I was instructed accordingly. Look at the influence that man must have. Is it not frightful?' They both agreed it was frightful, then made several bizarre remarks: 'Make rain and fine weather — one man — the Council — by the nose' — bits of absurd sentences that got the better of my drowsiness, so that I had pretty near the whole of my wits about me when the uncle said, 'The climate may do away with this difficulty for you. Is he alone there?' 'Yes,' answered the manager; 'he sent his assistant down the river with a note to me in these terms: "Clear this poor devil out of the country, and don't bother sending more of that sort. I had rather be alone than have the kind of men you can dispose of with me." It was more than a year ago. Can you imagine such impudence?' 'Anything since then?' asked the other hoarsely. 'Ivory,' jerked the nephew; 'lots of it — prime sort — lots — most annoying, from him.' 'And with that?' questioned the heavy rumble. 'Invoice,' was the reply fired out, so to speak. Then silence. They had been talking about Kurtz.

"I was broad awake by this time, but, lying perfectly at ease, remained still, having no inducement to change my position. 'How did that ivory come all this way?' growled the elder man, who seemed very vexed. The other explained that it had come with a fleet of canoes in charge of an English half-caste clerk Kurtz had with him; that Kurtz had apparently intended to return himself, the station being by that time bare of goods and stores, but after coming three hundred miles, had suddenly decided to go back, which he started to do alone in a small dugout with four paddlers, leaving the half-caste to continue down the river with the ivory. The two fellows there seemed astounded at anybody attempting such a thing. They were at a loss for an adequate motive. As for me, I seemed to see Kurtz for the first time. It was a distinct glimpse: the dugout, four paddling savages, and the lone white man turning his back suddenly on the headquarters, on relief, on thoughts of home — perhaps; setting his face towards the depths of the wilderness, towards his empty and desolate station. I did not know the motive. Perhaps he was just simply a fine fellow who stuck to his work for its own sake. His name, you understand, had not been pronounced once. He was 'that man.' The half-caste, who, as far as I could see, had conducted a difficult trip with great prudence and pluck, was invariably alluded to as 'that scoundrel.' The 'scoundrel' had reported that the 'man' had been very ill — had recovered imperfectly. . . . The two below me moved away then a few paces, and strolled back and forth at some little distance. I heard: 'Military post — doctor — two hundred miles — quite alone now — unavoidable delays — nine months — no news — strange rumours.' They approached again, just as the manager was saying, 'No one, as far as I know, unless a species of wandering trader — a pestilential fellow, snapping ivory from the natives.' Who was it they were talking about now? I gathered in snatches that this was some man supposed to be in Kurtz's district, and of whom the manager did not approve. 'We will not be free from unfair competition till one of these fellows is hanged for an example,' he said. 'Certainly,' grunted the other; 'get him hanged! Why not? Anything — anything can be done in this country. That's what I say; nobody here, you understand, *here*, can endanger your position. And why? You stand the climate — you outlast them all. The danger is in Europe; but there before I left I took care to —— ' They moved off and whispered, then their voices rose again. 'The extraordinary series of delays is not my fault. I did my possible.' The fat man sighed, 'Very sad.' 'And the pestiferous absurd- ity of his talk,' continued the other; 'he bothered me enough when he was here. "Each station should be like a beacon on the road towards better things, a centre for trade of course, but also for humanising, improving, instructing." Conceive you — that ass! And he wants to be manager! No, it's —— ' Here he got choked by excessive indig- nation, and I lifted my head the least bit. I was surprised to see how near they were — right under me. I could have spat upon their hats. They were looking on the ground, absorbed in thought. The manager was switching his leg with a slender twig: his sagacious relative lifted his head. 'You have been well since you came out this time?' he asked. The other gave a start. 'Who? I? Oh! Like a charm — like a charm. But the

rest — oh, my goodness! All sick. They die so quick, too, that I haven't
the time to send them out of the country — it's incredible.' 'H'm. Just
so,' grunted the uncle. 'Ah! my boy, trust to this — I say, trust to this.'
I saw him extend his short flipper of an arm for a gesture that took in
the forest, the creek, the mud, the river — seemed to beckon with a
dishonouring flourish before the sunlit face of the land a treacherous
appeal to the lurking death, to the hidden evil, to the profound darkness
of its heart. It was so startling that I leaped to my feet and looked back
at the edge of the forest, as though I had expected an answer of some
sort to that black display of confidence. You know the foolish notions
that come to one sometimes. The high stillness confronted these two
figures with its ominous patience, waiting for the passing away of a
fantastic invasion.

"They swore aloud together — out of sheer fright, I believe —
then, pretending not to know anything of my existence, turned back
to the station. The sun was low; and leaning forward side by side, they
seemed to be tugging painfully uphill their two ridiculous shadows of
unequal length, that trailed behind them slowly over the tall grass without bending a single blade.

"In a few days the Eldorado Expedition went into the patient
wilderness, that closed upon it as the sea closes over a diver. Long
afterwards the news came that all the donkeys were dead. I know
nothing as to the fate of the less valuable animals. They, no doubt, like
the rest of us, found what they deserved. I did not inquire. I was then
rather excited at the prospect of meeting Kurtz very soon. When I say
very soon I mean it comparatively. It was just two months from the day
we left the creek when we came to the bank below Kurtz's station.

"Going up that river was like travelling back to the earliest beginnings of the world, when vegetation rioted on the earth and the big trees
were kings. An empty stream, a great silence, and impenetrable forest.
The air was warm, thick, heavy, sluggish. There was no joy in the brilliance of sunshine. The long stretches of the waterway ran on, deserted,
into the gloom of overshadowed distances. On silvery sandbanks hippos
and alligators sunned themselves side by side. The broadening waters
flowed through a mob of wooded islands; you lost your way on that
river as you would in a desert, and butted all day long against shoals,
trying to find the channel, till you thought yourself bewitched and cut
off for ever from everything you had known once — somewhere — far
away — in another existence perhaps. There were moments when one's
past came back to one, as it will sometimes when you have not a moment to spare to yourself; but it came in the shape of an unrestful and

noisy dream, remembered with wonder amongst the overwhelming realities of this strange world of plants, and water, and silence. And this
stillness of life did not in the least resemble a peace. It was the stillness
of an implacable force brooding over an inscrutable intention. It looked
at you with a vengeful aspect. I got used to it afterwards; I did not see
it any more; I had no time. I had to keep guessing at the channel; I had
to discern, mostly by inspiration, the signs of hidden banks; I watched
for sunken stones; I was learning to clap my teeth smartly before my
heart flew out, when I shaved by a fluke some infernal sly old snag that
would have ripped the life out of the tin-pot steamboat and drowned
all the pilgrims; I had to keep a look-out for the signs of dead wood
we could cut up in the night for the next day's steaming. When you
have to attend to things of that sort, to the mere incidents of the
surface, the reality — the reality, I tell you — fades. The inner truth
is hidden — luckily, luckily. But I felt it all the same; I felt often its
mysterious stillness watching me at my monkey tricks, just as it watches
you fellows performing on your respective tight-ropes for — what is it?
half a crown a tumble —— "

"Try to be civil, Marlow," growled a voice, and I knew there
was at least one listener awake besides myself.

"I beg your pardon. I forgot the heartache which makes up the
rest of the price. And indeed what does the price matter, if the trick
be well done? You do your tricks very well. And I didn't do badly
either, since I managed not to sink that steamboat on my first trip. It's
a wonder to me yet. Imagine a blindfolded man set to drive a van over
a bad road. I sweated and shivered over that business considerably, I
can tell you. After all, for a seaman, to scrape the bottom of the thing
that's supposed to float all the time under his care is the unpardonable
sin. No one may know of it, but you never forget the thump — eh? A
blow on the very heart. You remember it, you dream of it, you wake
up at night and think of it — years after — and go hot and cold all
over. I don't pretend to say that steamboat floated all the time. More
than once she had to wade for a bit, with twenty cannibals splashing
around and pushing. We had enlisted some of these chaps on the way
for a crew. Fine fellows — cannibals — in their place. They were
men one could work with, and I am grateful to them. And, after
all, they did not eat each other before my face: they had brought
along a provision of hippo-meat which went rotten, and made the
mystery of the wilderness stink in my nostrils. Phoo! I can sniff it
now. I had the manager on board and three or four pilgrims with
their staves — all complete. Sometimes we came upon a station close

by the bank, clinging to the skirts of the unknown, and the white men
rushing out of a tumble-down hovel, with great gestures of joy and
surprise and welcome, seemed very strange — had the appearance of
being held there captive by a spell. The word 'ivory' would ring in
the air for a while — and on we went again into the silence, along
empty reaches, round the still bends, between the high walls of our
winding way, reverberating in hollow claps the ponderous beat of the
stern-wheel. Trees, trees, millions of trees, massive, immense, running
up high; and at their foot, hugging the bank against the stream, crept
the little begrimed steamboat, like a sluggish beetle crawling on the
floor of a lofty portico. It made you feel very small, very lost, and yet it
was not altogether depressing, that feeling. After all, if you were small,
the grimy beetle crawled on — which was just what you wanted it to
do. Where the pilgrims imagined it crawled to I don't know. To some
place where they expected to get something, I bet! For me it crawled
towards Kurtz — exclusively; but when the steam-pipes started leaking
we crawled very slow. The reaches opened before us and closed behind,
as if the forest had stepped leisurely across the water to bar the way for
our return. We penetrated deeper and deeper into the heart of darkness.
It was very quiet there. At night sometimes the roll of drums behind the
curtain of trees would run up the river and remain sustained faintly, as
if hovering in the air high over our heads, till the first break of day.
Whether it meant war, peace, or prayer we could not tell. The dawns
were heralded by the descent of a chill stillness; the woodcutters slept,
their fires burned low; the snapping of a twig would make you start.
We were wanderers on a prehistoric earth, on an earth that wore the
aspect of an unknown planet. We could have fancied ourselves the first
of men taking possession of an accursed inheritance, to be subdued at
the cost of profound anguish and of excessive toil. But suddenly, as
we struggled round a bend, there would be a glimpse of rush walls,
of peaked grass-roofs, a burst of yells, a whirl of black limbs, a mass
of hands clapping, of feet stamping, of bodies swaying, of eyes rolling,
under the droop of heavy and motionless foliage. The steamer toiled
along slowly on the edge of a black and incomprehensible frenzy. The
prehistoric man was cursing us, praying to us, welcoming us — who
could tell? We were cut off from the comprehension of our surroundings; we glided past like phantoms, wondering and secretly appalled, as
sane men would be before an enthusiastic outbreak in a madhouse. We
could not understand because we were too far and could not remember,
because we were travelling in the night of first ages, of those ages that
are gone, leaving hardly a sign — and no memories.

"The earth seemed unearthly. We are accustomed to look upon the shackled form of a conquered monster, but there — there you could look at a thing monstrous and free. It was unearthly, and the men were —— No, they were not inhuman. Well, you know, that was the worst of it — this suspicion of their not being inhuman. It would come slowly to one. They howled and leaped, and spun, and made horrid faces; but what thrilled you was just the thought of their humanity — like yours — the thought of your remote kinship with this wild and passionate uproar. Ugly. Yes, it was ugly enough; but if you were man enough you would admit to yourself that there was in you just the faintest trace of a response to the terrible frankness of that noise, a dim suspicion of there being a meaning in it which you — you so remote from the night of first ages — could comprehend. And why not? The mind of man is capable of anything — because everything is in it, all the past as well as all the future. What was there after all? Joy, fear, sorrow, devotion, valour, rage — who can tell? — but truth — truth stripped of its cloak of time. Let the fool gape and shudder — the man knows, and can look on without a wink. But he must at least be as much of a man as these on the shore. He must meet that truth with his own true stuff — with his own inborn strength. Principles? Principles won't do. Acquisitions, clothes, pretty rags — rags that would fly off at the first good shake. No; you want a deliberate belief. An appeal to me in this fiendish row — is there? Very well; I hear; I admit, but I have a voice too, and for good or evil mine is the speech that cannot be silenced. Of course, a fool, what with sheer fright and fine sentiments, is always safe. Who's that grunting? You wonder I didn't go ashore for a howl and a dance? Well, no — I didn't. Fine sentiments, you say? Fine sentiments be hanged! I had no time. I had to mess about with white-lead and strips of woollen blanket helping to put bandages on those leaky steam-pipes — I tell you. I had to watch the steering, and circumvent those snags, and get the tin-pot along by hook or by crook. There was surface-truth enough in these things to save a wiser man. And between whiles I had to look after the savage who was fireman. He was an improved specimen; he could fire up a vertical boiler. He was there below me, and, upon my word, to look at him was as edifying as seeing a dog in a parody of breeches and a feather hat, walking on his hind legs. A few months of training had done for that really fine chap. He squinted at the steam-gauge and at the water-gauge with an evident effort of intrepidity — and he had filed teeth too, the poor devil, and the wool of his pate shaved into queer patterns, and three ornamental scars on each of his cheeks. He ought to have been clapping his hands and stamping his feet on the bank, instead of which he was hard at work, a thrall to strange witchcraft, full of improving knowledge. He was useful because he had been instructed; and what he knew was this — that should the water in that transparent thing disappear, the evil spirit inside the boiler would get angry through the greatness of his thirst, and take a terrible vengeance. So he sweated and fired up and watched the glass fearfully (with an impromptu charm, made of rags, tied to his arm, and a piece of polished bone, as big as a watch, stuck flatways through his lower lip), while the wooded banks slipped past us slowly, the short noise was left behind, the interminable miles of silence — and we crept on, towards Kurtz. But the snags were thick, the water was treacherous and shallow, the boiler seemed indeed to have a sulky devil in it, and thus neither that fireman nor I had any time to peer into our creepy thoughts.

"Some fifty miles below the Inner Station we came upon a hut of reeds, an inclined and melancholy pole, with the unrecognisable tatters of what had been a flag of some sort flying from it, and a neatly stacked wood-pile. This was unexpected. We came to the bank, and on the stack of firewood found a flat piece of board with some faded pencil-writing on it. When deciphered it said: 'Wood for you. Hurry up. Approach cautiously.' There was a signature, but it was illegible — not Kurtz — a much longer word. Hurry up. Where? Up the river? 'Approach cautiously.' We had not done so. But the warning could not have been meant for the place where it could be only found after approach. Something was wrong above. But what — and how much? That was the question. We commented adversely upon the imbecility of that telegraphic style. The bush around said nothing, and would not let us look very far, either. A torn curtain of red twill hung in the doorway of the hut, and flapped sadly in our faces. The dwelling was dismantled; but we could see a white man had lived there not very long ago. There remained a rude table — a plank on two posts; a heap of rubbish reposed in a dark corner, and by the door I picked up a book. It had lost its covers, and the pages had been thumbed into a state of extremely dirty softness; but the back had been lovingly stitched afresh with white cotton thread, which looked clean yet. It was an extraordinary find. Its title was, *An Inquiry into some Points of Seamanship*, by a man Towser, Towson — some such name — Master in His Majesty's Navy. The matter looked dreary reading enough, with illustrative diagrams and repulsive tables of figures, and the copy was sixty years old. I handled this amazing antiquity with the greatest possible tenderness, lest it should dissolve in my hands. Within, Towson or Towser was inquiring earnestly into the breaking strain of ships' chains and tackle, and other such matters. Not a very enthralling book; but at the first glance you could see there a singleness of intention, an honest concern for the right way of going to work, which made these humble pages, thought out so many years ago, luminous with another than a professional light. The simple old sailor, with his talk of chains and purchases, made me forget the jungle and the pilgrims in a delicious sensation of having come upon something unmistakably real. Such a book being there was wonderful enough; but still more astounding were the notes pencilled in the margin, and plainly referring to the text. I couldn't believe my eyes! They were in cipher! Yes, it looked like cipher. Fancy a man lugging with him a book of that description into this nowhere and studying it — and making notes — in cipher at that! It was an extravagant mystery.

"I had been dimly aware for some time of a worrying noise, and when I lifted my eyes I saw the wood-pile was gone, and the manager, aided by all the pilgrims, was shouting at me from the river-side. I slipped the book into my pocket. I assure you to leave off reading was like tearing myself away from the shelter of an old and solid friendship.

"I started the lame engine ahead. 'It must be this miserable trader — this intruder,' exclaimed the manager, looking back malevolently at the place we had left. 'He must be English,' I said. 'It will not save him from getting into trouble if he is not careful,' muttered the manager darkly. I observed with assumed innocence that no man was safe from trouble in this world.

"The current was more rapid now, the steamer seemed at her last gasp, the stern-wheel flopped languidly, and I caught myself listening on tiptoe for the next beat of the float, for in sober truth I expected the wretched thing to give up every moment. It was like watching the last flickers of a life. But still we crawled. Sometimes I would pick out a tree a little way ahead to measure our progress towards Kurtz by, but I lost it invariably before we got abreast. To keep the eyes so long on one thing was too much for human patience. The manager displayed a beautiful resignation. I fretted and fumed and took to arguing with myself whether or no I would talk openly with Kurtz; but before I could come to any conclusion it occurred to me that my speech or my silence, indeed any action of mine, would be a mere futility. What did it matter what any one knew or ignored? What did it matter who was manager? One gets sometimes such a flash of insight. The essentials of this affair lay deep under the surface, beyond my reach, and beyond my power of meddling.

"Towards the evening of the second day we judged ourselves about eight miles from Kurtz's station. I wanted to push on; but the manager looked grave, and told me the navigation up there was so dangerous that it would be advisable, the sun being very low already, to wait where we were till next morning. Moreover, he pointed out that if the warning to approach cautiously were to be followed, we must approach in daylight — not at dusk, or in the dark. This was sensible enough. Eight miles meant nearly three hours' steaming for us, and I could also see suspicious ripples at the upper end of the reach. Nevertheless, I was annoyed beyond expression at the delay, and most unreasonably too, since one more night could not matter much after so many months. As we had plenty of wood, and caution was the word, I brought up in the middle of the stream. The reach was narrow, straight, with high sides like a railway cutting. The dusk came gliding into it long before the sun had set. The current ran smooth and swift, but a dumb immobility sat on the banks. The living trees, lashed together by the creepers and every living bush of the undergrowth, might have been changed into stone, even to the slenderest twig, to the lightest leaf. It was not sleep — it seemed unnatural, like a state of trance. Not the faintest sound of any kind could be heard. You looked on amazed, and began to suspect yourself of being deaf — then the night came suddenly, and struck you blind as well. About three in the morning some large fish leaped, and the loud splash made me jump as though a gun had been fired. When the sun rose there was a white fog, very warm and clammy, and more blinding than the night. It did not shift or drive; it was just there, standing all round you like something solid. At eight or nine, perhaps, it lifted as a shutter lifts. We had a glimpse of the towering multitude of trees, of the immense matted jungle, with the blazing little ball of the sun hanging over it — all perfectly still — and then the white shutter came down again, smoothly, as if sliding in greased grooves. I ordered the chain, which we had begun to heave in, to be paid out again. Before it stopped running with a muffled rattle, a cry, a very loud cry, as of infinite desolation, soared slowly in the opaque air. It ceased. A complaining clamour, modulated in savage discords, filled our ears. The sheer unexpectedness of it made my hair stir under my cap. I don't know how it struck the others: to me it seemed as though the mist itself had screamed, so suddenly, and apparently from all sides at once, did this tumultuous and mournful uproar arise. It culminated in a hurried outbreak of almost intolerably excessive shrieking, which stopped short, leaving us stiffened in a variety of silly attitudes, and obstinately listening to the nearly as appalling and excessive silence. 'Good God! What is the meaning —— ?' stammered at my elbow one of the pilgrims — a little fat man, with sandy hair and red whiskers, who wore side-spring boots, and pink pyjamas tucked into his socks. Two others remained open-mouthed a whole minute, then dashed into the little cabin, to rush out incontinently and stand darting scared glances, with Winchesters at 'ready' in their hands. What we could see was just the steamer we were on, her outlines blurred as though she had been on the point of dissolving, and a misty strip of water, perhaps two feet broad, around her — and that was all. The rest of the world was nowhere, as far as our eyes and ears were concerned. Just nowhere. Gone, disappeared; swept off without leaving a whisper or a shadow behind.

"I went forward, and ordered the chain to be hauled in short, so as to be ready to trip the anchor and move the steamboat at once if necessary. 'Will they attack?' whispered an awed voice. 'We will all be butchered in this fog,' murmured another. The faces twitched with the strain, the hands trembled slightly, the eyes forgot to wink. It was very curious to see the contrast of expressions of the white men and of the black fellows of our crew, who were as much strangers to that part of the river as we, though their homes were only eight hundred miles away. The whites, of course greatly discomposed, had besides a curious look of being painfully shocked by such an outrageous row. The others had an alert, naturally interested expression; but their faces were essentially quiet, even those of the one or two who grinned as they hauled at the chain. Several exchanged short, grunting phrases, which seemed to settle the matter to their satisfaction. Their head-man, a young, broad-chested black, severely draped in dark-blue fringed cloths, with fierce nostrils and his hair all done up artfully in oily ringlets, stood near me. 'Aha!' I said, just for good fellowship's sake. 'Catch 'im,' he snapped, with a bloodshot widening of his eyes and a flash of sharp teeth — 'catch 'im. Give 'im to us.' 'To you, eh?' I asked; 'what would you do with them?' 'Eat 'im!' he said curtly, and, leaning his elbow on the rail, looked out into the fog in a dignified and profoundly pensive attitude. I would no doubt have been properly horrified, had it not occurred to me that he and his chaps must be very hungry: that they must have been growing increasingly hungry for at least this month past. They had been engaged for six months (I don't think a single one of them had any clear idea of time, as we at the end of countless ages have. They still belonged to the beginnings of time — had no inherited experience

to teach them, as it were), and of course, as long as there was a piece
of paper written over in accordance with some farcical law or other
made down the river, it didn't enter anybody's head to trouble how
they would live. Certainly they had brought with them some rotten
hippo-meat, which couldn't have lasted very long, anyway, even if the
pilgrims hadn't, in the midst of a shocking hullabaloo, thrown a considerable quantity of it overboard. It looked like a high-handed proceeding; but it was really a case of legitimate self-defence. You can't breathe
dead hippo waking, sleeping, and eating, and at the same time keep
your precarious grip on existence. Besides that, they had given them
every week three pieces of brass wire, each about nine inches long; and
the theory was they were to buy their provisions with that currency in
river-side villages. You can see how *that* worked. There were either no
villages, or the people were hostile, or the director, who like the rest of
us fed out of tins, with an occasional old he-goat thrown in, didn't want
to stop the steamer for some more or less recondite reason. So, unless
they swallowed the wire itself, or made loops of it to snare the fishes
with, I don't see what good their extravagant salary could be to them.
I must say it was paid with a regularity worthy of a large and honour-
able trading company. For the rest, the only thing to eat — though
it didn't look eatable in the least — I saw in their possession was a
few lumps of some stuff like half-cooked dough, of a dirty lavender
colour, they kept wrapped in leaves, and now and then swallowed a
piece of, but so small that it seemed done more for the look of the
thing than for any serious purpose of sustenance. Why in the name of
all the gnawing devils of hunger they didn't go for us — they were thirty to five — and have a good tuck-in for once, amazes me now when
I think of it. They were big powerful men, with not much capacity to
weigh the consequences, with courage, with strength, even yet, though
their skins were no longer glossy and their muscles no longer hard.
And I saw that something restraining, one of those human secrets that
baffle probability, had come into play there. I looked at them with a
swift quickening of interest — not because it occurred to me I might
be eaten by them before very long, though I own to you that just then
I perceived — in a new light, as it were — how unwholesome the pilgrims looked, and I hoped, yes, I positively hoped, that my aspect was
not so — what shall I say? — so — unappetising: a touch of fantastic vanity which fitted well with the dream-sensation that pervaded all
my days at that time. Perhaps I had a little fever too. One can't live
with one's finger everlastingly on one's pulse. I had often 'a little fever,' or a little touch of other things — the playful paw-strokes of the

wilderness, the preliminary trifling before the more serious onslaught which came in due course. Yes; I looked at them as you would on any human being, with a curiosity of their impulses, motives, capacities, weaknesses, when brought to the test of an inexorable physical necessity. Restraint! What possible restraint? Was it superstition, disgust, patience, fear — or some kind of primitive honour? No fear can stand up to hunger, no patience can wear it out, disgust simply does not exist where hunger is; and as to superstition, beliefs, and what you may call principles, they are less than chaff in a breeze. Don't you know the devilry of lingering starvation, its exasperating torment, its black thoughts, its sombre and brooding ferocity? Well, I do. It takes a man all his inborn strength to fight hunger properly. It's really easier to face bereavement, dishonour, and the perdition of one's soul — than this kind of prolonged hunger. Sad, but true. And these chaps too had no earthly reason for any kind of scruple. Restraint! I would just as soon have expected restraint from a hyena prowling amongst the corpses of a battlefield. But there was the fact facing me — the fact dazzling, to be seen, like the foam on the depths of the sea, like a ripple on an unfathomable enigma, a mystery greater — when I thought of it — than the curious, inexplicable note of desperate grief in this savage clamour that had swept by us on the river-bank, behind the blind whiteness of the fog.

"Two pilgrims were quarrelling in hurried whispers as to which bank. 'Left.' 'No, no; how can you? Right, right, of course.' 'It is very serious,' said the manager's voice behind me; 'I would be desolated if anything should happen to Mr. Kurtz before we came up.' I looked at him, and had not the slightest doubt he was sincere. He was just the kind of man who would wish to preserve appearances. That was his restraint. But when he muttered something about going on at once, I did not even take the trouble to answer him. I knew, and he knew, that it was impossible. Were we to let go our hold of the bottom, we would be absolutely in the air — in space. We wouldn't be able to tell where we were going to — whether up or down stream, or across — till we fetched against one bank or the other — and then we wouldn't know at first which it was. Of course I made no move. I had no mind for a smash-up. You couldn't imagine a more deadly place for a shipwreck. Whether drowned at once or not, we were sure to perish speedily in one way or another. 'I authorise you to take all the risks,' he said, after a short silence. 'I refuse to take any,' I said shortly; which was just the answer he expected, though its tone might have surprised him. 'Well, I must defer to your judgment. You are captain,' he said, with marked civility. I turned my shoulder to him in sign of my appreciation, and looked into the fog. How long would it last? It was the most hope-less look-out. The approach to this Kurtz grubbing for ivory in the wretched bush was beset by as many dangers as though he had been an enchanted princess sleeping in a fabulous castle. 'Will they attack, do you think?' asked the manager, in a confidential tone.

"I did not think they would attack, for several obvious reasons. The thick fog was one. If they left the bank in their canoes they would get lost in it, as we would be if we attempted to move. Still, I had also judged the jungle of both banks quite impenetrable — and yet eyes were in it, eyes that had seen us. The river-side bushes were certain-ly very thick; but the undergrowth behind was evidently penetrable. However, during the short lift I had seen no canoes anywhere in the reach — certainly not abreast of the steamer. But what made the idea of attack inconceivable to me was the nature of the noise — of the cries we had heard. They had not the fierce character boding of immediate hostile intention. Unexpected, wild, and violent as they had been, they had given me an irresistible impression of sorrow. The glimpse of the steamboat had for some reason filled those savages with unrestrained grief. The danger, if any, I expounded, was from our proximity to a great human passion let loose. Even extreme grief may ultimately vent itself in violence — but more generally takes the form of apathy. . . .

"You should have seen the pilgrims stare! They had no heart to grin, or even to revile me; but I believe they thought me gone mad — with fright, maybe. I delivered a regular lecture. My dear boys, it was no good bothering. Keep a look-out? Well, you may guess I watched the fog for the signs of lifting as a cat watches a mouse; but for anything else our eyes were of no more use to us than if we had been buried miles deep in a heap of cotton-wool. It felt like it too — choking, warm, stifling. Besides, all I said, though it sounded extravagant, was absolutely true to fact. What we afterwards alluded to as an attack was really an attempt at repulse. The action was very far from being aggressive — it was not even defensive, in the usual sense: it was undertaken under the stress of desperation, and in its essence was purely protective.

"It developed itself, I should say, two hours after the fog lifted, and its commencement was at a spot, roughly speaking, about a mile and a half below Kurtz's station. We had just floundered and flopped round a bend, when I saw an islet, a mere grassy hummock of bright green, in the middle of the stream. It was the only thing of the kind; but as we opened the reach more, I perceived it was the head of a long sandbank, or rather of a chain of shallow patches stretching down the middle of the river. They were discoloured, just awash, and the whole lot was seen just under the water, exactly as a man's backbone is seen running down the middle of his back under the skin. Now, as far as I did see, I could go to the right or to the left of this. I didn't know either channel, of course. The banks looked pretty well alike, the depth appeared the same; but as I had been informed the station was on the west side, I naturally headed for the western passage.

"No sooner had we fairly entered it than I became aware it was much narrower than I had supposed. To the left of us there was the long uninterrupted shoal, and to the right a high steep bank heavily overgrown with bushes. Above the bush the trees stood in serried ranks. The twigs overhung the current thickly, and from distance to distance a large limb of some tree projected rigidly over the stream. It was then well on in the afternoon, the face of the forest was gloomy, and a broad strip of shadow had already fallen on the water. In this shadow we steamed up — very slowly, as you may imagine. I sheered her well inshore — the water being deepest near the bank, as the sounding-pole informed me.

"One of my hungry and forbearing friends was sounding in the bows just below me. This steamboat was exactly like a decked scow. On the deck there were two little teak-wood houses, with doors and windows. The boiler was in the fore-end, and the machinery right astern. Over the whole there was a light roof, supported on stanchions. The funnel projected through that roof, and in front of the funnel a small cabin built of light planks served for a pilot-house. It contained a couch, two camp-stools, a loaded Martini-Henry leaning in one corner, a tiny table, and the steering-wheel. It had a wide door in front and a broad shutter at each side. All these were always thrown open, of course. I spent my days perched up there on the extreme fore-end of that roof, before the door. At night I slept, or tried to, on the couch. An athletic black belonging to some coast tribe, and educated by my poor predecessor, was the helmsman. He sported a pair of brass earrings, wore a blue cloth wrapper from the waist to the ankles, and thought all the world of himself. He was the most unstable kind of fool I had ever seen. He steered with no end of a swagger while you were by; but if he lost sight of you, he became instantly the prey of an abject funk, and would let that cripple of a steamboat get the upper hand of him in a minute.

"I was looking down at the sounding-pole, and feeling much annoyed to see at each try a little more of it stick out of that river, when I saw my poleman give up the business suddenly, and stretch himself

flat on the deck, without even taking the trouble to haul his pole in.
He kept hold on it though, and it trailed in the water. At the same
time the fireman, whom I could also see below me, sat down abruptly
before his furnace and ducked his head. I was amazed. Then I had to
look at the river mighty quick, because there was a snag in the fairway. Sticks, little sticks, were flying about — thick: they were whizzing before my nose, dropping below me, striking behind me against
my pilot-house. All this time the river, the shore, the woods, were very
quiet — perfectly quiet. I could only hear the heavy splashing thump
of the stern-wheel and the patter of these things. We cleared the snag
clumsily. Arrows, by Jove! We were being shot at! I stepped in quickly
to close the shutter on the land-side. That fool-helmsman, his hands on
the spokes, was lifting his knees high, stamping his feet, champing his
mouth, like a reined-in horse. Confound him! And we were stagger-
ing within ten feet of the bank. I had to lean right out to swing the
heavy shutter, and I saw a face amongst the leaves on the level with
my own, looking at me very fierce and steady; and then suddenly, as
though a veil had been removed from my eyes, I made out, deep in
the tangled gloom, naked breasts, arms, legs, glaring eyes — the bush
was swarming with human limbs in movement, glistening, of bronze
colour. The twigs shook, swayed, and rustled, the arrows flew out of
them, and then the shutter came to. 'Steer her straight,' I said to the
helmsman. He held his head rigid, face forward; but his eyes rolled,
he kept on lifting and setting down his feet gently, his mouth foamed
a little. 'Keep quiet!' I said in a fury. I might just as well have ordered
a tree not to sway in the wind. I darted out. Below me there was a
great scuffle of feet on the iron deck; confused exclamations; a voice
screamed, 'Can you turn back?' I caught sight of a V-shaped ripple on
the water ahead. What? Another snag! A fusillade burst out under my
feet. The pilgrims had opened with their Winchesters, and were simply
squirting lead into that bush. A deuce of a lot of smoke came up and
drove slowly forward. I swore at it. Now I couldn't see the ripple or
the snag either. I stood in the doorway, peering, and the arrows came
in swarms. They might have been poisoned, but they looked as though
they wouldn't kill a cat. The bush began to howl. Our woodcutters
raised a warlike whoop; the report of a rifle just at my back deafened
me. I glanced over my shoulder, and the pilot-house was yet full of
noise and smoke when I made a dash at the wheel. The fool-nigger had
dropped everything, to throw the shutter open and let off that Martini-
Henry. He stood before the wide opening, glaring, and I yelled at
him to come back, while I straightened the sudden twist out of that

steamboat. There was no room to turn even if I had wanted to, the snag was somewhere very near ahead in that confounded smoke, there was no time to lose, so I just crowded her into the bank — right into the bank, where I knew the water was deep.

"We tore slowly along the overhanging bushes in a whirl of broken twigs and flying leaves. The fusillade below stopped short, as I had foreseen it would when the squirts got empty. I threw my head back to a glinting whiz that traversed the pilot-house, in at one shutter-hole and out at the other. Looking past that mad helmsman, who was shaking the empty rifle and yelling at the shore, I saw vague forms of men running bent double, leaping, gliding, distinct, incomplete, evanescent. Something big appeared in the air before the shutter, the rifle went overboard, and the man stepped back swiftly, looked at me over his shoulder in an extraordinary, profound, familiar manner, and fell upon my feet. The side of his head hit the wheel twice, and the end of what appeared a long cane clattered round and knocked over a little camp-stool. It looked as though after wrenching that thing from somebody ashore he had lost his balance in the effort. The thin smoke had blown away, we were clear of the snag, and looking ahead I could see that in another hundred yards or so I would be free to sheer off, away from the bank; but my feet felt so very warm and wet that I had to look down. The man had rolled on his back and stared straight up at me; both his hands clutched that cane. It was the shaft of a spear that, either thrown or lunged through the opening, had caught him in the side just below the ribs; the blade had gone in out of sight, after making a frightful gash; my shoes were full; a pool of blood lay very still, gleaming dark-red under the wheel; his eyes shone with an amazing lustre. The fusillade burst out again. He looked at me anxiously, gripping the spear like something precious, with an air of being afraid I would try to take it away from him. I had to make an effort to free my eyes from his gaze and attend to the steering. With one hand I felt above my head for the line of the steam whistle, and jerked out screech after screech hurriedly. The tumult of angry and warlike yells was checked instantly, and then from the depths of the woods went out such a tremulous and prolonged wail of mournful fear and utter despair as may be imagined to follow the flight of the last hope from the earth. There was a great commotion in the bush; the shower of arrows stopped, a few dropping shots rang out sharply — then silence, in which the languid beat of the sternwheel came plainly to my ears. I put the helm hard a-starboard at the moment when the pilgrim in pink pyjamas, very hot and agitated, appeared in the doorway. 'The manager sends me ——— ' he began in an official tone, and stopped short. 'Good God!' he said, glaring at the wounded man.

"We two whites stood over him, and his lustrous and inquiring glance enveloped us both. I declare it looked as though he would presently put to us some question in an understandable language; but he died without uttering a sound, without moving a limb, without twitching a muscle. Only in the very last moment, as though in response to some sign we could not see, to some whisper we could not hear, he frowned heavily, and that frown gave to his black death-mask an inconceivably sombre, brooding, and menacing expression. The lustre of inquiring glance faded swiftly into vacant glassiness. 'Can you steer?' I asked the agent eagerly. He looked very dubious; but I made a grab at his arm, and he understood at once I meant him to steer whether or no. To tell you the truth, I was morbidly anxious to change my shoes and socks. 'He is dead,' murmured the fellow, immensely impressed. 'No doubt about it,' said I, tugging like mad at the shoe-laces. 'And by the way, I suppose Mr. Kurtz is dead as well by this time.'

"For the moment that was the dominant thought. There was a sense of extreme disappointment, as though I had found out I had been striving after something altogether without a substance. I couldn't have been more disgusted if I had travelled all this way for the sole purpose of talking with Mr. Kurtz. Talking with . . . I flung one shoe overboard, and became aware that that was exactly what I had been looking forward to — a talk with Kurtz. I made the strange discovery that I had never imagined him as doing, you know, but as discoursing. I didn't say to myself, 'Now I will never see him,' or 'Now I will never shake him by the hand,' but, 'Now I will never hear him.' The man presented himself as a voice. Not of course that I did not connect him with some sort of action. Hadn't I been told in all the tones of jealousy and admiration that he had collected, bartered, swindled, or stolen more ivory than all the other agents together? That was not the point. The point was in his being a gifted creature, and that of all his gifts the one that stood out preeminently, that carried with it a sense of real presence, was his ability to talk, his words — the gift of expression, the bewildering, the illuminating, the most exalted and the most contemptible, the pulsating stream of light, or the deceitful flow from the heart of an impenetrable darkness.

"The other shoe went flying unto the devil-god of that river. I thought, By Jove! it's all over. We are too late; he has vanished — the gift has vanished, by means of some spear, arrow, or club. I will never hear that chap speak after all — and my sorrow had a startling extravagance of emotion, even such as I had noticed in the howling sorrow of these savages in the bush. I couldn't have felt more of lonely desolation somehow, had I been robbed of a belief or had missed my destiny in life. . . . Why do you sigh in this beastly way, somebody? Absurd? Well, absurd. Good Lord! mustn't a man ever —— Here, give me some tobacco." . . .

There was a pause of profound stillness, then a match flared, and Marlow's lean face appeared, worn, hollow, with downward folds and dropped eyelids, with an aspect of concentrated attention; and as he took vigorous draws at his pipe, it seemed to retreat and advance out of the night in the regular flicker of the tiny flame. The match went out.

"Absurd!" he cried. "This is the worst of trying to tell . . . Here you all are, each moored with two good addresses, like a hulk with two anchors, a butcher round one corner, a policeman round another, excellent appetites, and temperature normal — you hear — normal from year's end to year's end. And you say, Absurd! Absurd be — exploded! Absurd! My dear boys, what can you expect from a man who out of sheer nervousness had just flung overboard a pair of new shoes? Now I think of it, it is amazing I did not shed tears. I am, upon the whole, proud of my fortitude. I was cut to the quick at the idea of having lost the inestimable privilege of listening to the gifted Kurtz. Of course I was wrong. The privilege was waiting for me. Oh yes, I heard more than enough. And I was right, too. A voice. He was very little more than a voice. And I heard — him — it — this voice — other voices — all of them were so little more than voices — and the memory of that time itself lingers around me, impalpable, like a dying vibration of one immense jabber, silly, atrocious, sordid, savage, or simply mean, without any kind of sense. Voices, voices — even the girl herself — now —— "

He was silent for a long time.

"I laid the ghost of his gifts at last with a lie," he began suddenly. "Girl! What? Did I mention a girl? Oh, she is out of it — completely. They — the women I mean — are out of it — should be out of it. We must help them to stay in that beautiful world of their own, lest ours gets worse. Oh, she had to be out of it. You should have heard the disinterred body of Mr. Kurtz saying, 'My Intended.' You would have perceived directly then how completely she was out of it. And the lofty frontal bone of Mr. Kurtz! They say the hair goes on growing sometimes, but this — ah — specimen was impressively bald. The wilderness had patted him on the head, and, behold, it was like a ball — an ivory ball; it had caressed him, and — lo! — he had withered; it had taken him, loved him, embraced him, got into his veins, consumed his flesh, and sealed his soul to its own by the inconceivable ceremonies of some devilish initiation. He was its spoiled and pampered favourite. Ivory? I should think so. Heaps of it, stacks of it. The old mud shanty was bursting with it. You would think there was not a single tusk left either above or below the ground in the whole country. 'Mostly fossil,' the manager had remarked disparagingly. It was no more fossil than I am; but they call it fossil when it is dug up. It appears these niggers do bury the tusks sometimes — but evidently they couldn't bury this parcel deep enough to save the gifted Mr. Kurtz from his fate. We filled the steamboat with it, and had to pile a lot on the deck. Thus he could see and enjoy as long as he could see, because the appreciation of this favour had remained with him to the last. You should have heard him say, 'My ivory.' Oh yes, I heard him. 'My Intended, my ivory, my station, my river, my —— ' everything belonged to him. It made me hold my breath in expectation of hearing the wilderness burst into a prodigious peal of laughter that would shake the fixed stars in their places. Everything belonged to him — but that was a trifle. The thing was to know what he belonged to, how many powers of darkness claimed him for their own. That was the reflection that made you creepy all over. It was impossible — it was not good for one either — trying to imagine. He had taken a high seat amongst the devils of the land — I mean literally. You can't understand. How could you? — with solid pavement under your feet, surrounded by kind neighbours ready to cheer you or to fall on you, stepping delicately between the butcher and the policeman, in the holy terror of scandal and gallows and lunatic asylums — how can you imagine what particular region of the first ages a man's untrammelled feet may take him into by the way of solitude — utter solitude without a policeman — by the way of silence — utter silence, where no warning voice of a kind neighbour can be heard whispering of public opinion? These little things make all the great difference. When they are gone you must fall back upon your own innate strength, upon your own capacity for faithfulness. Of course you may be too much of a fool to go wrong — too dull even to know you are being assaulted by the powers of darkness. I take it, no fool ever made a bargain for his soul with the devil: the fool is too much of a fool, or the devil too much of a devil — I don't know which. Or you may be such a thunderingly exalted creature as to be altogether deaf and blind to anything but heavenly sights and sounds. Then the earth for you is only a standing place — and whether to be like this is your loss or your gain I won't pretend to say. But most of us are neither one nor the other. The earth for us is a place to live in, where we must put up with sights, with sounds, with smells, too, by Jove! — breathe dead hippo, so to speak, and not be contaminated. And there, don't you see? your strength comes in, the faith in your ability for the digging of unostentatious holes to bury the stuff in — your power of devotion, not to yourself, but to an obscure, back-breaking business. And that's difficult enough. Mind, I am not trying to excuse or even explain — I am trying to account to myself for — for — Mr. Kurtz — for the shade of Mr. Kurtz. This initiated wraith from the back of Nowhere honoured me with its amazing confidence before it vanished altogether. This was because it could speak English to me. The original Kurtz had been educated partly in England, and — as he was good enough to say himself — his sympathies were in the right place. His mother was half-English, his father was half-French. All Europe contributed to the making of Kurtz; and by and by I learned that, most appropriately, the International Society for the Suppression of Savage Customs had entrusted him with the making of a report, for its future guidance. And he had written it too. I've seen it. I've read it. It was eloquent, vibrating with eloquence, but too high-strung, I think. Seventeen pages of close writing he had found time for! But this must have been before his — let us say — nerves went wrong, and caused him to preside at certain midnight dances ending with unspeakable rites, which — as far as I reluctantly gathered from what I heard at various times — were offered up to him — do you understand? — to Mr. Kurtz himself. But it was a beautiful piece of writing. The opening paragraph, however, in the light of later information, strikes me now as ominous. He began with the argument that we whites, from the point of development we had arrived at, 'must necessarily appear to them [savages] in the nature of supernatural beings — we approach them with the might as of a deity,' and so on, and so on. 'By the simple exercise of our will we can exert a power for good practically unbounded,' etc. etc. From that point he soared and took me with him. The peroration was magnificent, though difficult to remember, you know. It gave me the notion of an exotic Immensity ruled by an august Benevolence. It made me tingle with enthusiasm. This was the unbounded power of eloquence — of words — of burning noble words. There were no practical hints to interrupt the magic current of phrases, unless a kind of note at the foot of the last page, scrawled evidently much later, in an unsteady hand, may be regarded as the exposition of a method. It was very simple, and at the end of that moving appeal to every altruistic sentiment it blazed at you, luminous and terrifying, like a flash of lightning in a serene sky: 'Exterminate all the brutes!' The curious part was that he had apparently forgotten all about that valuable postscriptum, because, later on, when he in a sense came to himself, he repeatedly entreated me to take good care of 'my pamphlet' (he called it), as it was sure to have in the future a good influence upon his career. I had full information about all these things, and, besides, as it turned out, I was to have the care of his memory. I've done enough for it to give me the indisputable right to lay it, if I choose, for an everlasting rest in the dust-bin of progress, amongst all the sweepings and, figuratively speaking, all the dead cats of civilisation. But then, you see, I can't choose. He won't be forgotten. Whatever he was, he was not common. He had the power to charm or frighten rudimentary souls into an aggravated witch-dance in his honour; he could also fill the small souls of the pilgrims with bitter misgivings: he had one devoted friend at least, and he had conquered one soul in the world that was neither rudimentary nor tainted with self-seeking. No; I can't forget him, though I am not prepared to affirm the fellow was exactly worth the life we lost in getting to him. I missed my late helmsman awfully — I missed him even while his body was still lying in the pilot-house. Perhaps you will think it passing strange this regret for a savage who was no more account than a grain of sand in a black Sahara. Well, don't you see, he had done something, he had steered; for months I had him at my back — a help — an instrument. It was a kind of partnership. He steered for me — I had to look after him, I worried about his deficiencies, and thus a subtle bond had been created, of which I only became aware when it was suddenly broken. And the intimate profundity of that look he gave me when he received his hurt remains to this day in my memory — like a claim of distant kinship affirmed in a supreme moment.

"Poor fool! If he had only left that shutter alone. He had no restraint, no restraint — just like Kurtz — a tree swayed by the wind. As soon as I had put on a dry pair of slippers, I dragged him out, after first jerking the spear out of his side, which operation I confess I performed with my eyes shut tight. His heels leaped together over the little doorstep; his shoulders were pressed to my breast; I hugged him from behind desperately. Oh! he was heavy, heavy; heavier than any man on earth, I should imagine. Then without more ado I tipped him overboard. The current snatched him as though he had been a wisp of grass, and I saw the body roll over twice before I lost sight of it for ever. All the pilgrims and the manager were then congregated on the awning-deck about the pilot-house, chattering at each other like a flock of excited magpies, and there was a scandalised murmur at my heartless promptitude. What they wanted to keep that body hanging about for I can't guess. Embalm it, maybe. But I had also heard another, and a very ominous, murmur on the deck below. My friends the wood-cutters were likewise scandalised, and with a better show of reason — though I admit that the reason itself was quite inadmissible. Oh, quite! I had made up my mind that if my late helmsman was to be eaten, the fishes alone should have him. He had been a very second-rate helmsman while alive, but now he was dead he might have become a first-class temptation, and possibly cause some startling trouble. Besides, I was anxious to take the wheel, the man in pink pyjamas showing himself a hopeless duffer at the business.

"This I did directly the simple funeral was over. We were going half-speed, keeping right in the middle of the stream, and I listened to the talk about me. They had given up Kurtz, they had given up the station; Kurtz was dead, and the station had been burnt — and so on, and so on. The red-haired pilgrim was beside himself with the thought that at least this poor Kurtz had been properly revenged. 'Say! We must have made a glorious slaughter of them in the bush. Eh? What do you think? Say?' He positively danced, the bloodthirsty little gingery beggar. And he had nearly fainted when he saw the wounded man! I could not help saying, 'You made a glorious lot of smoke, anyhow.' I had seen, from the way the tops of the bushes rustled and flew, that almost all the shots had gone too high. You can't hit anything unless you take aim and fire from the shoulder; but these chaps fired from the hip with their eyes shut. The retreat, I maintained — and I was right — was caused by the screeching of the steam-whistle. Upon this they forgot Kurtz, and began to howl at me with indignant protests.

"The manager stood by the wheel murmuring confidentially about the necessity of getting well away down the river before dark at all events, when I saw in the distance a clearing on the river-side and the outlines of some sort of building. 'What's this?' I asked. He clapped his hands in wonder. 'The station!' he cried. I edged in at once, still going half-speed.

"Through my glasses I saw the slope of a hill interspersed with rare trees and perfectly free from undergrowth. A long decaying building on the summit was half buried in the high grass; the large holes in the peaked roof gaped black from afar; the jungle and the woods made a background. There was no enclosure or fence of any kind; but there had been one apparently, for near the house half a dozen slim posts remained in a row, roughly trimmed, and with their upper ends ornamented with round carved balls. The rails, or whatever there had been between, had disappeared. Of course the forest surrounded all that. The river-bank was clear, and on the water side I saw a white man under a hat like a cart-wheel beckoning persistently with his whole arm. Examining the edge of the forest above and below, I was almost certain I could see movements — human forms gliding here and there. I steamed past prudently, then stopped the engines and let her drift down. The man on the shore began to shout, urging us to land. 'We have been attacked,' screamed the manager. 'I know — I know. It's all right,' yelled back the other, as cheerful as you please. 'Come along. It's all right. I am glad.'

"His aspect reminded me of something I had seen — something funny I had seen somewhere. As I manœuvred to get alongside, I was asking myself, 'What does this fellow look like?' Suddenly I got it. He looked like a harlequin. His clothes had been made of some stuff that was brown holland probably, but it was covered with patches all over, with bright patches, blue, red, and yellow — patches on the back, patches on the front, patches on elbows, on knees; coloured binding round his jacket, scarlet edging at the bottom of his trousers; and the sunshine made him look extremely gay and wonderfully neat withal, because you could see how beautifully all this patching had been done. A beardless, boyish face, very fair, no features to speak of, nose peeling, little blue eyes, smiles and frowns chasing each other over that open countenance like sunshine and shadow on a wind-swept plain. 'Look out, captain!' he cried; 'there's a snag lodged in here last night.' What! Another snag? I confess I swore shamefully. I had nearly holed my cripple, to finish off that charming trip. The harlequin on the bank turned his little pug-nose up to me. 'You English?' he asked, all smiles. 'Are you?' I shouted from the wheel. The smiles vanished, and he shook his head as if sorry for my disappointment. Then he brightened up. 'Never mind!' he cried encouragingly. 'Are we in time?' I asked. 'He is up there,' he replied, with a toss of the head up the hill, and becoming gloomy all of a sudden. His face was like the autumn sky, overcast one moment and bright the next.

"When the manager, escorted by the pilgrims, all of them armed to the teeth, had gone to the house, this chap came on board. 'I say, I don't like this. These natives are in the bush,' I said. He assured me earnestly it was all right. 'They are simple people,' he added; 'well, I am glad you came. It took me all my time to keep them off.' 'But you said it was all right,' I cried. 'Oh, they meant no harm,' he said; and as

I stared he corrected himself, 'Not exactly.' Then vivaciously, 'My faith, your pilot-house wants a clean-up!' In the next breath he advised me to keep enough steam on the boiler to blow the whistle in case of any trouble. 'One good screech will do more for you than all your rifles. They are simple people,' he repeated. He rattled away at such a rate he quite overwhelmed me. He seemed to be trying to make up for lots of silence, and actually hinted, laughing, that such was the case. 'Don't you talk with Mr. Kurtz?' I said. 'You don't talk with that man — you listen to him,' he exclaimed with severe exaltation. 'But now —— ' He waved his arm, and in the twinkling of an eye was in the uttermost depths of despondency. In a moment he came up again with a jump, possessed himself of both my hands, shook them continuously, while he gabbled: 'Brother sailor . . . honour . . . pleasure . . . delight . . . introduce myself . . . Russian . . . son of an archpriest . . . Government of Tambov . . . What? Tobacco! English tobacco; the excellent English tobacco! Now, that's brotherly. Smoke? Where's a sailor that does not smoke?'

"The pipe soothed him, and gradually I made out he had run away from school, had gone to sea in a Russian ship; ran away again; served some time in English ships; was now reconciled with the arch-priest. He made a point of that. 'But when one is young one must see things, gather experience, ideas; enlarge the mind.' 'Here!' I interrupted. 'You can never tell! Here I met Mr. Kurtz,' he said, youthfully solemn and reproachful. I held my tongue after that. It appears he had persuaded a Dutch trading-house on the coast to fit him out with stores and goods, and had started for the interior with a light heart, and no more idea of what would happen to him than a baby. He had been wandering about that river for nearly two years alone, cut off from everybody and everything. 'I am not so young as I look. I am twenty-five,' he said. 'At first old Van Shuyten would tell me to go to the devil,' he narrated with keen enjoyment; 'but I stuck to him, and talked and talked, till at last he got afraid I would talk the hind-leg off his favourite dog, so he gave me some cheap things and a few guns, and told me he hoped he would never see my face again. Good old Dutchman, Van Shuyten. I sent him one small lot of ivory a year ago, so that he can't call me a little thief when I get back. I hope he got it. And for the rest, I don't care. I had some wood stacked for you. That was my old house. Did you see?'

"I gave him Towson's book. He made as though he would kiss me, but restrained himself. 'The only book I had left, and I thought I had lost it,' he said, looking at it ecstatically. 'So many accidents happen to a man going about alone, you know. Canoes get upset sometimes — and sometimes you've got to clear out so quick when the people get angry.' He thumbed the pages. 'You made notes in Russian?' I asked. He nodded. 'I thought they were written in cipher,' I said. He laughed, then became serious. 'I had lots of trouble to keep these people off,' he said. 'Did they want to kill you?' I asked. 'Oh no!' he cried, and checked himself. 'Why did they attack us?' I pursued. He hesitated, then said shamefacedly, 'They don't want him to go.' 'Don't they?' I said curiously. He nodded a nod full of mystery and wisdom. 'I tell you,' he cried, 'this man has enlarged my mind.' He opened his arms wide, staring at me with his little blue eyes that were perfectly round."

III

"I looked at him, lost in astonishment. There he was before me, in motley, as though he had absconded from a troupe of mimes, enthusiastic, fabulous. His very existence was improbable, inexplicable, and altogether bewildering. He was an insoluble problem. It was inconceivable how he had existed, how he had succeeded in getting so far, how he had managed to remain — why he did not instantly disappear. 'I went a little farther,' he said, 'then still a little farther — till I had gone so far that I don't know how I'll ever get back. Never mind. Plenty time. I can manage. You take Kurtz away quick — quick — I tell you.' The glamour of youth enveloped his parti-coloured rags, his destitution, his loneliness, the essential desolation of his futile wanderings. For months — for years — his life hadn't been worth a day's purchase; and there he was gallantly, thoughtlessly alive, to all appearance indestructible solely by the virtue of his few years and of his unreflecting audacity. I was seduced into something like admiration — like envy. Glamour urged him on, glamour kept him unscathed. He surely wanted nothing from the wilderness but space to breathe in and to push on through. His need was to exist, and to move onwards at the greatest possible risk, and with a maximum of privation. If the absolutely pure, uncalculating, unpractical spirit of adventure had ever ruled a human being, it ruled this be-patched youth. I almost envied him the possession of this modest and clear flame. It seemed to have consumed all thought of self so completely, that, even while he was talking to you, you forgot that it was he — the man before your eyes — who had gone through these things. I did not envy him his devotion to Kurtz, though. He had not meditated over it. It came to him, and he accepted it with a sort of eager fatalism. I must say that to me it appeared about the most dangerous thing in every way he had come upon so far.

"They had come together unavoidably, like two ships becalmed near each other, and lay rubbing sides at last. I suppose Kurtz wanted an audience, because on a certain occasion, when encamped in the forest, they had talked all night, or more probably Kurtz had talked. 'We talked of everything,' he said, quite transported at the recollection. 'I forgot there was such a thing as sleep. The night did not seem to last an hour. Everything! Everything! . . . Of love too.' 'Ah, he talked to you of love!' I said, much amused. 'It isn't what you think,' he cried, almost passionately. 'It was in general. He made me see things — things.'

"He threw his arms up. We were on deck at the time, and the head-man of my wood-cutters, lounging near by, turned upon him his heavy and glittering eyes. I looked around, and I don't know why, but I assure you that never, never before, did this land, this river, this jungle, the very arch of this blazing sky, appear to me so hopeless and so dark, so impenetrable to human thought, so pitiless to human weakness. 'And, ever since, you have been with him, of course?' I said.

"On the contrary. It appears their intercourse had been very much broken by various causes. He had, as he informed me proudly, managed to nurse Kurtz through two illnesses (he alluded to it as you would to some risky feat), but as a rule Kurtz wandered alone, far in the depths of the forest. 'Very often coming to this station, I had to wait days and days before he would turn up,' he said. 'Ah, it was worth waiting for! — sometimes.' 'What was he doing? exploring or what?' I asked. 'Oh yes, of course'; he had discovered lots of villages, a lake too — he did not know exactly in what direction; it was dangerous to inquire too much — but mostly his expeditions had been for ivory. 'But he had no goods to trade with by that time,' I objected. 'There's a good lot of cartridges left even yet,' he answered, looking away. 'To speak plainly, he raided the country,' I said. He nodded. 'Not alone, surely!' He muttered something about the villages round that lake. 'Kurtz got the tribe to follow him, did he?' I suggested. He fidgeted a little. 'They adored him,' he said. The tone of these words was so extraordinary that I looked at him searchingly. It was curious to see his mingled eagerness and reluctance to speak of Kurtz. The man filled his life, occupied his thoughts, swayed his emotions. 'What can you expect?' he burst out; 'he came to them with thunder and lightning, you know — and they had never seen anything like it — and very terrible. He could be very terrible. You can't judge Mr. Kurtz as you would an ordinary man. No, no, no! Now — just to give you an idea — I don't mind telling you,

he wanted to shoot me too one day — but I don't judge him.' 'Shoot
you!' I cried. 'What for?' 'Well, I had a small lot of ivory the chief of
that village near my house gave me. You see I used to shoot game for
them. Well, he wanted it, and wouldn't hear reason. He declared he
would shoot me unless I gave him the ivory and then cleared out of
the country, because he could do so, and had a fancy for it, and there
was nothing on earth to prevent him killing whom he jolly well pleased.
And it was true too. I gave him the ivory. What did I care! But I didn't
clear out. No, no. I couldn't leave him. I had to be careful, of course,
till we got friendly again for a time. He had his second illness then.
Afterwards I had to keep out of the way; but I didn't mind. He was
living for the most part in those villages on the lake. When he came
down to the river, sometimes he would take to me, and sometimes
it was better for me to be careful. This man suffered too much. He
hated all this, and somehow he couldn't get away. When I had a chance
I begged him to try and leave while there was time; I offered to go back
with him. And he would say yes, and then he would remain; go off
on another ivory hunt; disappear for weeks; forget himself amongst
these people — forget himself — you know.' 'Why! he's mad,' I said.
He protested indignantly. Mr. Kurtz couldn't be mad. If I had heard
him talk, only two days ago, I wouldn't dare hint at such a thing. . . .
I had taken up my binoculars while we talked, and was looking at the
shore, sweeping the limit of the forest at each side and at the back
of the house. The consciousness of there being people in that bush,
so silent, so quiet — as silent and quiet as the ruined house on the
hill — made me uneasy. There was no sign on the face of nature of
this amazing tale that was not so much told as suggested to me in desolate exclamations, completed by shrugs, in interrupted phrases, in hints
ending in deep sighs. The woods were unmoved, like a mask — heavy,
like the closed door of a prison — they looked with their air of hidden knowledge, of patient expectation, of unapproachable silence. The
Russian was explaining to me that it was only lately that Mr. Kurtz had
come down to the river, bringing along with him all the fighting men
of that lake tribe. He had been absent for several months — getting
himself adored, I suppose — and had come down unexpectedly, with
the intention to all appearance of making a raid either across the river
or down stream. Evidently the appetite for more ivory had got the better of the — what shall I say? — less material aspirations. However, he
had got much worse suddenly. 'I heard he was lying helpless, and so
I came up — took my chance,' said the Russian. 'Oh, he is bad, very
bad.' I directed my glass to the house. There were no signs of life, but

there were the ruined roof, the long mud wall peeping above the grass, with three little square window-holes, no two of the same size; all this brought within reach of my hand, as it were. And then I made a brusque movement, and one of the remaining posts of that vanished fence leaped up in the field of my glass. You remember I told you I had been struck at the distance by certain attempts at ornamentation, rather remarkable in the ruinous aspect of the place. Now I had suddenly a nearer view, and its first result was to make me throw my head back as if before a blow. Then I went carefully from post to post with my glass, and I saw my mistake. These round knobs were not ornamental but symbol-ic; they were expressive and puzzling, striking and disturbing — food for thought and also for vultures if there had been any looking down from the sky; but at all events for such ants as were industrious enough to ascend the pole. They would have been even more impressive, those heads on the stakes, if their faces had not been turned to the house. Only one, the first I had made out, was facing my way. I was not so shocked as you may think. The start back I had given was really nothing but a movement of surprise. I had expected to see a knob of wood there, you know. I returned deliberately to the first I had seen — and there it was, black, dried, sunken, with closed eyelids — a head that seemed to sleep at the top of that pole, and, with the shrunken dry lips showing a narrow white line of the teeth, was smiling too, smiling continuously at some endless and jocose dream of that eternal slumber.

"I am not disclosing any trade secrets. In fact the manager said afterwards that Mr. Kurtz's methods had ruined the district. I have no opinion on that point, but I want you clearly to understand that there was nothing exactly profitable in these heads being there. They only showed that Mr. Kurtz lacked restraint in the gratification of his various lusts, that there was something wanting in him — some small matter which, when the pressing need arose, could not be found under his magnificent eloquence. Whether he knew of this deficiency himself I can't say. I think the knowledge came to him at last — only at the very last. But the wilderness had found him out early, and had tak-en on him a terrible vengeance for the fantastic invasion. I think it had whispered to him things about himself which he did not know, things of which he had no conception till he took counsel with this great solitude — and the whisper had proved irresistibly fascinating. It echoed loudly within him because he was hollow at the core. . . . I put down the glass, and the head that had appeared near enough to be spoken to seemed at once to have leaped away from me into inaccessible distance.

"The admirer of Mr. Kurtz was a bit crestfallen. In a hurried, indistinct voice he began to assure me he had not dared to take these — say, symbols — down. He was not afraid of the natives; they would not stir till Mr. Kurtz gave the word. His ascendancy was extraordinary. The camps of these people surrounded the place, and the chiefs came every day to see him. They would crawl . . . 'I don't want to know anything of the ceremonies used when approaching Mr. Kurtz,' I shouted. Curious, this feeling that came over me that such details would be more intolerable than those heads drying on the stakes under Mr. Kurtz's windows. After all, that was only a savage sight, while I seemed at one bound to have been transported into some lightless region of subtle horrors, where pure, uncomplicated savagery was a positive relief, being something that had a right to exist — obviously — in the sunshine. The young man looked at me with surprise. I suppose it did not occur to him that Mr. Kurtz was no idol of mine. He forgot I hadn't heard any of these splendid monologues on, what was it? on love, justice, conduct of life — or what not. If it had come to crawling before Mr. Kurtz, he crawled as much as the veriest savage of them all. I had no idea of the conditions, he said: these heads were the heads of rebels. I shocked him excessively by laughing. Rebels! What would be the next definition I was to hear? There had been enemies, criminals, workers — and these were rebels. Those rebellious heads looked very subdued to me on their sticks. 'You don't know how such a life tries a man like Kurtz,' cried Kurtz's last disciple. 'Well, and you?' I said. 'I! I! I am a simple man. I have no great thoughts. I want nothing from anybody. How can you compare me to . . . ?' His feelings were too much for speech, and suddenly he broke down. 'I don't understand,' he groaned. 'I've been doing my best to keep him alive, and that's enough. I had no hand in all this. I have no abilities. There hasn't been a drop of medicine or a mouthful of invalid food for months here. He was shamefully abandoned. A man like this, with such ideas. Shamefully! Shamefully! I — I — haven't slept for the last ten nights. . . .'

"His voice lost itself in the calm of the evening. The long shadows of the forests had slipped downhill while we talked, had gone far beyond the ruined hovel, beyond the symbolic row of stakes. All this was in the gloom, while we down there were yet in the sunshine, and the stretch of the river abreast of the clearing glittered in a still and dazzling splendour, with a murky and overshadowed bend above and below. Not a living soul was seen on the shore. The bushes did not rustle.

"Suddenly round the corner of the house a group of men appeared, as though they had come up from the ground. They waded waist-deep in the grass, in a compact body, bearing an improvised stretcher in their midst. Instantly, in the emptiness of the landscape, a cry arose whose shrillness pierced the still air like a sharp arrow flying straight to the very heart of the land; and, as if by enchantment, streams of human beings — of naked human beings — with spears in their hands, with bows, with shields, with wild glances and savage movements, were poured into the clearing by the dark-faced and pensive forest. The bushes shook, the grass swayed for a time, and then everything stood still in attentive immobility.

"'Now, if he does not say the right thing to them we are all done for,' said the Russian at my elbow. The knot of men with the stretcher had stopped too, half-way to the steamer, as if petrified. I saw the man on the stretcher sit up, lank and with an uplifted arm, above the shoulders of the bearers. 'Let us hope that the man who can talk so well of love in general will find some particular reason to spare us this time,' I said. I resented bitterly the absurd danger of our situation, as if to be at the mercy of that atrocious phantom had been a dishonouring necessity. I could not hear a sound, but through my glasses I saw the thin arm extended commandingly, the lower jaw moving, the eyes of that apparition shining darkly far in its bony head that nodded with grotesque jerks. Kurtz — Kurtz — that means 'short' in German — don't it? Well, the name was as true as everything else in his life — and death. He looked at least seven feet long. His covering had fallen off, and his body emerged from it pitiful and appalling as from a winding-sheet. I could see the cage of his ribs all astir, the bones of his arm waving. It was as though an animated image of death carved out of old ivory had been shaking its hand with menaces at a motionless crowd of men made of dark and glittering bronze. I saw him open his mouth wide — it gave him a weirdly voracious aspect, as though he had wanted to swallow all the air, all the earth, all the men before him. A deep voice reached me faintly. He must have been shouting. He fell back suddenly. The stretcher shook as the bearers staggered forward again, and almost at the same time I noticed that the crowd of savages was vanishing without any perceptible movement of retreat, as if the forest that had ejected these beings so suddenly had drawn them in again as the breath is drawn in a long aspiration.

"Some of the pilgrims behind the stretcher carried his arms — two shot-guns, a heavy rifle, and a light revolver-carbine — the thunderbolts of that pitiful Jupiter. The manager bent over him murmuring as he walked beside his head. They laid him down in one of the little cabins — just a room for a bed-place and a camp-stool or two, you know.

We had brought his belated correspondence, and a lot of torn envelopes and open letters littered his bed. His hand roamed feebly amongst these papers. I was struck by the fire of his eyes and the composed languor of his expression. It was not so much the exhaustion of disease. He did not seem in pain. This shadow looked satiated and calm, as though for the moment it had had its fill of all the emotions.

"He rustled one of the letters, and looking straight in my face said, 'I am glad.' Somebody had been writing to him about me. These special recommendations were turning up again. The volume of tone he emitted without effort, almost without the trouble of moving his lips, amazed me. A voice! a voice! It was grave, profound, vibrating, while the man did not seem capable of a whisper. However, he had enough strength in him — factitious no doubt — to very nearly make an end of us, as you shall hear directly.

"The manager appeared silently in the doorway; I stepped out at once and he drew the curtain after me. The Russian, eyed curiously by the pilgrims, was staring at the shore. I followed the direction of his glance.

"Dark human shapes could be made out in the distance, flitting indistinctly against the gloomy border of the forest, and near the river two bronze figures, leaning on tall spears, stood in the sunlight under fantastic head-dresses of spotted skins, warlike and still in statuesque repose. And from right to left along the lighted shore moved a wild and gorgeous apparition of a woman.

"She walked with measured steps, draped in striped and fringed cloths, treading the earth proudly, with a slight jingle and flash of barbarous ornaments. She carried her head high; her hair was done in the shape of a helmet; she had brass leggings to the knee, brass wire gauntlets to the elbow, a crimson spot on her tawny cheek, innumerable necklaces of glass beads on her neck; bizarre things, charms, gifts of witch-men, that hung about her, glittered and trembled at every step. She must have had the value of several elephant tusks upon her. She was savage and superb, wild-eyed and magnificent; there was something ominous and stately in her deliberate progress. And in the hush that had fallen suddenly upon the whole sorrowful land, the immense wilderness, the colossal body of the fecund and mysterious life seemed to look at her, pensive, as though it had been looking at the image of its own tenebrous and passionate soul.

"She came abreast of the steamer, stood still, and faced us. Her long shadow fell to the water's edge. Her face had a tragic and fierce aspect of wild sorrow and of dumb pain mingled with the fear of some struggling, half-shaped resolve. She stood looking at us without a stir, and like the wilderness itself, with an air of brooding over an inscrutable purpose. A whole minute passed, and then she made a step forward. There was a low jingle, a glint of yellow metal, a sway of fringed draperies, and she stopped as if her heart had failed her. The young fellow by my side growled. The pilgrims murmured at my back. She looked at us all as if her life had depended upon the unswerving steadiness of her glance. Suddenly she opened her bared arms and threw them up rigid above her head, as though in an uncontrollable desire to touch the sky, and at the same time the swift shadows darted out on the earth, swept around on the river, gathering the steamer in a shadowy embrace. A formidable silence hung over the scene.

"She turned away slowly, walked on, following the bank, and passed into the bushes to the left. Once only her eyes gleamed back at us in the dusk of the thickets before she disappeared.

" 'If she had offered to come aboard I really think I would have tried to shoot her,' said the man of patches nervously. 'I had been risking my life every day for the last fortnight to keep her out of the house. She got in one day and kicked up a row about those miserable rags I picked up in the storeroom to mend my clothes with. I wasn't decent. At least it must have been that, for she talked like a fury to Kurtz for an hour, pointing at me now and then. I don't understand the dialect of this tribe. Luckily for me, I fancy Kurtz felt too ill that day to care, or there would have been mischief. I don't understand. . . . No — it's too much for me. Ah, well, it's all over now.'

"At this moment I heard Kurtz's deep voice behind the curtain: 'Save me! — save the ivory, you mean. Don't tell me. Save *me*! Why, I've had to save you. You are interrupting my plans now. Sick! Sick! Not so sick as you would like to believe. Never mind. I'll carry my ideas out yet — I will return. I'll show you what can be done. You with your little peddling notions — you are interfering with me. I will return. I . . .'

"The manager came out. He did me the honour to take me under the arm and lead me aside. 'He is very low, very low,' he said. He considered it necessary to sigh, but neglected to be consistently sorrowful. 'We have done all we could for him — haven't we? But there is no disguising the fact, Mr. Kurtz has done more harm than good to the Company. He did not see the time was not ripe for vigorous action. Cautiously, cautiously — that's my principle. We must be cautious yet. The district is closed to us for a time. Deplorable! Upon the whole, the trade will suffer. I don't deny there is a remarkable quantity of ivory — mostly fossil. We must save it, at all events — but look how precarious the position is — and why? Because the method is unsound.' 'Do you,' said I, looking at the shore, 'call it "unsound method"?' 'Without doubt,' he exclaimed hotly. 'Don't you?' . . . 'No method at all,' I murmured after a while. 'Exactly,' he exulted. 'I anticipated this. Shows a complete want of judgment. It is my duty to point it out in the proper quarter.' 'Oh,' said I, 'that fellow — what's his name? — the brickmaker, will make a readable report for you.' He appeared confounded for a moment. It seemed to me I had never breathed an atmosphere so vile, and I turned mentally to Kurtz for relief — positively for relief. 'Nevertheless, I think Mr. Kurtz is a remarkable man,' I said with emphasis. He started, dropped on me a cold heavy glance, said very quietly, 'He *was*,' and turned his back on me. My hour of favour was over; I found myself lumped along with Kurtz as a partisan of methods for which the time was not ripe: I was unsound! Ah! but it was something to have at least a choice of nightmares.

"I had turned to the wilderness really, not to Mr. Kurtz, who, I was ready to admit, was as good as buried. And for a moment it seemed to me as if I also were buried in a vast grave full of unspeakable secrets. I felt an intolerable weight oppressing my breast, the smell of the damp earth, the unseen presence of victorious corruption, the darkness of an impenetrable night. . . . The Russian tapped me on the shoulder. I heard him mumbling and stammering something about 'brother seaman — couldn't conceal — knowledge of matters that would affect Mr. Kurtz's reputation.' I waited. For him evidently Mr. Kurtz was not in his grave; I suspect that for him Mr. Kurtz was one of the immortals. 'Well!' said I at last, 'speak out. As it happens, I am Mr. Kurtz's friend — in a way.'

"He stated with a good deal of formality that had we not been 'of the same profession,' he would have kept the matter to himself without regard to consequences. He suspected 'there was an active ill-will towards him on the part of these white men that ——' ' You are right,' I said, remembering a certain conversation I had overheard. 'The manager thinks you ought to be hanged.' He showed a concern at this intelligence which amused me at first. 'I had better get out of the way quietly,' he said earnestly. 'I can do no more for Kurtz now, and they would soon find some excuse. What's to stop them? There's a military post three hundred miles from here.' 'Well, upon my word,' said I, 'perhaps you had better go if you have any friends amongst the savages near by.' 'Plenty,' he said. 'They are simple people — and I want nothing, you know.' He stood biting his lip, then: 'I don't want any harm to happen to these whites here, but of course I was thinking of Mr. Kurtz's reputation — but you are a brother seaman and —— ' 'All right,' said I, after a time. 'Mr. Kurtz's reputation is safe with me.' I did not know how truly I spoke.

"He informed me, lowering his voice, that it was Kurtz who had ordered the attack to be made on the steamer. 'He hated sometimes the idea of being taken away — and then again . . . But I don't understand these matters. I am a simple man. He thought it would scare you away — that you would give it up, thinking him dead. I could not stop him. Oh, I had an awful time of it this last month.' 'Very well,' I said. 'He is all right now.' 'Ye-e-es,' he muttered, not very convinced apparently. 'Thanks,' said I; 'I shall keep my eyes open.' 'But quiet — eh?' he urged anxiously. 'It would be awful for his reputation if anybody here — ' I promised a complete discretion with great gravity. 'I have a canoe and three black fellows waiting not very far. I am off. Could you give me a few Martini-Henry cartridges?' I could, and did, with proper secrecy. He helped himself, with a wink at me, to a handful of my tobacco. 'Between sailors — you know — good English tobacco.' At the door of the pilot-house he turned round — 'I say, haven't you a pair of shoes you could spare?' He raised one leg. 'Look.' The soles were tied with knotted strings sandal-wise under his bare feet. I rooted out an old pair, at which he looked with admiration before tucking it under his left arm. One of his pockets (bright red) was bulging with cartridges, from the other (dark blue) peeped 'Towson's Inquiry,' etc. etc. He seemed to think himself excellently well equipped for a renewed encounter with the wilderness. 'Ah! I'll never, never meet such a man again. You ought to have heard him recite poetry — his own too it was, he told me. Poetry!' He rolled his eyes at the recollection of these delights. 'Oh, he enlarged my mind!' 'Good-bye,' said I. He shook hands and vanished in the night. Sometimes I ask myself whether I had ever really seen him — whether it was possible to meet such a phenomenon! . . .

"When I woke up shortly after midnight his warning came to my mind with its hint of danger that seemed, in the starred darkness, real enough to make me get up for the purpose of having a look round. On the hill a big fire burned, illuminating fitfully a crooked corner of the station-house. One of the agents with a picket of a few of our blacks, armed for the purpose, was keeping guard over the ivory; but deep within the forest, red gleams that wavered, that seemed to sink and rise from the ground amongst confused columnar shapes of intense blackness, showed the exact position of the camp where Mr. Kurtz's adorers were keeping their uneasy vigil. The monotonous beating of a big drum filled the air with muffled shocks and a lingering vibration. A steady droning sound of many men chanting each to himself some weird incantation came out from the black, flat wall of the woods as the humming of bees comes out of a hive, and had a strange narcotic effect upon my half-awake senses. I believe I dozed off leaning over the rail, till an abrupt burst of yells, an overwhelming outbreak of a pent-up and mysterious frenzy, woke me up in a bewildered wonder. It was cut short all at once, and the low droning went on with an effect of audible and soothing silence. I glanced casually into the little cabin. A light was burning within, but Mr. Kurtz was not there.

"I think I would have raised an outcry if I had believed my eyes. But I didn't believe them at first — the thing seemed so impossible. The fact is, I was completely unnerved by a sheer blank fright, pure abstract terror, unconnected with any distinct shape of physical danger. What made this emotion so overpowering was — how shall I define it? — the moral shock I received, as if something altogether monstrous, intolerable to thought and odious to the soul, had been thrust upon me unexpectedly. This lasted of course the merest fraction of a second, and then the usual sense of commonplace, deadly danger, the possibility of a sudden onslaught and massacre, or something of the kind, which I saw impending, was positively welcome and composing. It pacified me, in fact, so much, that I did not raise an alarm.

"There was an agent buttoned up inside an ulster and sleeping on a chair on deck within three feet of me. The yells had not awakened him; he snored very slightly; I left him to his slumbers and leaped ashore. I did not betray Mr. Kurtz — it was ordered I should never betray him — it was written I should be loyal to the nightmare of my choice. I was anxious to deal with this shadow by myself alone — and to this day I don't know why I was so jealous of sharing with any one the peculiar blackness of that experience.

"As soon as I got on the bank I saw a trail — a broad trail through the grass. I remember the exultation with which I said to myself, 'He can't walk — he is crawling on all-fours — I've got him.' The grass was wet with dew. I strode rapidly with clenched fists. I fancy I had some vague notion of falling upon him and giving him a drubbing. I don't know. I had some imbecile thoughts. The knitting old woman with the cat obtruded herself upon my memory as a most improper person to be sitting at the other end of such an affair. I saw a row of pilgrims squirting lead in the air out of Winchesters held to the hip. I thought I would never get back to the steamer, and imagined myself living alone and unarmed in the woods to an advanced age. Such silly things — you know. And I remember I confounded the beat of the drum with the beating of my heart, and was pleased at its calm regularity.

"I kept to the track though — then stopped to listen. The night was very clear; a dark blue space, sparkling with dew and starlight, in which black things stood very still. I thought I could see a kind of motion ahead of me. I was strangely cocksure of everything that night. I actually left the track and ran in a wide semicircle (I verily believe chuckling to myself) so as to get in front of that stir, of that motion I had seen — if indeed I had seen anything. I was circumventing Kurtz as though it had been a boyish game.

"I came upon him, and, if he had not heard me coming, I would have fallen over him too, but he got up in time. He rose, unsteady, long, pale, indistinct, like a vapour exhaled by the earth, and swayed slightly, misty and silent before me; while at my back the fires loomed between the trees, and the murmur of many voices issued from the forest. I had cut him off cleverly; but when actually confronting him I seemed to come to my senses, I saw the danger in its right proportion. It was by no means over yet. Suppose he began to shout? Though he could hardly stand, there was still plenty of vigour in his voice. 'Go away — hide yourself,' he said, in that profound tone. It was very awful. I glanced back. We were within thirty yards from the nearest fire. A black figure stood up, strode on long black legs, waving long black arms, across the glow. It had horns — antelope horns, I think — on its head. Some sorcerer, some witch-man, no doubt: it looked fiend-like enough. 'Do you know what you are doing?' I whispered. 'Perfectly,' he answered, raising his voice for that single word: it sounded to me far off and yet loud, like a hail through a speaking-trumpet. If he makes a row we are lost, I thought to myself. This clearly was not a case for fisticuffs, even apart from the very natural aversion I had to beat that Shadow — this wandering and tormented thing. 'You will be lost,' I said — 'utterly lost.' One gets sometimes such a flash of inspiration, you know. I did say the right thing, though indeed he could not have been more irretrievably lost than he was at this very moment, when the foundations of our intimacy were being laid — to endure — to endure — even to the end — even beyond.

" 'I had immense plans,' he muttered irresolutely. 'Yes,' said I; 'but if you try to shout I'll smash your head with ——— ' There was not a stick or a stone near. 'I will throttle you for good,' I corrected myself. 'I was on the threshold of great things,' he pleaded, in a voice of longing, with a wistfulness of tone that made my blood run cold. 'And now for this stupid scoundrel ——— ' 'Your success in Europe is assured in any case,' I affirmed steadily. I did not want to have the throttling of him, you understand — and indeed it would have been very little use for any practical purpose. I tried to break the spell — the heavy, mute spell of the wilderness — that seemed to draw him to its pitiless breast by the awakening of forgotten and brutal instincts, by the memory of gratified and monstrous passions. This alone, I was convinced, had driven him out to the edge of the forest, to the bush, towards the gleam of fires, the throb of drums, the drone of weird incantations; this alone had beguiled his unlawful soul beyond the bounds of permitted aspirations. And, don't you see, the terror of the position was not in being knocked on the head — though I had a very lively sense of that danger too — but in this, that I had to deal with a being to whom I could not appeal in the name of anything high or low. I had, even like the niggers, to invoke him — himself — his own exalted and incredible degradation. There was nothing either above or below him, and I knew it. He had kicked himself loose of the earth. Confound the man! he had kicked the very earth to pieces. He was alone, and I before him did not know whether I stood on the ground or floated in the air. I've been telling you what we said — repeating the phrases we pronounced — but what's the good? They were common everyday words — the familiar, vague sounds exchanged on every waking day of life. But what of that? They had behind them, to my mind, the terrific suggestiveness of words heard in dreams, of phrases spoken in nightmares. Soul! If anybody had ever struggled with a soul, I am the man. And I wasn't arguing with a lunatic either. Believe me or not, his intelligence was perfectly clear — concentrated, it is true, upon himself with horrible intensity, yet clear; and therein was my only chance — barring, of course, the killing him there and then, which wasn't so good, on account of unavoidable noise. But his soul was mad. Being alone in the wilderness, it had looked within itself, and, by Heavens! I tell you, it had gone mad. I had — for my sins, I suppose, to go through the ordeal of looking into it myself. No eloquence could have been so withering to one's belief in mankind as his final burst of sincerity. He struggled with himself too. I saw it — I heard it. I saw the inconceivable mystery of a soul that knew no restraint, no faith, and no fear, yet struggling blindly with itself. I kept my head pretty well; but when I had him at last stretched on the couch, I wiped my forehead, while my legs shook under me as though I had carried half a ton on my back down that hill. And yet I had only supported him, his bony arm clasped round my neck — and he was not much heavier than a child.

"When next day we left at noon, the crowd, of whose presence behind the curtain of trees I had been acutely conscious all the time, flowed out of the woods again, filled the clearing, covered the slope with a mass of naked, breathing, quivering, bronze bodies. I steamed up a bit, then swung downstream, and two thousand eyes followed the evolutions of the splashing, thumping, fierce river-demon beating the water with its terrible tail and breathing black smoke into the air. In front of the first rank, along the river, three men, plastered with bright red earth from head to foot, strutted to and fro restlessly. When we came abreast again, they faced the river, stamped their feet, nodded their horned heads, swayed their scarlet bodies; they shook towards the fierce river-demon a bunch of black feathers, a mangy skin with a pendent tail — something that looked like a dried gourd; they shouted periodically together strings of amazing words that resembled no sounds of human language; and the deep murmurs of the crowd, interrupted suddenly, were like the responses of some satanic litany.

"We had carried Kurtz into the pilot-house: there was more air there. Lying on the couch, he stared through the open shutter. There was an eddy in the mass of human bodies, and the woman with helmeted head and tawny cheeks rushed out to the very brink of the stream. She put out her hands, shouted something, and all that wild mob took up the shout in a roaring chorus of articulated, rapid, breathless utterance.

" 'Do you understand this?' I asked.

"He kept on looking out past me with fiery, longing eyes, with a mingled expression of wistfulness and hate. He made no answer, but I saw a smile, a smile of indefinable meaning, appear on his colourless lips that a moment after twitched convulsively. 'Do I not?' he said slowly, gasping, as if the words had been torn out of him by a supernatural power.

"I pulled the string of the whistle, and I did this because I saw the pilgrims on deck getting out their rifles with an air of anticipating a jolly lark. At the sudden screech there was a movement of abject terror through that wedged mass of bodies. 'Don't! don't you frighten them away,' cried some one on deck disconsolately. I pulled the string time after time. They broke and ran, they leaped, they crouched, they swerved, they dodged the flying terror of the sound. The three red chaps had fallen flat, face down on the shore, as though they had been shot dead. Only the barbarous and superb woman did not so much as flinch, and stretched tragically her bare arms after us over the sombre and glittering river.

"And then that imbecile crowd down on the deck started their little fun, and I could see nothing more for smoke.

"The brown current ran swiftly out of the heart of darkness, bearing us down towards the sea with twice the speed of our upward progress; and Kurtz's life was running swiftly too, ebbing, ebbing out of his heart into the sea of inexorable time. The manager was very placid, he had no vital anxieties now, he took us both in with a comprehensive and satisfied glance: the 'affair' had come off as well as could be wished. I saw the time approaching when I would be left alone of the party of 'unsound method.' The pilgrims looked upon me with disfavour. I was, so to speak, numbered with the dead. It is strange how I accepted this unforeseen partnership, this choice of nightmares forced upon me in the tenebrous land invaded by these mean and greedy phantoms.

"Kurtz discoursed. A voice! a voice! It rang deep to the very last. It survived his strength to hide in the magnificent folds of eloquence the barren darkness of his heart. Oh, he struggled! he struggled! The wastes of his weary brain were haunted by shadowy images now — images of wealth and fame revolving obsequiously round his unextinguishable gift of noble and lofty expression. My Intended, my station, my career, my ideas — these were the subjects for the occasional utterances of elevated sentiments. The shade of the original Kurtz frequented the bedside of the hollow sham, whose fate it was to be buried presently in the mould of primeval earth. But both the diabolic love and the unearthly hate of the mysteries it had penetrated fought for the possession of that soul satiated with primitive emotions, avid of lying fame, of sham distinction, of all the appearances of success and power.

"Sometimes he was contemptibly childish. He desired to have kings meet him at railway stations on his return from some ghastly Nowhere, where he intended to accomplish great things. 'You show them you have in you something that is really profitable, and then there will be no limits to the recognition of your ability,' he would say. 'Of course you must take care of the motives — right motives — always.' The long reaches that were like one and the same reach, monotonous bends that were exactly alike, slipped past the steamer with their multitude of secular trees looking patiently after this grimy fragment of another world, the forerunner of change, of conquest, of trade, of massacres, of blessings. I looked ahead — piloting. 'Close the shutter,' said Kurtz suddenly one day; 'I can't bear to look at this.' I did so. There was a silence. 'Oh, but I will wring your heart yet!' he cried at the invisible wilderness.

"We broke down — as I had expected — and had to lie up for repairs at the head of an island. This delay was the first thing that shook Kurtz's confidence. One morning he gave me a packet of papers and a photograph — the lot tied together with a shoe-string. 'Keep this for me,' he said. 'This noxious fool' (meaning the manager) 'is capable of prying into my boxes when I am not looking.' In the afternoon I saw him. He was lying on his back with closed eyes, and I withdrew quietly, but I heard him mutter, 'Live rightly, die, die . . .' I listened. There was nothing more. Was he rehearsing some speech in his sleep, or was it a fragment of a phrase from some newspaper article? He had been writing for the papers and meant to do so again, 'for the furthering of my ideas. It's a duty.'

"His was an impenetrable darkness. I looked at him as you peer down at a man who is lying at the bottom of a precipice where the sun never shines. But I had not much time to give him, because I was helping the engine-driver to take to pieces the leaky cylinders, to straighten a bent connecting-rod, and in other such matters. I lived in an infernal mess of rust, filings, nuts, bolts, spanners, hammers, ratchet-drills — things I abominate, because I don't get on with them. I tended the little forge we fortunately had aboard; I toiled wearily in a wretched scrap-heap — unless I had the shakes too bad to stand.

"One evening coming in with a candle I was startled to hear him say a little tremulously, 'I am lying here in the dark waiting for death.' The light was within a foot of his eyes. I forced myself to murmur, 'Oh, nonsense!' and stood over him as if transfixed.

"Anything approaching the change that came over his features I have never seen before, and hope never to see again. Oh, I wasn't touched. I was fascinated. It was as though a veil had been rent. I saw on that ivory face the expression of sombre pride, of ruthless power, of craven terror — of an intense and hopeless despair. Did he live his life again in every detail of desire, temptation, and surrender during that supreme moment of complete knowledge? He cried in a whisper at some image, at some vision — he cried out twice, a cry that was no more than a breath:

" 'The horror! The horror!'

"I blew the candle out and left the cabin. The pilgrims were dining in the mess-room, and I took my place opposite the manager, who lifted his eyes to give me a questioning glance, which I successfully ignored. He leaned back, serene, with that peculiar

smile of his sealing the unexpressed depths of his meanness. A continuous shower of small flies streamed upon the lamp, upon the cloth,
upon our hands and faces. Suddenly the manager's boy put his inso-
lent black head in the doorway, and said in a tone of scathing contempt:

" 'Mistah Kurtz — he dead.'

"All the pilgrims rushed out to see. I remained, and went on
with my dinner. I believe I was considered brutally callous. However,
I did not eat much. There was a lamp in there — light, don't you
know — and outside it was so beastly, beastly dark. I went no more
near the remarkable man who had pronounced a judgment upon the
adventures of his soul on this earth. The voice was gone. What else
had been there? But I am of course aware that next day the pilgrims
buried something in a muddy hole.

"And then they very nearly buried me.

"However, as you see, I did not go to join Kurtz there and
then. I did not. I remained to dream the nightmare out to the end,
and to show my loyalty to Kurtz once more. Destiny. My destiny!
Droll thing life is — that mysterious arrangement of merciless logic for
a futile purpose. The most you can hope from it is some knowledge of
yourself — that comes too late — a crop of unextinguishable regrets.
I have wrestled with death. It is the most unexciting contest you can
imagine. It takes place in an impalpable greyness, with nothing underfoot, with nothing around, without spectators, without clamour, without glory, without the great desire of victory, without the great fear of
defeat, in a sickly atmosphere of tepid scepticism, without much belief
in your own right, and still less in that of your adversary. If such is the
form of ultimate wisdom, then life is a greater riddle than some of us
think it to be. I was within a hair's-breadth of the last opportunity for
pronouncement, and I found with humiliation that probably I would
have nothing to say. This is the reason why I affirm that Kurtz was
a remarkable man. He had something to say. He said it. Since I
had peeped over the edge myself, I understand better the meaning
of his stare, that could not see the flame of the candle, but was wide
enough to embrace the whole universe, piercing enough to penetrate
all the hearts that beat in the darkness. He had summed up — he had
judged. 'The horror!' He was a remarkable man. After all, this was the
expression of some sort of belief; it had candour, it had conviction, it
had a vibrating note of revolt in its whisper, it had the appalling face of
a glimpsed truth — the strange commingling of desire and hate. And
it is not my own extremity I remember best — a vision of greyness

without form filled with physical pain, and a careless contempt for the evanescence of all things — even of this pain itself. No! It is his extremity that I seem to have lived through. True, he had made that last stride, he had stepped over the edge, while I had been permitted to draw back my hesitating foot. And perhaps in this is the whole difference; perhaps all the wisdom, and all truth, and all sincerity, are just compressed into that inappreciable moment of time in which we step over the threshold of the invisible. Perhaps! I like to think my summing-up would not have been a word of careless contempt. Better his cry — much better. It was an affirmation, a moral victory paid for by innumerable defeats, by abominable terrors, by abominable satisfactions. But it was a victory! That is why I have remained loyal to Kurtz to the last, and even beyond, when a long time after I heard once more, not his own voice, but the echo of his magnificent eloquence thrown to me from a soul as translucently pure as a cliff of crystal.

"No, they did not bury me, though there is a period of time which I remember mistily, with a shuddering wonder, like a passage through some inconceivable world that had no hope in it and no desire. I found myself back in the sepulchral city resenting the sight of people hurrying through the streets to filch a little money from each other, to devour their infamous cookery, to gulp their unwholesome beer, to dream their insignificant and silly dreams. They trespassed upon my thoughts. They were intruders whose knowledge of life was to me an irritating pretence, because I felt so sure they could not possibly know the things I knew. Their bearing, which was simply the bearing of commonplace individuals going about their business in the assurance of perfect safety, was offensive to me like the outrageous flauntings of folly in the face of a danger it is unable to comprehend. I had no particular desire to enlighten them, but I had some difficulty in restraining myself from laughing in their faces, so full of stupid importance. I daresay I was not very well at that time. I tottered about the streets — there were various affairs to settle — grinning bitterly at perfectly respectable persons. I admit my behaviour was inexcusable, but then my temperature was seldom normal in these days. My dear aunt's endeavours to 'nurse up my strength' seemed altogether beside the mark. It was not my strength that wanted nursing, it was my imagination that wanted soothing. I kept the bundle of papers given me by Kurtz, not knowing exactly what to do with it. His mother had died lately, watched over, as I was told, by his Intended. A clean-shaved man, with an official manner and wearing gold-rimmed spectacles, called on me one day and made inquiries, at first circuitous, afterwards suavely pressing, about what he was pleased to denominate certain 'documents.' I was not surprised, because I had had two rows with the manager on the subject out there. I had refused to give up the smallest scrap out of that package, and I took the same attitude with the spectacled man. He became darkly menacing at last, and with much heat argued that the Company had the right to every bit of information about its 'territories.' And, said he, 'Mr. Kurtz's knowledge of unexplored regions must have been necessarily extensive and peculiar — owing to his great abilities and to the deplorable circumstances in which he had been placed: therefore — ' I assured him Mr. Kurtz's knowledge, however extensive, did not bear upon the problems of commerce or administration. He invoked then the name of science. 'It would be an incalculable loss if,' etc. etc. I offered him the report on the 'Suppression of Savage Customs,' with the postscriptum torn off. He took it up eagerly, but ended by sniffing at it with an air of contempt. 'This is not what we had a right to expect,' he remarked. 'Expect nothing else,' I said. 'There are only private letters.' He withdrew upon some threat of legal proceedings, and I saw him no more; but another fellow, calling himself Kurtz's cousin, appeared two days later, and was anxious to hear all the details about his dear relative's last moments. Incidentally he gave me to understand that Kurtz had been essentially a great musician. 'There was the making of an immense success,' said the man, who was an organist, I believe, with lank grey hair flowing over a greasy coat-collar. I had no reason to doubt his statement; and to this day I am unable to say what was Kurtz's profession, whether he ever had any — which was the greatest of his talents. I had taken him for a painter who wrote for the papers, or else for a journalist who could paint — but even the cousin (who took snuff during the interview) could not tell me what he had been — exactly. He was a universal genius — on that point I agreed with the old chap, who thereupon blew his nose noisily into a large cotton handkerchief and withdrew in senile agitation, bearing off some family letters and memoranda without importance. Ultimately a journalist anxious to know something of the fate of his 'dear colleague' turned up. This visitor informed me Kurtz's proper sphere ought to have been politics 'on the popular side.' He had furry straight eyebrows, bristly hair cropped short, an eyeglass on a broad ribbon, and, becoming expansive, confessed his opinion that Kurtz really couldn't write a bit — 'but Heavens! how that man could talk! He electrified large meetings. He had faith — don't you see? — he had the faith. He could get himself to believe anything — anything.

He would have been a splendid leader of an extreme party.' 'What party?' I asked. 'Any party,' answered the other. 'He was an — an — extremist.' Did I not think so? I assented. Did I know, he asked, with a sudden flash of curiosity, 'what it was that had induced him to go out there?' 'Yes,' said I, and forthwith handed him the famous Report for publication, if he thought fit. He glanced through it hurriedly, mumbling all the time, judged 'it would do,' and took himself off with this plunder.

"Thus I was left at last with a slim packet of letters and the girl's portrait. She struck me as beautiful — I mean she had a beautiful expression. I know that the sunlight can be made to lie too, yet one felt that no manipulation of light and pose could have conveyed the delicate shade of truthfulness upon those features. She seemed ready to listen without mental reservation, without suspicion, without a thought for herself. I concluded I would go and give her back her portrait and those letters myself. Curiosity? Yes; and also some other feeling perhaps. All that had been Kurtz's had passed out of my hands: his soul, his body, his station, his plans, his ivory, his career. There remained only his memory and his Intended — and I wanted to give that up too to the past, in a way — to surrender personally all that remained of him with me to that oblivion which is the last word of our common fate. I don't defend myself. I had no clear perception of what it was I really wanted. Perhaps it was an impulse of unconscious loyalty, or the fulfilment of one of those ironic necessities that lurk in the facts of human existence. I don't know. I can't tell. But I went.

"I thought his memory was like the other memories of the dead that accumulate in every man's life — a vague impress on the brain of shadows that had fallen on it in their swift and final passage; but before the high and ponderous door, between the tall houses of a street as still and decorous as a well-kept alley in a cemetery, I had a vision of him on the stretcher, opening his mouth voraciously, as if to devour all the earth with all its mankind. He lived then before me; he lived as much as he had ever lived — a shadow insatiable of splendid appearances, of frightful realities; a shadow darker than the shadow of the night, and draped nobly in the folds of a gorgeous eloquence. The vision seemed to enter the house with me — the stretcher, the phantom-bearers, the wild crowd of obedient worshippers, the gloom of the forests, the glitter of the reach between the murky bends, the beat of the drum, regular and muffled like the beating of a heart — the heart of a conquering darkness. It was a moment of triumph for the wilderness, an invading and vengeful rush which, it seemed to me, I would have to keep back alone for the salvation of another soul. And the memory of what I had heard him say afar there, with the horned shapes stirring at my back, in the glow of fires, within the patient woods, those broken phrases came back to me, were heard again in their ominous and terrifying simplicity. I remembered his abject pleading, his abject threats, the colossal scale of his vile desires, the meanness, the torment, the tempestuous anguish of his soul. And later on I seemed to see his collected languid manner, when he said one day, 'This lot of ivory now is really mine. The Company did not pay for it. I collected it myself at a very great personal risk. I am afraid they will try to claim it as theirs though. H'm. It is a difficult case. What do you think I ought to do — resist? Eh? I want no more than justice.' . . . He wanted no more than justice — no more than justice. I rang the bell before a mahogany door on the first floor, and while I waited he seemed to stare at me out of the glassy panel — stare with that wide and immense stare embracing, condemning, loathing all the universe. I seemed to hear the whispered cry, 'The horror! The horror!'

"The dusk was falling. I had to wait in a lofty drawing-room with three long windows from floor to ceiling that were like three luminous and bedraped columns. The bent gilt legs and backs of the furniture shone in indistinct curves. The tall marble fireplace had a cold and monumental whiteness. A grand piano stood massively in a corner; with dark gleams on the flat surfaces like a sombre and polished sarcophagus. A high door opened — closed. I rose.

"She came forward, all in black, with a pale head, floating towards me in the dusk. She was in mourning. It was more than a year since his death, more than a year since the news came; she seemed as though she would remember and mourn for ever. She took both my hands in hers and murmured, 'I had heard you were coming.' I noticed she was not very young — I mean not girlish. She had a mature capacity for fidelity, for belief, for suffering. The room seemed to have grown darker, as if all the sad light of the cloudy evening had taken refuge on her forehead. This fair hair, this pale visage, this pure brow, seemed surrounded by an ashy halo from which the dark eyes looked out at me. Their glance was guileless, profound, confident, and trustful. She carried her sorrowful head as though she were proud of that sorrow, as though she would say, I — I alone know how to mourn for him as he deserves. But while we were still shaking hands, such a look of awful desolation came upon her face that I perceived she was one of those creatures that are not the playthings of Time. For her he had died only yesterday. And, by Jove! the impression was so powerful that for me too he seemed to have died only yesterday — nay, this very minute. I saw her and him in the same instant of time — his death and her sorrow — I saw her sorrow in the very moment of his death. Do you understand? I saw them together — I heard them together. She had said, with a deep catch of the breath, 'I have survived'; while my strained ears seemed to hear distinctly, mingled with her tone of despairing regret, the summing-up whisper of his eternal condemnation. I asked myself what I was doing there, with a sensation of panic in my heart as though I had blundered into a place of cruel and absurd mysteries not fit for a human being to behold. She motioned me to a chair. We sat down. I laid the packet gently on the little table, and she put her hand over it. . . . 'You knew him well,' she murmured, after a moment of mourning silence.

" 'Intimacy grows quickly out there,' I said. 'I knew him as well as it is possible for one man to know another.'

" 'And you admired him,' she said. 'It was impossible to know him and not to admire him. Was it?'

" 'He was a remarkable man,' I said unsteadily. Then before the appealing fixity of her gaze, that seemed to watch for more words on my lips, I went on, 'It was impossible not to —— '

" 'Love him,' she finished eagerly, silencing me into an appalled dumbness. 'How true! how true! But when you think that no one knew him so well as I! I had all his noble confidence. I knew him best.'

" 'You knew him best,' I repeated. And perhaps she did. But with every word spoken the room was growing darker, and only her forehead, smooth and white, remained illumined by the unextinguishable light of belief and love.

" 'You were his friend,' she went on. 'His friend,' she repeated, a little louder. 'You must have been, if he had given you this, and sent you to me. I feel I can speak to you — and oh! I must speak. I want you — you who have heard his last words — to know I have been worthy of him. . . . It is not pride. . . . Yes! I am proud to know I understood him better than any one on earth — he told me so himself. And since his mother died I have had no one — no one — to — to —— '

"I listened. The darkness deepened. I was not even sure whether he had given me the right bundle. I rather suspect he wanted me to take care of another batch of his papers which, after his death, I saw the manager examining under the lamp. And the girl talked, easing her pain in the certitude of my sympathy; she talked as thirsty men drink. I had heard that her engagement with Kurtz had been disapproved by her people. He wasn't rich enough or something. And indeed I don't know whether he had not been a pauper all his life. He had given me some reason to infer that it was his impatience of comparative poverty that drove him out there.

" '. . . Who was not his friend who had heard him speak once?' she was saying. 'He drew men towards him by what was best in them.' She looked at me with intensity. 'It is the gift of the great,' she went on, and the sound of her low voice seemed to have the accompaniment of all the other sounds, full of mystery, desolation, and sorrow, I had ever heard — the ripple of the river, the soughing of the trees swayed by the wind, the murmurs of the crowds, the faint ring of incomprehensible words cried from afar, the whisper of a voice speaking from beyond the threshold of an eternal darkness. 'But you have heard him! You know!' she cried.

" 'Yes, I know,' I said with something like despair in my heart, but bowing my head before the faith that was in her, before that great and saving illusion that shone with an unearthly glow in the darkness, in the triumphant darkness from which I could not have defended her — from which I could not even defend myself.

" 'What a loss to me — to us!' — she corrected herself with beautiful generosity; then added in a murmur, 'To the world.' By the last gleams of twilight I could see the glitter of her eyes, full of tears — of tears that would not fall.

" 'I have been very happy — very fortunate — very proud,' she went on. 'Too fortunate. Too happy for a little while. And now I am unhappy for — for life.'

"She stood up; her fair hair seemed to catch all the remaining light in a glimmer of gold. I rose too.

" 'And of all this,' she went on mournfully, 'of all his promise, and of all his greatness, of his generous mind, of his noble heart, nothing remains — nothing but a memory. You and I —— '

" 'We shall always remember him,' I said hastily.

" 'No!' she cried. 'It is impossible that all this should be lost — that such a life should be sacrificed to leave nothing — but sorrow. You know what vast plans he had. I knew of them too — I could not perhaps understand — but others knew of them. Something must remain. His words, at least, have not died.'

" 'His words will remain,' I said.

" 'And his example,' she whispered to herself. 'Men looked up to him — his goodness shone in every act. His example —— '

" 'True,' I said; 'his example too. Yes, his example. I forgot that.'

" 'But I do not. I cannot — I cannot believe — not yet. I cannot believe that I shall never see him again, that nobody will see him again, never, never, never.'

"She put out her arms as if after a retreating figure, stretching them back and with clasped pale hands across the fading and narrow sheen of the window. Never see him! I saw him clearly enough then. I shall see this eloquent phantom as long as I live, and I shall see her too, a tragic and familiar Shade, resembling in this gesture another one, tragic also, and bedecked with powerless charms, stretching bare brown arms over the glitter of the infernal stream, the stream of darkness. She said suddenly very low, 'He died as he lived.'

" 'His end,' said I, with dull anger stirring in me, 'was in every way worthy of his life.'

" 'And I was not with him,' she murmured. My anger subsided before a feeling of infinite pity.

" 'Everything that could be done —— ' I mumbled.

" 'Ah, but I believed in him more than any one on earth — more than his own mother, more than — himself. He needed me! Me! I would have treasured every sigh, every word, every sign, every glance.'

"I felt like a chill grip on my chest. 'Don't,' I said, in a muffled voice.

" 'Forgive me. I — I — have mourned so long in silence — in silence. . . . You were with him — to the last? I think of his loneliness. Nobody near to understand him as I would have understood. Perhaps no one to hear . . .'

" 'To the very end,' I said shakily. 'I heard his very last words. . . .' I stopped in a fright.

" 'Repeat them,' she murmured in a heartbroken tone. 'I want — I want — something — something — to — to live with.'

"I was on the point of crying at her, 'Don't you hear them?' The dusk was repeating them in a persistent whisper all around us, in a whisper that seemed to swell menacingly like the first whisper of a rising wind. 'The horror! The horror!'

" 'His last word — to live with,' she insisted. 'Don't you understand I loved him — I loved him — I loved him!'

"I pulled myself together and spoke slowly.

" 'The last word he pronounced was — your name.'

"I heard a light sigh and then my heart stood still, stopped dead short by an exulting and terrible cry, by the cry of inconceivable triumph and of unspeakable pain. 'I knew it — I was sure!' . . . She knew. She was sure. I heard her weeping; she had hidden her face in her hands.

It seemed to me that the house would collapse before I could escape, that the heavens would fall upon my head. But nothing happened. The heavens do not fall for such a trifle. Would they have fallen, I wonder, if I had rendered Kurtz that justice which was his due? Hadn't he said he wanted only justice? But I couldn't. I could not tell her. It would have been too dark — too dark altogether. . . ."

Marlow ceased, and sat apart, indistinct and silent, in the pose of a meditating Buddha. Nobody moved for a time. "We have lost the first of the ebb," said the Director suddenly. I raised my head. The offing was barred by a black bank of clouds, and the tranquil waterway leading to the uttermost ends of the earth flowed sombre under an overcast sky — seemed to lead into the heart of an immense darkness.

PART TWO

Heart of Darkness: A Case Study in Contemporary Criticism

Introduction:
The Critical Background

Heart of Darkness was published serially in *Blackwood's Magazine* in 1899. But it was not seriously reviewed until 1902, when it was reprinted in a hard-cover volume entitled *Youth*. Even then, the other two works published in the collection, *Youth* and *The End of the Tether*, were received more favorably. In an unsigned 1902 review Edward Garnett both explained and deplored the fact that *Heart of Darkness* was the least popular of the three tales. Calling it "too strong" a piece of "meat for the ordinary reader," he insisted that it was nonetheless "the high water mark" of Conrad's "talent," a "psychological masterpiece" relating "the sub-conscious life within us . . . to our conscious actions, feelings, and outlook." As such, Garnett concluded, it offers an "analysis of the deterioration of the white man's *morale,* when he is let loose from European restraint, and planted down in the tropics as an emissary of light armed to the teeth, to make trade profits out of the subject races."[1] Responding to Garnett's review in a personal letter, Conrad wrote: "My dearest fellow you quite overcome me. And your brave attempt to grapple with the foggishness of *Heart of Darkness,* to explain what I myself tried to shape blindfold, as it were, touched me profoundly."[2]

[1]Edward Garnett, unsigned review in *Academy and Literature,* 6 December 1902. Collected in *Conrad: The Critical Heritage,* ed. Norman Sherry (London: Routledge & Kegan Paul, 1973), pp. 132–33.
[2]Laurence Davies and Frederick R. Karl, eds., *The Collected Letters of Joseph Conrad* (Cambridge: Cambridge University Press, 1983), 2:467–68.

The tone of Conrad's response is treacherously difficult to determine. But of this we can be sure: Garnett was right in declaring the novel to be about the immorality of whites in Africa. The idea behind *Heart of Darkness,* Conrad had written to William Blackwood one month before the first installment of the novel had appeared in *Blackwood's Magazine,* is "the criminality of inefficiency and pure selfishness when tackling the civilizing work in Africa." This much, too, we can feel certain of: Conrad knew that the theme of his book was not obvious, and that serious readers like Garnett *would* have to reflect before being rewarded by the discovery of meaning. "The idea is so wrapped up in secondary notions," he had admitted in an 1899 letter to R. B. Cunninghame Graham, "that You — even You! may miss it."[3]

Conrad, of course, may be trying to sound humble in these letters, suggesting that his idea is obscured by "secondary notions" in a novel that is, consequently, "foggish." On the other hand, he may be asserting that meaning *should* lie beyond the details that enshroud it in a work of novelistic art, that the idea of a work should only emerge as the *product* of a reader's experience of more immediate, if secondary, details. "You must remember," Conrad goes on to say in the letter to Graham, "that I don't start with an abstract notion. I start with definite images and as their rendering is true some little effect is produced."[4]

Some early readers of Conrad, however, failed to find Conrad's images any more definite than his ideas. E. M. Forster, best known for his novel *A Passage to India* (1924), once wrote that "sentence after sentence" in Conrad "discharges its smoke screen into our abashed eyes," and he went on to accuse the author of being "misty" at "the edges" as well as "in the middle."[5] Forster was not the only artist-critic who found Conrad a little *too* fuzzy. The poet John Masefield (later to become poet laureate) declared that there is "too much cobweb" in *Heart of Darkness,* that Conrad's style, in general, is neither "vigorous, direct, effective, like that of Mr. [Rudyard] Kipling," nor "clear and fresh like that of [Robert Louis] Stevenson."[6]

Not all the reviewers who commented on style, though, found the novel notable for its lack of directness, precision, or clarity. The reviewer for the *Athenaeum* commented on Conrad's atmosphere but

[3]Ibid., 2:139–40, 157.
[4]Ibid., 2:157–58.
[5]E. M. Forster in *Abinger Harvest* (London: Edward Arnold, 1936), p. 138.
[6]John Masefield in *The Speaker,* 31 January 1903. Collected in Sherry, *Conrad: The Critical Heritage,* p. 142.

did so in order to praise, not fault, it: "He presents the atmosphere in which his characters move and act with singular fidelity, by means of watchful and careful building in which the craftsman's methods are never obtrusive, and after turning to the last page of one of his books, we rise saturated by the very air they breathed."[7] And an anonymous reviewer writing in the *Manchester Guardian* found in *Heart of Darkness* not atmosphere at all but, instead, "a great expression of adventure and romance."[8]

Was *Heart of Darkness* — is *Heart of Darkness* — a political novel, a psychological novel, or a simple adventure tale designed to give us a thrill? Is it primarily an atmospheric work and, if so, is the atmosphere so precisely evoked that we feel we breathe it, right alongside the characters? Or are Conrad's words like so much cobweb? The debate over these and other questions was intense during the decades that followed the publication of *Heart of Darkness,* and to a great extent, the various critical positions taken by reviewers in the first half of our century still guide us as we ask questions of the novel and arrive at interpretations of it. After all, no work is approached in a vacuum, and the interpretive history of a work is part of the context in which we read it. When we publish our views, even if we do so only in a comment to a few other readers of a particular work, we add to and alter slightly the language in which that work is and will be discussed. Those who follow are likely to locate their respective positions vis-à-vis our own.

Not surprisingly, then, when F. R. Leavis set out critically to assess *Heart of Darkness* fifty years after its serial publication, he praised strengths and attacked weaknesses in ways that had been prepared for him by previous critics. In his influential study of English fiction, *The Great Tradition,* Leavis begins by asserting that E. M. Forster was correct to fault Conrad for obscurity and a vaporous style. However, Leavis then insists that other critics were correct, too, in praising Conrad's ability to describe things and actions precisely, thereby creating an "overwhelming sinister and fantastic 'atmosphere.' "[9] Leavis has it both ways by arguing that Conrad pictures places — such as the grove "greenish" with "gloom" in which Marlow stumbles upon diseased,

[7]Unsigned review in *Athenaeum,* 20 December 1902. Collected in Sherry, *Conrad: The Critical Heritage,* p. 198.

[8]Unsigned review in *The Manchester Guardian,* 10 December 1902. Reprinted in Sherry, *Conrad: The Critical Heritage,* p. 134.

[9]F. R. Leavis, *The Great Tradition* (New York: New York University Press, 1963), p. 177.

starving Africans (p. 31) — with description that can be terribly vivid. But the novelist becomes vague and foggy, according to Leavis, when he steps back to philosophize.

Part of the problem, Leavis concludes, is that Conrad tends to overburden philosophical passages with adjectives that obscure rather than describe. "There are places in *Heart of Darkness*," he points out, where Conrad has already "overworked" words like " 'inscrutable,' 'inconceivable,' 'unspeakable.' . . . Yet still they recur." Quoting Conrad's sentence, "It was the stillness of an implacable force brooding over an inscrutable intention" (p. 49), Leavis goes on to remark that Conrad's vocabulary often backfires, particularly when it tries to express a sense of profundity or horror. Conrad repeatedly uses words such as "inexpressible" and "incomprehensible," Leavis hypothesizes, in order to "magnify" a "thrilled sense of the unspeakable potentialities of the human soul." But "the actual effect is not to magnify but rather to muffle."[10]

Giving as an example the scene in which human heads are found mounted on posts surrounding the house of Kurtz, Leavis praises the image, which he says tells us all we need to know, but faults Conrad for supplementing such images with what he calls the "adjectival and worse than supererogatory insistence on 'unspeakable rites,' 'unspeakable secrets,' 'monstrous passions.' " Conrad tries too hard, Leavis thinks, to "impose . . . a 'significance' that is merely an emotional insistence on the presence of what he can't produce. . . . He is intent on making a virtue out of not knowing what he means."[11]

These are strong words coming from a critic who ranks Conrad as one of the four great novelists in a great tradition of British fiction. They are words, nonetheless, that express what other, earlier readers felt. More important, though, they are words that later critics have found useful. For what Leavis unwittingly gave to later critics was the language that, with revision, could be used to discuss not the flaws of *Heart of Darkness* but rather the special nature of the novel's greatness.

Albert J. Guerard, in his much-acclaimed 1958 study *Conrad the Novelist,* reaffirms but also drastically revises the views of *Heart of Darkness* afforded by Leavis. One way Guerard differs significantly

[10]Ibid., p. 179.
[11]Ibid., p. 180.

from Leavis is in the attention he pays not to Kurtz but to Marlow. "F. R. Leavis," Guerard writes, "seems to regard him as a narrator only, providing a 'specific and concretely realized point of view.' "[12] Indeed, Marlow *was* to Leavis a mere agent, the character whose primary purpose in the narrative is to provide those "details and circumstances of the voyage" that make palpable the fantastic "atmosphere" Kurtz inhabits.[13] "But Marlow," Guerard asserts to the contrary, "is recounting a spiritual voyage of self-discovery," and it is that voyage and that discovery that should interest readers of *Heart of Darkness*. For Guerard the story is like a "powerful dream" in which Marlow meets up with his own, dark, passional nature. Marlow feels the excitement of what he calls the "wild and passionate uproar," finds himself fascinated by abominations, and, most important, meets a strange alter ego or double. The most important stage in Marlow's journey within, according to Guerard, is the one in which he comes to recognize his kinships with Kurtz, "a white man and sometime idealist who had fully responded to the wilderness: a potential and fallen self. . . . At the climax Marlow follows Kurtz ashore, confounds the beat of the drum with the beating of his heart, . . . and brings [Kurtz] back to the ship. He returns to Europe a changed and more knowing man."[14]

By seeing the novel as a dream of self-discovery, Guerard not only expands upon what Edward Garnett said when he called *Heart of Darkness* a psychological masterpiece but also explains why the world has been so taken with this story that *is,* at least in some ways, fuzzy, smoky, misty, unclear. *Heart of Darkness* is ambiguous as a *dream* is ambiguous; it is powerful precisely to the extent that it is *not* precise. "If my summary [of the novel as a dream] has even a partial validity," Guerard concludes, "it should explain and to an extent justify some of the 'adjectival and worse than supererogatory insistence' to which F. R. Leavis . . . objects. I am willing to grant that the unspeakable rites and unspeakable secrets become wearisome, but the fact — at once literary and psychological — is that they must remain *unspoken*."[15] In other words, if *Heart of Darkness* were perfectly precise in its profoundest passages, it would not be dreamlike; more important, it could not seem like *our* dream. To say "murder" or "death" or "greed" or "lust," instead of using that more "misty" phrase, "The horror" (p. 85),

[12]Albert J. Guerard, *Conrad the Novelist* (Cambridge, Mass.: Harvard University Press, 1958), p. 38.
[13]Leavis, *The Great Tradition,* p. 176.
[14]Guerard, *Conrad the Novelist,* pp. 39, 38.
[15]Ibid., p. 42.

would be to distance most readers from that horror. Thus Guerard makes use of Leavis even while seeming to reject him. He turns a vocabulary of critical objection into a language of critical analysis, a language that may be used to explain just why *Heart of Darkness* is so haunting.

Thomas Moser, who in 1957 published an important study entitled *Joseph Conrad: Achievement and Decline,* begins with two ideas: that Conrad "is as great as F. R. Leavis believe[s] him to be, and as serious and subtle as . . . Albert J. Guerard" has shown him to be. It is Guerard, though, who seems to have influenced Moser most directly. *"Heart of Darkness,* 'The Secret Sharer,' and *Lord Jim* are all principally concerned with the theme of self-knowledge," Moser asserts, sounding like Guerard. "We must recognize our potential weaknesses, our plague spots, in order to achieve a perceptive, moral life."[16]

Moser, however, does more than repeat Guerard's reading of the novel; like Guerard and Leavis before him, he bends and adapts a strong predecessor's language in order to make it useful in a new way. In stating that Conrad's early works show us that "we must recognize our plague spots," Moser has already developed an idea only latent in Guerard, namely, that Marlow in the jungle is like the reader in the text, that somehow Marlow's quest for self-knowledge must be doubled by our own. "It is difficult to discuss Conrad's technique without referring to its effect upon the reader," Moser writes, "for Conrad's masterly control of the reader's responses is one of the most significant results of his unorthodox methods. By holding back information and moving forward and backward in time, Conrad catches up and involves the reader in a moral situation, makes the reader's emotions follow a course analogous to that of the characters."[17]

In addition to expanding on Guerard's view of the novel as one of self-discovery, Moser develops a still older view of the novel: that it is a work critical of racist European imperialism. Unlike early reviewers, however, Moser sees the theme of anti-imperialism as being inseparable from the novel's imagery, and he discusses the connection to show that it was thematically useful to Conrad to create superficially confusing imagery. In *Heart of Darkness,* Moser points out, the usual pattern is reversed and "darkness means truth, whiteness

[16]Thomas Moser, *Joseph Conrad: Achievement and Decline* (Cambridge, Mass.: Harvard University Press, 1957), pp. 1, 24.
[17]Ibid., p. 42.

means falsehood."[18] The reversal tells simultaneously a political truth about races in the Congo, a psychological truth about Marlow and all of us (the truth is within, therefore dark and obscure), and any number of moral truths (the trade in ivory is dark and dirty). One pair of colors can suggest all these different kinds of meanings, Moser adds, because *Heart of Darkness* was written by "Conrad the artist," who happened also to be "Conrad the moralist, . . . Conrad the psychologist," and "Conrad the commentator on politics."[19]

Moser's reminder that Conrad was an *artist* was made time and time again by the New Critics, who dominated Anglo-American academic criticism in the middle decades of the twentieth century. The New Criticism — or formalism, as it is now usually called — was a reaction against the tendency to see poems and novels as products of the author's personal and historical experience. Formalists such as William K. Wimsatt warned against trying to discern an author's intention; our time as readers is better spent, they suggested, in describing the way the parts of the work interrelate to form beautiful artistic unities. Albert Guerard prepared the way for formalist readings of *Heart of Darkness* by focusing attention on Marlow — a tale-teller — and his narrative, rather than on its subjects: Africa, ivory, battle scenes, Kurtz. Guerard also showed a formalist tendency in believing that Conrad's dreamlike ambiguity may be part of the meaning, not just a fault of Conrad's that gets in the way of some other meaning that Conrad surely intended us to see.

Numerous critics writing since 1960 have paid attention to the artistic form or unity of *Heart of Darkness*. Leo Gurko reminds us that "the novel . . . begins and ends on a yawl, on the deck of which Marlow is telling his story to four men." The unity provided by that opening and closing scene, moreover, is reinforced by descriptions of the scene. ("The sea-reach of the Thames stretched before us like the beginning of an interminable waterway"; "the sea and the sky were welded together without a joint" [p. 17].) Together, Gurko argues, Conrad's images lead us to view nature as a continuum, to see the story as a continuum like nature, and to conclude that the "theme of all experience being one experience . . . underlies the story, and appears in several variations."[20] Marlow's lie to the Intended, for instance, is like Europe's imperialistic dealings in Africa. "The lie, like the imperialism,

[18]Ibid., p. 47.
[19]Ibid., p. 38.
[20]Leo Gurko, *Joseph Conrad: Giant in Exile* (New York: Macmillan, 1962), p. 148.

is an evil thing." But both are "redeemed," according to Gurko, "by a benevolent and idealistic motivation."[21]

In taking this rather tolerant view of imperialism, and in suggesting that Conrad took such a view, Gurko differs from most later critics who have written on the subject. For instance, in *Conrad's Politics,* published in 1967, Avrom Fleishman insists that "In Africa as well as in the Indies, the disruptive effects of imperialism on native society were clear to Conrad."[22] Whereas previous critics had emphasized the breakdown of the mores of white men sent to the tropics armed and in search of profits, Fleishman discusses the moral decay of Africans once Europeans have been loosed upon them. Several of Fleishman's predecessors had implied that *Heart of Darkness* tells how imperialism reduces white emissaries from a civilized to a primitive state, leaving them no better morally than the savages whom they exploit. Against this view, Fleishman responds correctively. The natives unspeakably treated by a degenerating Kurtz were not barbarians prone to committing unprovoked atrocities. Or, rather, they were not until Kurtz came among them and prompted them "to organized warfare in order to obtain ivory for export."[23]

Although he makes no mention of Fleishman's views, Bruce Johnson concurs with many of them in *Conrad's Models of Mind,* published four years after *Conrad's Politics.* Like Fleishman, Johnson disagrees with the notion that Conrad held tribal life in low esteem. And like Gurko, to whom he several times refers, Johnson finds in *Heart of Darkness* the view that nature is a unity, a continuum. Indeed, for Johnson, unity with nature is what the African natives have until "civilized" whites — who do not have this unity — disrupt and destroy it. Conrad, Johnson argues, held the Victorian view "that the savage is one with nature, while the civilized white man has fallen — for better or worse — from the primal unity."[24] According to this view of Africans, the native "feels no sense of alienation" and, therefore, no "need to create his own contingent values and sanctions." Europeans, who *do* feel alienated from that "something great and invincible" we call nature, *do* create such values and sanctions. The combination, as

[21]Ibid., p. 151.

[22]Avrom Fleishman, *Conrad's Politics* (Baltimore: Johns Hopkins University Press, 1967), p. 89.

[23]Ibid., p. 90.

[24]Bruce Johnson, *Conrad's Models of Mind* (Minneapolis: University of Minnesota Press, 1971), p. 71.

Johnson sees it, can literally be deadly. The unalienated native tends "readily to accept what presents itself convincingly," as if it had "divine sanction."[25] An alienated European like Kurtz, who shapes rather than accepts the world, exploits precisely this tendency. By presenting himself convincingly, Kurtz becomes a people's disruptive, destructive, even murderous god.

In analyzing the process by which Europeans create artificial roles and laws, Johnson raises an issue — language — that had received scant attention from earlier critics. Because the nature from which "civilized" people feel alienated is immense, language cannot explain it. Consequently, Kurtz — in spite of his "magnificent eloquence" (p. 87) — cannot "show Marlow the kind of naming that will constitute a 'victory.' " The "West," which Kurtz represents, has a "taste for decisiveness, endings, stories with kernels of meaning and definitions." But it was "no match for the intractable immensity confronting it."[26]

Kurtz (and his culture) responded to that truth, according to Johnson, by repressing it — by pretending that language *is* an adequate tool for understanding complex truths. And the repression turned out to be destructive. Kurtz sets himself up among the natives as a god and creates the *illusion* of having a wholly adequate language, for anyone worshipped as a God may name and define at will, without being questioned or contradicted. Marlow, though, sees through the illusion, inwardly challenges Kurtz's language. The severed heads on Kurtz's fence posts are said by the man in motley, Kurtz's "disciple," to be those of "rebels." "Rebels!" Marlow exclaims to himself. "What would be the next definition I was to hear? There had been enemies, criminals, workers — and these were rebels" (p. 74).

Johnson, unlike his predecessors, places Conrad in a philosophical tradition leading from Immanuel Kant to Arthur Schopenhauer to Jean-Paul Sartre. He suggests that Conrad anticipated existentialist thought by showing how the alienated self, when confronted with the meaninglessness of existence, has both the freedom and the responsibility to create its own values and even reality. That is what Kurtz has (irresponsibly) done; that is what Marlow does when he makes both a myth and a reality for Kurtz's Intended by telling what Johnson calls the "responsible and articulate lie that Kurtz's last word was her name."[27]

[25]Ibid., p. 72.
[26]Ibid., pp. 84, 76.
[27]Ibid., p. 88.

Critics who have written on *Heart of Darkness* since 1971 have tended to see in the novel the development of literary rather than philosophical ideas and traditions. David Thorburn, in *Conrad's Romanticism* (1974), goes back to an idea expressed by the early reviewer in the *Manchester Guardian* that *Heart of Darkness* is a modified adventure tale. "The young hero, dragged unready into a world of moral and physical menace, is both a cliché of the adventure mode and a figure of seminal importance in Conrad's finest books," Thorburn writes.[28] Even Conrad's first-person narrative style is said to be "common in the adventure mode, so common, indeed, that Henry James seems to have assumed that only in romance was such a narrative technique acceptable."[29] But Conrad, Thorburn shows, uses the first-person narrative technique artistically, to show how the imagination of an innocent hero responds to the trials of real experience.

Conrad, according to Thorburn, makes us realize that his adventurer has grown through experience by having the hero tell of an adventure in the distant past. By doing so, the author shows an awareness of the tradition of British Romantic poetry as well as that of the romance adventure. "It is striking," Thorburn writes, "how closely Conrad's most characteristic works resemble what M. H. Abrams has identified as the greater Romantic lyric, a poetic form whose defining features are the play of memory across time and the juxtaposition of an older poet with his younger self."[30] Marlow, then, is not unlike Samuel Taylor Coleridge's Ancient Mariner, who relives the horrors of a voyage on which he shot an albatross by telling the tale of his past to a wedding guest. Marlow bears a resemblance, as well, to the poet Wordsworth, who lyrically recaptures and reflects his former selves.

Using his awareness of literary history, Thorburn develops a notion first outlined in the 1950s: "Guerard and others were surely correct," he says, "in their claim that the novel is fundamentally Marlow's story: a journey into regions where Marlow confronts, as it were, an aspect of himself."[31] That self-confrontation, Thorburn points out, owes much to the traditions of the adventure tale and of Romantic poetry, which showed Conrad how a narrator may

[28]David Thorburn, *Conrad's Romanticism* (New Haven, Conn.: Yale University Press, 1974), p. 42.

[29]Ibid., p. 120. The remark by Henry James that Thorburn refers to was made in a letter to H. G. Wells.

[30]Ibid., p. 103.

[31]Ibid., p. 122.

confront himself, both in another character and in telling the story of his own past.

Romantic poetry, Thorburn also suggests, led Conrad to that concern with the use and inadequacy of language identified by Johnson:

> Conrad, like the English Romantic poets, holds to a meager but partly sustaining faith in the power of language to make sense of the world . . . , however imperfectly. . . . "I cannot paint / What then I was [Wordsworth writes]." But I will try and I will come close.[32]

Conrad's Romantic or Wordsworthian "preoccupation with the limits of language" causes the author to use his own words to reveal those limits in *Heart of Darkness*. Thus Conrad gives to Marlow a stuttering diction and a "vocabulary of uncertainty" — a language, in other words, that exposes as well as explores the limits of language. "In *Lord Jim,* as in *Heart of Darkness,*" Thorburn writes, "the famous adjectival insistence which has so disturbed Leavis and others is for the most part an essential aspect of the novel's meaning." The vagueness of Marlow's adjectives, in other words, "reinforces his stated conviction that his telling must fall short of perfect truth."[33]

By 1980 most of the assumptions about literature shared by the formalists had been set aside by young Conrad scholars and critics. Gone, certainly, was the predilection for looking at individual works as if they were hermetically sealed. Critics such as Johnson and Thorburn had interpreted *Heart of Darkness* in the light of philosophical and literary traditions. Claire Rosenfield, writing in *Paradise of Snakes: An Archetypal Analysis of Conrad's Political Novels,* had argued that "the artist does not write in a vacuum but as part of social order within historical time." An "archetypal" or "myth" critic in the school of Northrop Frye, Rosenfield had gone on to explain that "the problem for the archetypal critic . . . is to show how [a] novel is related to the rest of literature and to the culture in which it participates," and to do so by "show[ing] how mythical structures and patterns enable [an] author

---

[32]Ibid., p. 127.
[33]Ibid., p. 118.

to communicate his vision of reality."[34] For Rosenfield, the general cultural myths underlying all of Conrad's works are those of the Fall from Paradise and of the night-sea voyage, in which a hero journeys to the center of the earth or underneath the sea to encounter the forces of evil and to be reborn.

Gone too by 1980 was the formalist reluctance to speak of an author as well as of a text. Even authorial intention could once again be discussed. When Daniel R. Schwarz turned his attentions to *Heart of Darkness,* he went a long way toward equating Conrad with Marlow and Marlow's self-discovery (of which Guerard spoke) with Conrad's night-sea journey to new life. Schwarz quotes a letter to Ford Madox Ford in which Conrad writes, "How fine it would be if the thought did not escape — if the expression did not hide underground, if the idea had a substance and words a magic power, if the invisible could be snared into a shape."[35] Since *Heart of Darkness* is, in Schwarz's view, partly about Marlow's "effort to find the appropriate words" with which to "come to terms with the Congo experience, especially Kurtz," Marlow is a stand-in for his author and *Heart of Darkness* is, in part, about Conrad's challenge as a writer "to discover the signs and symbols which make . . . experience intelligible."[36]

Among the factors contributing to the tendency of recent critics like Schwarz to revisit the biographical dimensions of Conrad's fiction were two biographies published in 1979. A year before Schwarz published his view that Kurtz represents the apparently eloquent artist whereas Marlow represents that self-doubting side of Conrad, Frederick Karl made the claim, in *Joseph Conrad: The Three Lives,* that while writing *Heart of Darkness,* "Conrad began to split into pieces, and the result was Charley Marlow, a middle-aged seaman." Later, Karl suggests that some of the disparities between Marlow and Kurtz — "between Marlow's moderation and Kurtz's anarchy," for instance — are not unlike "divisions" that existed "within [Conrad] himself."[37]

Karl wrote his biography in a climate that for a decade had been favorable both to "myth" critics and to literary historians — to critics,

[34]Claire Rosenfield, *Paradise of Snakes: An Archetypical Analysis of Conrad's Political Novels* (Chicago: University of Chicago Press, 1967), p. 5.
    [35]Daniel R. Schwarz, *Conrad: "Almayer's Folly" to "Under Western Eyes"* (Ithaca, N.Y.: Cornell University Press, 1980), p. 63. The letter to which Schwarz refers may be found in *The Collected Letters of Joseph Conrad,* 2:119.
    [36]Ibid.
    [37]Frederick Karl, *Joseph Conrad: The Three Lives* (New York: Farrar, Straus and Giroux, 1979), pp. 425, 488.

in other words, interested in the family tree of literature and legend. As a result, he can see the books Conrad read and the myths he knew as being as much among his life experiences as his marriage or his trip to the Congo. Karl freely relates a text like *Heart of Darkness* not just to the adventures in Conrad's life but also to texts and fables that formed the author's verbal and literary experiences and education. The scene in which Marlow sees "a wasted landscape of industrial junk" in which "a chain gang of indentured Africans . . . clink, deathlike, indifferent" is said to be "Inferno-like, a descent, whether that of Dante, Odysseus, or Aeneas, into the underworld of human existence."[38] The Inner Station, Karl ventures to say, "has a totemic value as the lair for a dragon or primitive beast, as the mythical hiding place for Loke or another satanic figure of evil."[39] Kurtz, the particular figure who waits there for Marlow, is a particular kind of evil agent, namely, a latter-day Faust figure who has sold his soul in return for forbidden knowledge, experience, power. Marlow, who encounters and struggles with Kurtz, is in Karl's view a latter-day Ulysses.

The same year Karl published his biography of Conrad, Ian Watt published an account of the author's early life and work entitled *Conrad in the Nineteenth Century*. Watt, like Karl, sees *Heart of Darkness* as a product of Conrad's experiences as a reader, but whereas Karl sees the novel as an expression of mythic themes to which Conrad was drawn psychologically, Watt finds in the book a reaction against the Victorian religion of progress, and he identifies the poet Tennyson as one of the authors of that optimistic religion. Whereas Tennyson had, in a famous phrase, foreseen humanity "Mov[ing] upward, working out the beast," Conrad suspected that the beast will always reside within and that humankind may not survive, let alone evolve. Watt pays attention to scientists as well as poets in his biography, for the Victorian religion of progress cannot be seen apart from Social Darwinism or, ultimately, from the various theories of evolution formulated during the mid-nineteenth century.

The influence Watt downplays is that of impressionism, the late-nineteenth-century artistic movement in which painters such as Claude Monet sought to render their perceptions of a scene rather than to represent it objectively. Whereas Guerard had suggested in 1958 that the impressionists' aesthetic principles help explain the hazy indefiniteness of some of Conrad's word pictures, Watt suspects that

[38]Ibid., p. 290.
[39]Ibid., p. 296.

impressionism is a term more fruitfully used to describe French pictorial art than literature in English. As for the painters who are properly viewed as representatives of the impressionist movement, they were not much appreciated by Conrad, according to Watt. "Conrad's tastes in painting, as in music," Watt writes, "were distinctly old fashioned; he apparently disliked Van Gogh and Cezanne, and the only painter he ever mentioned as a model for his own writing was the peasant realist Jean-François Millet."[40]

To describe those moments that seem impressionistic in Conrad, especially in *Heart of Darkness,* Watt coins a new concept and phrase: "delayed decoding." Decoding has been "delayed," for instance, in passages like the one in which Marlow describes a sky full of deadly arrows: "sticks, little sticks, were flying about — thick: they were whizzing before my nose, dropping below me, striking behind me against my pilot house" (p. 60). Conrad, according to Watt, was trying to show the gap between initial perception and ultimate conception or understanding. The novelist, in other words, uses narrative to show that it takes consciousness awhile to decode or categorize raw experience fully and intelligently.

In 1985, Bruce Johnson responded to Watt's argument, not by disagreeing with the biographer's claim that Conrad is interested in "delayed decoding" but by insisting that *all* impressionist artists were interested in it. According to Johnson, impressionistic painters, not unlike Conrad, were aware of the gap between impression and conscious understanding; like Conrad, according to Johnson, they wondered whether understanding really clarifies — really *is* understanding. Johnson, in effect, argues that Watt, unlike Conrad and other impressionistic painters and writers, overvalues the act of decoding. He suggests that Conrad, like all impressionists, was most interested in exploring the integrity of sensations unspoiled by rational concepts and categories. When the mind decodes "sticks" into "arrows" it may lose more than it gains in understanding, for Kurtz's natives may think white men are gods who cannot be harmed by mere arrows ("little sticks"); their only thought in shooting at the boat may be to delay or prevent the departure of a divinity. Johnson puts it this way: "The fact that arrows seem at first to be 'little sticks' may reveal more about the ambiguous attitude of [the] natives . . . , and about Kurtz's functioning among

[40]Ian Watt, *Conrad in the Nineteenth Century* (Berkeley: University of California Press, 1979), p. 173.

them as a god, than the subsequently official and rather self-limiting definition of this very complex set of events and feelings as, simply, 'an attack.' "[41]

From Johnson's viewpoint it is only a short step to that provided by Hunt Hawkins in his essay, "Conrad and the Psychology of Colonialism." Hawkins thinks that imperialistic colonialism causes and is caused by interpretations of a foreign world that *seem* rational, but that in fact are erroneous and harmful decodings of impressions that cannot be decoded by Western assumptions. Taking political, anthropological, and sociological theorists rather than literary critics as his intellectual allies, Hawkins sees Conrad as a writer who anticipates the social theories of thinkers like Hannah Arendt and, especially, O. Mannoni, author of a seminal study of the colonial situation entitled *Prospero and Caliban* (1956). Conrad, like Mannoni, dramatizes the lives of white men who see themselves as living in a world without other human beings. What they really live in, of course, is a world violently emptied by pejorative interpretations of native peoples and biased decodings of their cultures — wrongheaded interpretations and decodings that make native peoples and cultures seem subhuman. Conrad's understanding, both of white emissaries and of their subjugated victims, has drawn the praise of non-Western writers such as D. C. R. A. Goonetilleke, a Sri Lankan quoted by Hawkins as saying that Conrad's Malayan world is "predominantly authentic," rendered without "conventional Western prejudices."[42]

It is tempting to think that recent Conrad criticism has brought us full circle. Frederick Karl's analysis of Conrad's divided psyche has helped explain why Edward Garnett called *Heart of Darkness* a "psychological masterpiece" in 1902, and Hunt Hawkins has refocused critical attention on what Conrad himself called the "criminality" and "pure selfishness" of white, Western conquerors. But just as literature did not come full circle in 1922, when T. S. Eliot turned Chaucer's great line about April's sweet, rejuvenating showers into an equally memorable one in *The Waste Land* about "the cruellest month, breeding / Lilacs out of the dead land," so the circle traced by Conrad critics is just that — an apparent circle. Frederick Karl is, after all, cannily and self-consciously Freudian; he has been influenced, furthermore, by post-Freudian theories of the

[41]Bruce Johnson, "Conrad's Impressionism and Watt's 'Delayed Decoding,' " in *Conrad Revisited: Essays for the Eighties,* ed. Ross C Murfin (University, Ala.: University of Alabama Press, 1985), p. 57.

[42]Hunt Hawkins, "Conrad and the Psychology of Colonialism," in Murfin, *Conrad Revisited: Essays for the Eighties,* p. 82.

unconscious and of writing that Edward Garnett could never have imagined when he used the word "psychological." Hunt Hawkins, like Garnett and Conrad, is reviving an old discussion of imperialism in *Heart of Darkness,* but he would never speak, as Conrad does, of "the criminality of [imperialists] . . . tackling the *civilizing* work in Africa" (italics mine). Rather, Hawkins uses the thinking of anthropologists and sociologists — of Third World anthropologists and sociologists at that — to demystify, to deconstruct, and to rewrite the history of the white man's "civilizing work."

The essays that follow demonstrate just how changing and vital Conrad criticism is today. They also demonstrate, by their distinct differences, something of the variety of critical options available. One by Brook Thomas, a new historicist critic, develops the interdisciplinary, global perspective of critics like Hawkins. Another — by Frederick Karl, Conrad's biographer — invokes the psychoanalytic theories of Sigmund Freud. J. Hillis Miller, a celebrated post-structuralist critic, deconstructs not imperialism but rather Conrad's own novel, showing deep contradictions in its language and purpose. A feminist critic, Johanna M. Smith, critiques Conrad's social critique, and a reader-response critic, Adena Rosmarin, develops, in surprising new ways, Thomas Moser's claim that Conrad's readers are adventuring through the text much as his characters experience Africa. Critical thought, as these essays demonstrate, is occasionally more like a coiled spring than like a circle; it comes almost, but not quite, back to a place it has been before, but it is the "not quite," the difference, that gives it resiliency, strength — and a future. Great works of literature seem naturally to produce these unending, near-cycles of strong thought. They produce, for each of us, the possibility of saying something entirely new while speaking of something quite old in a language that our predecessors seem to have been *almost* ready to use.

Psychoanalytic Criticism
and
Heart of Darkness

WHAT IS PSYCHOANALYTIC CRITICISM?

It seems natural to think about novels in terms of dreams. Like dreams, novels are fictions, inventions of the mind that, though based on reality, are by definition not exactly and literally true. Like a novel, a dream may have some truth to tell, but, like a novel, it may have to be interpreted before that truth can be grasped.

There are other reasons why it seems natural to make an analogy between dreams and novels. We can live vicariously through romantic fictions, much as we do in pleasant dreams. Terrifying novels and nightmares affect us in much the same way, plunging us into an atmosphere that continues to cling, even after the last chapter has been read — or the alarm clock has sounded. Thus, it is not surprising to hear someone say that William Golding's *Lord of the Flies* is like a nightmare. Nor will most readers be surprised by the claim of Conrad biographer Frederick Karl that "Conrad penetrated . . . the darkness entered into when people sleep, when they are free to pursue secret wishes"; that, like the content of a dream, *Heart of Darkness* "forms itself around distortion, condensation, and displacement"; that the riverboat setting of the novel is a nightmarish one. But Karl refers to *Heart of Darkness* and Sigmund Freud's seminal psychoanalytic essay *Interpretation of Dreams* (1900) in the same breath. Is the reader

who classifies *Lord of the Flies* as a nightmarish tale a Freudian as well?
Is he or she, too, a psychoanalytic critic?

To an extent, the answer to both questions has to be yes. Freud's
work is one reason it *seems* natural to think of literary works in terms
of dreams. We are all Freudians, really, whether we have read a single
work by the Austrian psychoanalyst or not. Most of us have referred,
at one time or another, to ego, libido, complexes, unconscious desires,
and sexual repression. The premises of Freud's thought have changed
the way the Western world thinks about itself. To a lesser extent, we
are all psychoanalytic interpreters as well. Psychoanalytic criticism
has influenced the teachers our teachers studied from, the works of
scholarship and criticism they read, and the critical and creative writers
we read as well.

Freud's theories are directly or indirectly concerned with the nature
of the unconscious mind. Freud didn't invent the unconscious; others
before him had suggested that even the sane human mind was only
conscious and rational at times, and even then on only one level. But
Freud went further, suggesting that the powers motivating men and
women are *mainly* and *normally* unconscious.

Freud, then, powerfully developed an old idea: that the human
mind is essentially dual in nature. He called the predominantly passional, irrational, unknown, and unconscious part of the psyche the *id,*
or "it." The *ego,* or "I," was his term for the predominantly rational,
logical, orderly, conscious part. Another part, which he called the
superego, is really a projection of the ego. That part which makes
moral judgments, which tells us to make sacrifices for good causes
even though self-sacrifice may not be quite logical or rational, the
superego almost seems to be outside of the self. And, in a sense, it
is, for much of what it tells us to do or think is what we have learned
from our parents, our schools, or our religious institutions.

What the ego and superego tell us *not* to do or think is
repressed into the unconscious mind. One of Freud's most important
contributions to the study of the psyche, the theory of repression,
goes something like this: much of what lies in the unconscious
mind has been put there by consciousness, which acts as a censor,
driving underground, as it were, unconscious or conscious thoughts
or instincts that it deems unacceptable. Censored materials often
involve infantile sexual desires, Freud postulated. Repressed to an
unconscious state, they only emerge in disguised forms: in dreams,
in language (such as through so-called Freudian slips), in creative

activity that may produce art (including literature), and in neurotic behavior.

All of us, according to Freud, have repressed wishes and fears; we all have dreams in which repressed materials emerge disguised, and thus we all could, in theory, have our dreams analyzed. One of the unconscious wishes we have all supposedly repressed is the childhood wish to displace the parent of our own sex and to take his or her place in the affections of the parent of the opposite sex. This wish really involves a number of different but related wishes and fears (a boy may fear that his father will castrate him, and he may wish that his mother would go back to nursing him). Freud referred to the whole complex of feelings by the word "oedipal," naming the complex after the Greek tragic hero Oedipus, who unwittingly killed his father and married his mother.

Why are oedipal wishes and fears repressed by the conscious side of the mind? And what happens to them after they have been censored? As Roy P. Basler puts it in *Sex, Symbolism, and Psychology in Literature*: "From the beginning of recorded history such wishes have been restrained by the most powerful religious and social taboos, and as a result have come to be regarded as 'unnatural,' " even though "Freud found that such wishes are more or less characteristic of normal human development":

> In dreams, particularly, Freud found ample evidence that such wishes persisted. . . . Hence he conceived that natural urges, when identified as "wrong," may be repressed but not obliterated. . . . In the unconscious, these urges take on symbolic garb, regarded as nonsense by the waking mind that does not recognize their significance.[1]

Freud's belief in the significance of dreams was no more original than his belief that there is an unconscious side to the psyche. Again, it was the extent to which he developed a theory of how dreams work — and the extent to which that theory helped him, by analogy, to understand far more than just dreams — that made him unusual, important, and influential beyond the perimeters of medical schools and psychiatrists' offices.

The psychoanalytic approach to literature not only rests on the theories of Freud, it may even be said to have *begun* with Freud,

---

[1]Roy P. Basler makes this point in *Sex, Symbolism, and Psychology in Literature* (New York: Octagon Books, 1975), p. 14. I am indebted to his general summary of Freud's achievement, especially on p. 15.

who was interested in writers — especially those who relied heavily on symbols. Such writers regularly cloak or mystify things and ideas in figures that only make sense once interpreted, much as the unconscious mind of a neurotic disguises secret thoughts in dream stories or bizarre actions that need to be figured out by an analyst. Freud's interest in literary artists led him to make some unfortunate generalizations about creativity; for example, in the twenty-third lecture in *Introductory Lectures on Psycho-Analysis,* he defines the artist as "one urged on by instinctive needs that are too clamorous."[2] But it also led him to write creative literary criticism of his own, including an influential essay, "The Relation of a Poet to Daydreaming" (1908), and "The Uncanny" (1919), a provocative psychoanalytic reading of E. T. A. Hoffmann's supernatural tale, "The Sandman."

Freud's application of psychoanalytic theory to literature quickly caught on. In 1909, only a year after Freud had published "The Relation of a Poet to Daydreaming," the psychoanalyst Otto Rank published *The Myth of the Birth of the Hero.* In it, Rank subscribes to the notion that the artist turns a powerful, secret wish into a literary fantasy, and he uses Freud's notion about the oedipal complex to explain why the popular stories of so many heroes in literature are so similar. A year after Rank had published his psychoanalytic account of heroic texts, Ernest Jones, Freud's student and eventual biographer, turned his attention to a tragic text: Shakespeare's *Hamlet.* In an essay first published in the *American Journal of Psychology,* Jones, like Rank, makes use of the oedipal concept; he suggests that Hamlet is a victim of strong feelings toward his mother, the queen.

Between 1909 and 1949 numerous other critics decided that psychological and psychoanalytic theory could assist in the understanding of literature. I. A. Richards, Kenneth Burke, and Edmund Wilson were among the most influential to become interested in the new approach. Not all of the early critics were totally committed to the approach, and neither were all of them Freudians; some followed Alfred Adler, who believed that writers wrote out of inferiority complexes, and even more were persuaded by the writings of Carl Gustav Jung, who had broken with Freud over Freud's emphasis on sex and who had developed a theory of the *collective* unconscious. (A great novel like *Heart of Darkness,* the Jungian would say, is not a disguised expression of Conrad's

[2]Sigmund Freud, *Introductory Lectures on Psycho-Analysis,* trans. Joan Riviere (London: Allen & Unwin, 1922), p. 314.

personal, repressed wishes; it is rather a manifestation of desires the whole human race once had but repressed upon becoming civilized.)

It is important to point out that among those who relied on Freud's models were a number of critics who were poets and novelists as well. Conrad Aiken wrote a Freudian study of American literature, and poets such as Robert Graves and W. H. Auden relied on Freudian insights when writing critical prose. William Faulkner, Henry James, James Joyce, D. H. Lawrence, Marcel Proust, and Dylan Thomas are only a few of the novelists who have either written criticism influenced by Freud or who have written novels that conceive of character, conflict, and creative writing itself in Freudian terms. The poet H. D. (Hilda Doolittle) was actually a patient of Freud and provided an account of her analysis in her book, *Tribute to Freud*. By giving Freudian theory a credibility among students of literature that only they could bestow, such writers helped give psychoanalytic criticism the largely Freudian orientation that, one could argue, it still exhibits today.

The willingness, even eagerness, of writers to use Freudian models in producing literature and criticism of their own consummated a relationship that, to Freud and other pioneering psychoanalytic theorists, had seemed fated from the beginning; after all, therapy involves the close analysis of language. Books *about* psychoanalytic criticism even began to appear, such as F. J. Hoffman's *Freudianism and the Literary Mind* (1945). In 1942 René Wellek and Austin Warren had been ready to include "psychological" criticism as one of the five "extrinsic" approaches to literature described in their influential book, *Theory of Literature*. Psychological criticism, they suggest, typically attempts to do at least one of the following things: provide a psychological study of an individual writer; explore the nature of the creative process; generalize about "types and laws present within works of literature"; or theorize about the psychological "effects of literature upon its readers."[3]

Probably because of Freud's characterization of the creative mind as "clamorous" if not ill, psychoanalytic criticism written before 1950 tended to psychoanalyze the individual author. Poems were read as fantasies that allowed authors to indulge repressed wishes, to protect themselves from deep-seated anxieties, or both. A perfect example of author analysis would be Marie Bonaparte's 1949 study of Edgar Allan

---

[3]René Wellek and Austin Warren, *Theory of Literature* (New York: Harcourt, Brace, and World, 1942), p. 81.

Poe, whom she found to be so fixated on his mother that his repressed longing emerges in his stories in images such as the white spot on a black cat's breast, which is said to represent mother's milk.

Novels and plays, of course, contain characters, and early psycho-analytic critics would often pause to analyze them before proceeding to their authors. But not for long, since characters, evil and good, tended to be seen by early psychoanalytic critics as the author's potential selves, projections of various repressed aspects of his or her psyche. For instance, in *A Psychoanalytic Study of the Double in Literature,* Robert Rogers begins with the view that human beings are at least double in nature. Using this assumption, plus the psychoanalytic concept of "dissociation" (best known by its result, the dual or multiple personality), Rogers concludes that writers reveal instinctual or repressed selves in their books, often without realizing that they have done so. One of the writers Rogers discusses is Conrad; he analyzes "The Secret Sharer," suggesting not only that the criminal hidden and aided by a ship's captain is the captain's dark double but also that *both* characters are projections of the complex psyche of Conrad. "Legatt and the captain," Rogers suggests, "reflect contradictions which Conrad's biographers see in him, those between loyalty and rebellion, patriotism and exile, maturity and youth, order and passion, realism and idealism, and so on; as Albert Guerard puts it, 'the dreamer, adventurer, audacious seaman, and innovating subjective writer was also a cool rationalist, political conservative, and withdrawn spectator.' "[4]

In the view of critics attempting to arrive at more psychological insights into an author than biographical materials can provide, a work of literature is a fantasy or a dream — or, at least, it is something so analogous to daydream or dream that Freudian analysis can help explain the nature of the mind that produced it. The author's purpose in writing is to gratify secretly some forbidden wish, in particular an infantile wish or desire that has been repressed into the unconscious mind. To discover what the wish is, the psychoanalytic critic employs many of the terms and procedures developed by Freud to analyze dreams.

The literal surface of a work is sometimes spoken of as its "manifest content" and treated as a "manifest dream" or "dream story" would be treated by a Freudian analyst. Just as the analyst tries to figure out

[4]Robert Rogers, *A Psychoanalytic Study of the Double in Literature* (Detroit: Wayne State University Press, 1970), p. 43.

the "dream thought" behind the dream story — that is, the latent content hidden in the manifest dream — so the psychoanalytic literary critic tries to expose the latent, underlying content of a work. Freud used the words "condensation" and "displacement" to explain two of the mental processes whereby the mind disguises its wishes and fears in dream stories. In condensation several thoughts or persons may be condensed into a single manifestation or image in a dream story; in displacement, an anxiety or wish or person may also be displaced onto the image of another, with which or whom it is loosely connected through a string of associations that only an analyst can untangle. Psychoanalytic critics treat metaphors as if they were dream condensations; they treat metonyms — figures of speech based on extremely loose, arbitrary associations — as if they were dream displacements. Thus, figurative literary language in general is treated as something that evolves as the writer's conscious mind resists what the unconscious tells it to picture or describe. A symbol is, in Daniel Weiss's words, "a meaningful concealment of truth as the truth promises to emerge as some frightening or forbidden idea."[5]

In a 1970 article entitled "The Unconscious of Literature: The Psychoanalytic Approach," Norman Holland, a literary critic trained in psychoanalysis, succinctly sums up the attitudes held by critics who would psychoanalyze authors. He does so, though, without quite saying that it is the author *per se* being analyzed by the psychoanalytic critic. "When one looks at a poem psychoanalytically," Holland writes, "one considers it as though it was a dream or as though some ideal patient [was speaking] from the couch in iambic pentameter." One "looks for the general level or levels of fantasy associated with the language. By level I mean the familiar stages of childhood development — oral, anal, urethral, phallic, oedipal."[6] Holland goes on to analyze not Robert Frost but Frost's poem, "Mending Wall," as a specifically oral fantasy that is

[5]Daniel Weiss, *The Critic Agonistes: Psychology, Myth, and the Art of Fiction,* eds. Eric Solomon and Stephen Arkin (Seattle: University of Washington Press, 1985), p. 20.

[6]Norman Holland's essay, "The 'Unconscious' of Literature," is the chapter devoted to the psychoanalytic approach to literature in *Contemporary Criticism,* eds. Malcolm Bradbury and David Palmer, Stratford-upon-Avon Series, vol. 12 (New York: St. Martin's Press, 1971), p. 136. The oral stage refers to that period of development in which desires for nourishment and infantile sexual desires overlap; eating, consequently, satisfies undeveloped sexual longings. During the anal stage, infants supposedly receive their primary pleasure from defecation; during the urethral stage, urinary functions are the locus of sexual feelings and pleasure. The phallic stage, which usually follows the anal stage, is marked by interest in the penis, or, in girls, some symbolic penis substitute.

not particular to its author. "Mending Wall" is "about breaking down the wall which marks the separated or individuated self so as to return to a state of closeness to some Other" — including and perhaps essentially the nursing mother.[7]

Once psychoanalytic critics stopped assuming that artists are borderline neurotics and that consciously fabricated characters can be psychoanalyzed to find out what is "wrong" with their authors, they came to understand that artists are skilled creators of works that appeal to *our* repressed wishes and fancies. So they shifted their focus somewhat — away from the minds of characters, away from the psyche of the author, and toward the psychology of the reader and text. Holland's theories, which have concerned themselves more with the reader than with the text, have helped to establish another school of critical theory: reader-response criticism. Elizabeth Wright explains Holland's brand of modern psychoanalytic criticism this way: "What draws us as readers to a text is the secret expression of what we desire to hear, much as we protest we do not. The disguise must be good enough to fool the censor into thinking that the text is respectable, but bad enough to allow the unconscious to glimpse the unrespectable."[8]

Whereas Holland increasingly came to focus on the reader more than on the work being read, others who have turned away from character and author diagnosis have preferred to concentrate on texts; they have remained skeptical that readers regularly fulfill wishes by reading. Following the theories of D. W. Winnicott, a psychoanalytic theorist who argues that even very young babies have relationships as well as raw wishes, these textually oriented psychoanalytic critics argue that the relationship between reader and text depends greatly upon the text. Some works, to be sure, fulfill the reader's secret wishes, but others — maybe most — do not. The texts created by some authors effectively resist the reader's involvement.

In determining the nature of the text, such critics may think of the text in terms of a dream. But no longer do they assume that dreams are meaningful in the way that works of literature are. Rather, they assume something different, something more complex. "If we move outward" from one "scene to others in the [same] novel," Meredith Skura writes, "as Freud moves from the dream to its associations, we find that the

---

[7]Ibid., p. 139.
[8]Elizabeth Wright, "Modern Psychoanalytic Criticism," in *Modern Literary Theory: A Comparative Introduction,* eds. Ann Jefferson and David Robey (Totowa, N.J.: Barnes and Noble, 1982), p. 117.

paths of movement are really quite similar."[9] Dreams are viewed more as a language than as symptoms of repression. In fact, the French structuralist psychoanalyst, Jacques Lacan, treats the unconscious *as* a language, a form of discourse. Thus, dreams are something we may study psychoanalytically to learn about literature, even as we may study literature to learn more about the unconscious. In Lacan's seminar on Poe's "The Purloined Letter," a pattern of repetition like that used by psychoanalysts in their analyses is used to arrive at a reading of Poe's detective tale. "The new psychoanalytic structural approach to literature," Wright tells us, employs "analogies from psychoanalysis . . . to explain the workings of the text as distinct from the workings of a particular author's, character's, or even reader's mind."[10]

Frederick Karl, whose essay follows, is not the only critic who has used Freudian concepts in coming to terms with Conrad's fiction. Robert Rogers's work has already been mentioned; Bernard C. Meyer, an analyst, has written on the subject in *Conrad: A Psychoanalytic Biography* (1967); and Frederick Crews has found *Heart of Darkness* to be an expression of the oedipus complex. In a chapter of *Out of My System* entitled "Conrad's Uneasiness — and Ours," Crews writes that if "the plot were recounted to a psychoanalyst as a dream," Kurtz, the "exposed sinner," would be "an image of the father, accused of sexual 'rites' with the mother," and that Marlow the "dreamer" interrupts the "primal scene" by making his "journey" into the "maternal body."[11] Donald M. Kartiganer has taken a somewhat different view of Marlow and Kurtz, preferring to look on the latter as the "outlaw" alter-ego projected by the fantasy of the former. He compares the story to the actual case history of one of Freud's most famous patients, the so-called Wolf-Man.[12]

Karl, who unlike Crews finds no oedipal "uneasiness" for us to share with Conrad, would seem to agree with Kartiganer that Kurtz represents one side of Marlow. But Karl's goal is not, finally, that of

---

[9]Meredith Anne Skura, *The Literary Use of the Psychoanalytic Process* (New Haven, Conn.: Yale University Press, 1981), p. 181. Skura's book, it should be noted, is especially clear in explaining why neither characters nor authors (from textual evidence) can be legitimately psychoanalyzed (see p. 167).

[10]Wright, "Modern Psychoanalytic Criticism," p. 125.

[11]Frederick Crews, *Out of My System: Psychoanalysis, Ideology, and Critical Methodology* (Oxford: Oxford University Press, 1975), p. 56.

[12]Donald M. Kartiganer, "Freud's Reading Process: The Divided Protagonist Narrative and the Case of the Wolf-Man," in *The Psychoanalytic Study of Literature* (Hillsdale, N.J.: The Analytic Press, 1985), p. 8.

Kartiganer, who psychoanalyzes a literary character. Nor is his method that of Crews, which is to psychoanalyze the author by treating the text as if it were made of words Conrad spoke from an analyst's couch. Rather it is to look upon Kurtz's psyche, the "savage" mind, Marlow's mind, the collective mentality of European imperialism, the mind of the reader, and the general human soul as if they were an interlocking set of blocks — each one different from and yet a characteristic extension of the others. Thus, ultimately, Karl sees Marlow's condition (and Kurtz's by extension) as the human one, representing "the collective neuroses" of "a people," indeed, representing "a world irrational and out of focus" in spite of its "seeming rationality."

One of the irrational forces driving the human will is sexual. Karl writes of a desire for orgiastic, uncontrolled sexual expression that is represented not only by the "jungle woman, by her wanton, demanding display of sex," but also by the river and jungle, the penetration of each representing some "unspeakable" sexual encounter with the female. But it is not just an unconscious, uncontrollable will to sex that, according to Karl, Conrad depicts in *Heart of Darkness*. In Kurtz Conrad represents an extreme form of the will to power, the desire for mastery which the German philosopher Friedrich Nietzsche believed characterizes all human behavior. Kurtz's "savage career," Karl says, "is every man's wish fulfillment." In Freudian terms, it fulfills the desire of the id to get out from under the censoring controls of the ego and superego, those censoring agents of the psyche that have learned to tell it: thou shalt not have orgies; thou shalt not kill those who resist thee; thou shalt not ornament thy fence posts with their skulls.

Karl is indebted to Jung's notion of the collective unconscious, as well as to Nietzsche's writings on the will to power. But his deepest debt, clearly, is to Freud. He views Conrad, Freud's contemporary, as a writer who meant by "darkness" what Freud meant by "unconscious" and who, like Freud, believed human beings to be largely motivated by the irrational side of the mind. Whereas Freud came to understand that side by analyzing dreams, Conrad explored it by creating images usually experienced only in dreams or war. Again: Karl doesn't analyze these images as if they were symptoms of Conrad's illness; Conrad was carefully controlling the images he was making. It is on that control, which produces an artistic *text*, that Karl's focus remains.

Karl's title is revealing. In it, he refers to the *danse macabre*, the medieval dance of death. The image conveyed, of a skeleton leading the living or other skeletons toward the grave, is like a scene from a nightmare. And yet the noun in the phrase, "dance," reminds us that Conrad's novel is a carefully choreographed work of art. *Heart of Darkness* may well be a *danse macabre*, but it is, finally, not a dream but a dance.

A PSYCHOANALYTIC CRITIC AT WORK

FREDERICK R. KARL

Introduction to the *Danse Macabre:* Conrad's *Heart of Darkness*

Heart of Darkness is possibly the greatest short novel in English and is one of the greatest in any language. Like all great fiction, it involves the reader in dramatic, crucially difficult moral decisions which parallel those of the central characters. It asks troublesome questions, disturbs preconceptions, forces curious confrontations, and possibly changes us. With one of the two central characters, Kurtz, we sense the allure of great power. With the other, Marlow, we edge toward an abyss and return different.

Conrad himself recognized that this novella penetrated to those areas of darkness and dream — indeed nightmare — with which he tried to define the substance of his world. Written when he was still a fledgling novelist, *Heart of Darkness* helped solidify a vision that rarely wavered in Conrad's later work, and one we now accept as uniquely modern. In it he limned the images one usually encounters in dreams or in war, and here he found that discontinuous, inexplicable, existentially absurd experience which was to haunt his letters and his work.

Based on personal impressions, his own Congo journey, *Heart of Darkness* welled out. As he wrote apologetically and hesitatingly to Elsie Hueffer in December, 1902: "What I distinctly admit is the fault of having made Kurtz too symbolic or rather symbolic at all. But the story being mainly a vehicle for conveying a batch of personal impressions I gave the rein to my mental laziness and took the line of least resistance."[1] The novella, then, contains a vision so powerful that Conrad excuses himself for being unable (he thought) to control it. It contains also that which Sigmund Freud suggests may be found in his own *Interpretation of Dreams*,[2] namely an insight that falls to one but once in a lifetime.

The reference to Freud and to *Dreams* is not fortuitous. It was of course chance that Freud and Conrad were contemporaries, but chance ends when we note the extraordinary parallelism of their achievements. Freud did his major work on dreams in the 1890s, the same time that Conrad was fermenting ideas about the Congo and personal and political expedience in a quicksand, nightmarish world. Freud's book, the culmination of his observations, appeared in 1900, only months after Conrad's *Heart of Darkness*.

Chance is further reduced when we recognize that literature and a new style of psychological exploration have been first cousins for more than a hundred years, that both Conrad and Freud were pioneers in stressing the irrational elements in human behavior which resisted orthodox interpretation. Conrad's great contribution to political thought is his insight into the irrationality of politics, its nightmarish qualities which depend on the neurosis of a leader, in turn upon the collective neuroses of a people. Such an insight is timeless, but it is particularly helpful to those of us seeking to understand historical developments since 1900. For when has humankind tried so carefully to preserve life while also squandering it so carelessly? Conrad caught not only hypocrisy (an old-fashioned value) but the illogic of human behavior which tries to justify itself with precision, only to surrender to explosive inner needs. "Exterminate all the brutes," Kurtz scrawled at the bottom of his report (p. 66). This is the politics of personal disintegration, uncontrollable personal needs, ultimately paranoia.

Confronting similar material, the scientist Freud was concerned to analyze logically the seeming illogic, the apparent irrationality, of dreams and, on occasion, of nightmares. Both he and Conrad penetrated into the darkness, the darkness entered into when people sleep or when their consciences sleep, when they are free to pursue secret wishes, whether in dreams, like Freud's analysands, or in actuality,

---

[1]Frederick R. Karl and Laurence Davies, eds., *The Collected Letters of Joseph Conrad* (Cambridge: Cambridge University Press, 1983), 2:460.

[2]In the Foreword to *The Interpretation of Dreams*, 3rd English edition, Sigmund Freud (London: Allen and Unwin, 1923).

like Kurtz and his followers. The key word is *darkness*; the black of the
jungle for Conrad is the dark of the sleeping consciousness for Freud.

In still another sense, Marlow, in his trip up the Congo, has
suffered through a nightmare, an experience that sends him back a
different man, now aware of depths in himself that he cannot hide.
The tale he narrates on the *Nellie* is one he is unable to suppress; a
modern version of Coleridge's Ancient Mariner, he has discovered a
new world and must relate his story to regain stability. The account is
a form of analysis — for him and for Conrad. In a way, it provides a
defense against Kurtz's vision.

Freud, too, returned from the world of dreams — an equally dark
Congo — with an interpretation and a method, an attempt to convey
order. His great discovery, like Conrad's, was surely that dreams, despite
the various barriers the conscious mind erects, are wish-fulfillments of
the hidden self. This sense of wish-fulfillment is evidently never far from
Marlow — for the very qualities in Kurtz that horrify him are those
he finds masked in himself. Kurtz's great will to power, Nietzschean
and ruthless in its thrust, is also Marlow's. The latter, however, can
hold back — his restraint, for Conrad, a mark of his Englishness.
Marlow, however, only barely restrains himself, for, irresistibly, he
is drawn toward Kurtz, readily accepting the latter's ruthlessness as
preferable to the bland hypocrisy of the station manager. Even Marlow
is seduced — he, too, hides secret wishes and desires, his dreams
curiously close to Kurtz's; and so are the dreams of us all, Conrad
suggests. Kurtz's savage career is every man's wish-fulfillment, although
by dying he conveniently disappears before we all become his disciples.

But *not* before we are filled with a sense of the absurd — a sense
of the absurd gap between what we profess to be and what we are,
a sense of our consequently and inevitably skewed relationship with
objects, with our milieu, with the universe itself. In this respect *Heart
of Darkness* is one of our archetypal existential literary documents. The
images of the narrative, like images of a poem, intensify man's sense
of absurdity — and alienation; in the appearances of the pale, white-
skulled, ailing, then dying Kurtz, we confront an elongated image
of wasted power and fruitless endeavor, the humanitarian become
inhuman. Possibly it is this sense of absurdity and discontinuity which
so impresses Marlow that he returns a changed man.

Whether it is or not, this gnarled seaman is surely one of the
keys to the story; he is a modern rendition of Everyman, the flawed
representative of mankind in late-medieval drama, an updated version
of Christian, the imperfect voyager whose story Bunyan tells in *Pilgrim's*

Progress. Conrad made Marlow sentient, somewhat intelligent, but, most of all, courageous — about himself, about life, about man's social responsibilities — yet at the same time sufficiently cynical; in brief, very much like Conrad himself. But the two are not congruent; among other things, Conrad possessed a literary intelligence that his narrator did not. He surrounds Marlow as well as enters him. But even if he is foremost a man of action, Marlow should not be taken too lightly. His intelligence is displayed in his moral sensibility. With a certain dogged charm, reminiscent of many American presidents and statesmen, he wishes to see the world based on English (or American) democracy. He accepts private enterprise — with personal restraints. He believes that imperialism must justify itself with good deeds. He expects all men to be fair and decent. Such are Marlow's preoccupations, and here Conrad demonstrated to good purpose the absurd contradictions and rifts between modern belief and modern practice. And here also is the source of Conrad's irony — a quality that gives him considerable advantage over Marlow.

Since he is a man of order and moral courage, Marlow expects similar restraints to prevail elsewhere. As a captain he of course knows that such qualities are essential to preserve life at sea. Carrying them over into civilian life, they become for him psychological expectations. Marlow looks upon the world's work as being basically just and fundamentally good, even necessary, provided it is done by enlightened men. Like Conrad, he accepts the status quo, but as one maintained, he trusts, by just men. Marlow rarely questions whether particular work is necessary; for example, he never asks whether white men should be in the Congo — for whatever reason. Rather, he assumes they should be, since they are, and that they must come as friends, as helpers, as bringers of enlightenment.

Marlow's great revelation comes when he sees that the world is not arranged this way — and here the Congo is a microcosm of the great world in which those who can, plunder those who cannot. Marlow's awareness of evil comes when he notes that many men, and those the most willful, do not share his belief in an orderly, enlightened society. Theirs is one of chaos, anarchy, "unspeakable rites" (p. 65). They approve human sacrifice, and they eat their victims. This is what Conrad's novel is about. A law-abiding morally sensitive man enters an avaricious, predatory, almost psychopathic world. For the moment he sees that civilization brings dubious rewards. He learns the harsh vocabulary of reality. He matures. The nineteenth century becomes the twentieth.

Clearly, every facet of Marlow's experience in the Congo, including his preliminary interview in the Brussels office, contains elements of the absurd, that is to say, elements that become a wedge between man's seeming rationality and a world suddenly irrational and out of focus. The question is not Hamlet's — whether to be or not to be — but how one should live. If absurdity is acknowledged, what are a man's guidelines? Does one concern oneself with morality or conscience? And even so, what sustains a man when tempted by the devil within, by corruption without? What is restraint if it isolates?

In a letter to Cunninghame Graham, written while *Heart of Darkness* was welling up in 1898, Conrad reveals his most personal fears: that in a world of ever-shifting illusions nothing, finally, matters and no one, ultimately, cares:

> In a dispassionate view the ardour for reform, improvement for virtue, for knowledge, and even for beauty is only a vain sticking up for appearances as though one were anxious about the cut of one's clothes in a community of blind men. Life knows us not and we do not know life — we don't know even our own thoughts. Half the words we use have no meaning whatever and of the other half each man understands each word after the fashion of his own folly and conceit. Faith is a myth and beliefs shift like mists on the shore; thoughts vanish; words, once pronounced, die; and the memory of yesterday is as shadowy as the hope of to-morrow — only the string of my platitudes seems to have no end. As our [Polish] peasants say: "Pray, brother, forgive me for the love of God." And we don't know what forgiveness is, nor what is love, nor where God is. Assez.[3]

Heart of Darkness, then, is concerned with moral issues in their most troubling sense: not only as philosophical imperatives, but practically as they work out in human behavior.

In another letter to Cunninghame Graham, written a year later, Conrad seems less to reflect philosophically than to discuss the sources of his imagery. He stresses apropos of *Heart of Darkness* that he didn't start "with an abstract notion" but with "definite images."[4] Such images abound: from the ludicrous French gunboat to its shells lobbed indiscriminately into the bush, then the metal of nuts and bolts and decaying, overturned equipment, the rusted steamboat settled in the mud, even the polished, unnatural accountant at the station, with the

[3]Karl and Davies, *The Collected Letters,* 2:17.
[4]Ibid., 2:157–58.

land itself silhouetted by withered natives, shades of themselves, victims of an imperialist Inferno, now dried, inhuman, lacking flesh or spirit, too soft for modern life. These definite images, however, suggest moral issues, as well as a philosophical position. The profusion of metallic and mechanical images indicates that resistant objects have superseded softness, flexibility, humanity itself; that, clearly, one must become an object, tough and durable, in order to survive.

The sense of human waste that pervades the story is best unfolded in the smoothly metallic, white luxurious ivory itself. It is an object for the rich — in decorations, for piano keys, for bibelots — hardly necessary for physical or mental survival. In a way, it is like art, a social luxury, and it is for art that the Congo is plundered and untold numbers slaughtered brutally, or casually. This view of ivory as art was surely part of Conrad's conception; a utilitarian object would have had its own *raison d'être.* A relatively useless item or ne selective in its market only points up the horror; surely this, too, is part of Kurtz's vision. Possibly Kurtz's artistic propensities (he paints, he collects human heads, he seeks ivory) make him so contemptuous of individual lives; for art and life have always warred. In the name of art (pyramids, churches, tombs, monuments, palaces), how many have died, gone without, worked as slaves? Traditionally, beauty for the few is gained with blood of the many.

Where art rules, artifacts are a form of power. The art object takes on magical significance, becoming a kind of totem, the fairytale golden egg. Knowing this, Kurtz gains his power, indeed his identity and being, from the ivory he covets. In a world of art, the most greedy collector is often supreme; matter, not manner, counts. One source of Kurtz's fascination for Marlow is the former's will to power, Nietzschean, superhuman, and brutal. Kurtz has risen above the masses — of natives, station managers, even of directors back in Brussels. He must continue to assert himself, a megalomaniac in search of further power. Marlow has never met anyone like him, this Kurtz who represents all of Europe. The insulated Englishman now faces east, toward the continent. "I took great care to give a cosmopolitan origin to Kurtz," Conrad noted in a 1903 letter to K. Waliszewski.[5] "All Europe contributed to the making of Kurtz," we read (p. 65).

He is indeed Europe, searching for power, maneuvering for advantage; and he finds the lever in the colonial adventure of ivory. No

---

[5]December 16, 1903, in *Lettres Françaises,* ed. G. Jean-Aubry (Paris: Gallimard, 1929); Karl's translation.

wonder, then, that Kurtz's hunger for acquisition is so overwhelming. Supremacy over all is all he seeks: supremacy over things, people, and, finally, values. Having gratified forbidden desires, he is free of civilized taboos. In the Congo, he can do anything. His only prescription: produce results, send back ivory. Indeed, his very will to power and confident brutality make him appear a kind of god to the natives and other agents who fear him and to the Russian sailor who believes in him.

The ultimate corruption is that Kurtz can go his way without restraint. All human barriers are down. Only power counts — no matter whether political or economic. In the jungle, as in enterprise, only the strong survive, and Kurtz obviously is one of the strong. He brings European power — all of Europe — into the jungle; his weapons encompass 2,000 years of Western civilization. And the consequence: corruption of self and death to "inferiors" on a monumental scale.

When a journalist informs Marlow that Kurtz would have been a "splendid leader of an extreme party," Marlow understandably asks, "What party?" "Any party," his visitor answers, "he was an — an — extremist" (p. 89). With that Conrad presents his grandest insight into the politics of our time — totalitarian politics especially but democratic politics as well. The absence of social morality, the desire to rise at everyone's expense, the manipulation of whole peoples for purely selfish ends, the obsession with image and consensus, and personal power, the absence of meaningful beliefs, the drive for advancement and aggrandizement without larger considerations, the career built on manipulation and strategies, not ideas: these are the traits that have characterized the leaders of our age, that have become the expected burden of the ruled in our century. The rapists have been Belgian, German, Russian, and American — though they have, to be sure, raped and plundered in different ways and to varying degrees. Too often power is vested in the chameleon, the politician who claims to be all things to all people. "The best lack all conviction," as William Butler Yeats expresses it in "The Second Coming," "while the worst are full of passionate intensity."

In this conception of Kurtz Conrad's powers as an artistic thinker were at their strongest. In reading Conrad it is often necessary to discriminate between pure thought and thought embodied in a work of art. As a political and social theorist, he was antagonistic to modern developments, deeply conservative in the sense that he suspected or mocked new departures or experiments. As an artistic thinker, however, he was at once caustic, subtle, broad. His conception of Kurtz, slim on the surface, broadening beneath, is a Cassandra's view of Western progress, a view both realistic and ironic.

Conrad was concerned with the rape of a people. The Congo had been, since 1875, the private preserve of Leopold II of Belgium, a medieval kingdom for personal use, organized under the deceptive title of the International Association for the Civilization of Central Africa. Demographists estimate that hundreds of thousands, possibly millions, of Congolese died in slavery or through brutality. Kurtz, or his type of exploiter, was the rule, not the exception. Kurtz himself was based roughly and loosely on one Georges-Antoine Klein (Klein = small, Kurtz = short), whom Conrad had taken aboard his steamer during his Congo days. Conrad's journey, as he relates in his Congo diary, was real; Kurtz and his type prevailed; the land and the natives existed; the facts are undisputed. Even if Conrad used symbols to excess, as he feared, each symbol is solidly grounded in fact. Here is white against black, entrenched against primitive, have against have-not, machine against spear, civilization against tribe.

If Conrad's novella is to have artistic as well as political significance, it must make broad reference to human motivation and behavior. One evident part of the application comes with Kurtz's double shriek of "The horror! The horror!" (p. 85). The cry is far richer and more ambiguous than most readers make it. We must remember that Marlow is reporting, and Marlow has a particular view and need of Kurtz. As Marlow understands the scream, it represents a moral victory; that is, on the threshold of death, Kurtz has reviewed his life with all its horror and in some dying part of him has repented. Marlow hears the words as a victory of moral sensibility over a life of brutality and prostituted ideals. This "Christian" reading of the words is, of course, what Marlow himself wishes to hear; he is a moral man, and he believes, with this kind of bourgeois religiosity, that all men ultimately repent when confronted by the great unknown. Kurtz's cry, in this interpretation, fits in with what Marlow wants to know of human nature.

We are not all Marlows, however, and we should not be seduced into agreeing with him, even if he is partially right. More ambiguously and ironically, Kurtz's cry might be a shriek of despair that after having accomplished so little he must now perish. His horror is the anguish of one who dies with his work incomplete. In this view, Kurtz does not repent; rather, he bewails a fate which frustrates his plans. Indeed, at the very moment of death, he challenges life and death and tries to make his baffled will prevail. Like Satan in Milton's *Paradise Lost,* he prefers hell to compromise.

Just because Marlow fails to see Kurtz as a devil, however, does not mean that his author did. Conrad always harked back to the individual devil in each man — perhaps as part of his Catholic background. He believed that men deceived themselves to the very end: about the evil in others and in themselves. "Our refuge is in stupidity, in drunkenness of all kinds, in lies, in beliefs, in murder, thieving, reforming — in negation, in contempt," he wrote in 1898, in yet another letter to Cunninghame Graham. "There is no morality, no knowledge and no hope; there is only the consciousness of ourselves which drives us about a world that whether seen in a convex or a concave mirror is always but a vain and floating appearance."[6]

Marlow cannot, or will not, admit the truth of what Conrad here suggests. Returning from the world of the dead, Marlow — our twentieth-century Everyman — cannot even admit the full impact of the indecency he has witnessed, of the feelings he has experienced. Even this most honest of men must disguise what he has seen and felt. Like a politician he must bed down with lies. Marlow, that pillar of truth and morality, does Kurtz's work at the end, lies to protect the lie of Kurtz's existence, ultimately lies to preserve his (Marlow's) own illusions. In an impure, dirty world, he desperately seeks a compromise — and finds it in the pretty illusions of naive women. Only Conrad, who is outside both Marlow and Kurtz, can admit the truth, can limn the lie and see it as a lie. Only the artist, and his art, can triumph; all else is dragged down or forced to exist by virtue of untruths. Marlow, the narrator, controlled in turn by Conrad, the creator, can transform the horror of his experience into the human terms necessary for continued life. Conrad has succeeded in constructing a form which can, so to speak, hold the horror at arm's length and yet also touch us deeply.

In this and other respects, *Heart of Darkness* is a masterpiece of concealment. Just as Marlow has concealed from himself the true nature of his own needs, so too we can find concealment — in art, in nature, in people — in virtually every other aspect of the novella. The jungle itself, that vast protective camouflage barring the light of sun and sky, masks and hides, becoming part of the psychological as well as physical landscape. Like the dream content, it forms itself around distortion, condensation, and displacement.

Post-Darwinian and overpowering, the jungle is not Wordsworth's gentle landscape, by no means the type of nature which gives

[6]Karl and Davies, *The Collected Letters*, 2:30.

strength and support in our darkest hours. Rather, it runs parallel to our anxieties, becomes the repository of our fears. The darkness of the jungle approximates darkness everywhere, adumbrating the blackness of Conrad's humor, the despair of his irony.

The persistence of darkness, and especially of the color black, sets the tone and elicits our response. We first meet the Romans, who penetrate *their* Congo — the English swamp, the "dark" and "savage" Thames (p. 20). Then we encounter the women in the Brussels office who knit black wool, suitable for Fates who send gladiators out to die in the jungle for the glory of empire. It is significant that Marlow encounters only two Fates (they could be Clotho and Lachesis, who in classical mythology spin and measure the thread of human life), for the presence of a third (Atropos, who cuts the thread) would indicate his imminent death. Their black is indeed morbid against Brussels, called a "whited sepulchre." Later, when Kurtz paints in oils, he represents a woman, draped and blindfolded, carrying a torch, all against the somber background. She emerges from the dark, but only partially, for dark nourishes her. She is, in fact, a symbolic Kurtz — one contiguous with and defined by blackness. Then, just before Kurtz dies, he lies in dim light awaiting the end, his face writhing with despair, the blackness of the past merging with the mystery of the future. Once dead, Kurtz returns to the black of the Congo, his epitaph spoken by the manager's boy: "Mistah Kurtz — he dead" (p. 86).

The sarcastic understatement of the boy, his cruel indifference to Kurtz's prestige, all stress the contrast between Kurtz's desires and the blackness which receives him. The jungle itself will conceal him. Beyond every wish is the force of fate, the dark power which is both within and without, psychological needs and physical consequences. "Mistah Kurtz — he dead" becomes the epitaph of all those who die in jungles, their careers curtly reviewed in the contemptuous words of the boy, a bleak and black destiny.

Attached to each of these events — Kurtz's final words, his death, the report by the manager's boy, the darkness surrounding all, the frantic run out of the Congo, the meeting with Kurtz's Brussels fiancée — connected to all such events is the shimmer and nightmare of dream, Conrad's definition of modern life. No less than Kafka, he saw existence as forms of unreality stubbled with real events. And no little part of the dreamlike substance of the tale is the Russian follower of Kurtz, like Marlow a mariner. Dressed in motley, he seems a figure from another world, and yet with his ludicrous appearance he is a perfect symbol for Marlow's Congo experience. Befitting someone who worships Kurtz like a god, the Russian forgives his worst behavior and argues that a common man like himself needs someone to follow. He is persuaded that Kurtz's will to power draws in all those less capable, conveys hope and substance to them.

There is, in his view, a void in every man that only someone like Kurtz can fill. Without Kurtz, the sailor says, he is nothing. "He made me see things — things" (p. 71). The sailor's own ordinariness is balanced by Kurtz's superiority — every disciple needs a god. Like the natives, like the superb native mistress who forgives Kurtz everything, the sailor follows power. Conrad's prescience was never more trenchant.

To Marlow's accusation that Kurtz is insane, simply mad, the Russian offers Kurtz's great intelligence, his ability to talk brilliantly, his charismatic qualities. To our objection that the sailor himself is mad, Conrad offers his influence upon Marlow — he strikes in Marlow precisely the note of love-hate that Conrad's narrator has come to feel for Kurtz. Although Marlow would like to anchor himself solidly in the Russian's sea manual and reject the vapidity of the Russian, he too is drawn into Kurtz's orbit. He senses what the sailor voices.

In this strangely insane world, all alignments defy logic. Loyalties, beliefs, love, women themselves take on new shapes and attractions. Marlow, that neuter bachelor, is fascinated by the jungle woman, by her wanton, demanding display of sex, by the "fecund and mysterious life" she embodies (p. 76), by the deliberate provocation of her measured walk. He is further drawn to her sense of reality; without illusion, without question, she accepts Kurtz for what he is, as integrated with the very savagery which enfolds her.

Though the reticent, chivalrous Marlow never speaks directly of sex, it lies heavily on the story, in every aspect of nature, in *his* fears, in *its* demands. Like the Styx, the mythological river that winds nine times about the underworld, the long river that informs this world is described by Marlow in treacherous, serpentine terms — "deadly — like a snake," "resembling an immense snake uncoiled" (p. 24, p. 22). The river is essentially a woman: dangerous, dark, mysterious, concealed, with the jungle also feminine, personified by Kurtz's savage mistress. Marlow is overwhelmed; his ideal of womanhood is clearly the girl back in Brussels, or his aunt — the brainwashed public — that naive woman who believes "the labourer is worthy of his hire" (p. 27). Such womanly illusions Marlow wishes to preserve. But his experience includes a treacherous, feminine river, an equally perfidious jungle that conceals its terrors, and, finally, a savage mistress — in all, an unspeakable sexual experience. And so it is that Marlow remains silent. As much as he fears the attraction of power, he shies away from the temptation of orgiastic, uncontrollable sex. He retreats into neutral shock.

But what of those things he can and does speak of — of those other anarchic forces and terrible things he has witnessed in the heart of darkness? Again and again, he breaks off his narrative to assure his listeners that all this really happened. Even while he talks, this modern mariner, he must convey the depth of his experience, try to convince that it was as profound as he claims. Marlow knows what happened — yet to find the precise words is almost impossible. Returning from the dead, like Eliot's J. Alfred Prufrock, he now has to convince his audience that there is really a hell.

The problem of Marlow, as we saw earlier, is the problem of Conrad's art: to communicate the weight and depth of an experience which is uniquely felt. Some of the criticism of Conrad's treatment, particularly F. R. Leavis's, has been directed toward his "excessive" use of descriptives to suggest mysteriousness and unspeakable events. Possibly in some areas the language is too heavy, but to labor this point is to lose sight of the story as a whole. One might, in fact, argue the very opposite: that the words — adjectives and all — beat upon us, creating drumlike rhythms entirely appropriate to the thick texture of the jungle, a more sophisticated version of Vachel Lindsay's poem "Congo," with its repetitive refrain of "Boomlay, boomlay, BOOM." When one confronts the artistry of *Heart of Darkness* as a whole, Conrad's reliance on verbal embellishment appears a minor consideration.

The story in fact has form: from the opening frame, with Marlow's somewhat ingenuous listeners, to the closing sequence, with Kurtz's innocent fiancée confirming her illusions. The use of a first-person narrative, through the agency of Marlow, was necessary so that Conrad could gain aesthetic distance and the reader could identify with an average man thrown into an abnormal situation. We must, Conrad realized, go through it with him and Marlow. Lacking the narrator, the story would appear too distant from the immediate experience — as though it had happened and was now over, like ancient history. From this safe distance, everyone was saved, and the evil force, Kurtz, rightfully had perished. But that is not at all Conrad's story; to make a morality play out of the tale is to destroy its felt sense. The story is concerned with hidden terrors in the normal heart, with the attractions of the unspeakable which we all experience, with the sense of power we wish to exert or identify with, ultimately with the underground existence each sentient being recognizes in himself. In this respect, Marlow as direct participant through his narration becomes indispensable.

So, too, in other respects did Conrad work out the shape of the story, in large and in details: through doubling of scenes and characters, through repetition, analogy, duplicating images, through difference of tone. From the beginning, when the ancient Romans on the Thames are contrasted with the modern Europeans on the Congo, Conrad used heightening and foreshortening, contrast and comparison to give the novella form. Most obviously, Marlow's peaceful setting on the *Nellie* is set off against his nightmarish Congo riverboat setting; in a different way, Kurtz's two fiancées are contrasted, each one standing for certain values, indeed for entire cultures, in conflict; further, the jungle is set off against the river, with jungle as death, river as possible relief; in another way, Kurtz is compared with other forms of evil, with the deceptive smoothness of the station manager, with the hypocrisy of the pilgrims; the pilgrims in turn are ironically compared with the savages they condemn, with the pilgrims less Christian than the pagan natives; within the natives, the tribal savages are contrasted with those exposed to civilization, detribalized as it were, the latter already full of wiles and deceit; light and dark, the painter's chiaroscuro, hover over the entire story, no less important here than in Milton's Christian epic, *Paradise Lost*; day dream and night dream form contrasts, worked out in the play between expectation and consequence, between professed ideals and realistic behavior, between Kurtz's humanitarianism and his barbarism, between Marlow's middle-class sense of English justice and the Congo reality, between the fluctuating love-and-hate which fill both Kurtz and Marlow.

Out of the infinite possibilities facing Conrad, he chose these to give unity to his language and ideas. Such devices shape our thoughts and give form to our responses; they, too, become the substance of our awareness. Only in *Nostromo,* with his use of silver, or in *The Secret Agent,* with London city streets, did Conrad find comparable central images to the Congo.

To discover the rightful place of *Heart of Darkness* in European culture, we must leave English literature and compare it with Dostoyevsky's *Notes from Underground,* Kafka's *Metamorphosis,* Thomas Mann's *Death in Venice,* Camus's *The Stranger* — all relatively short fictions concerned with "underground" men, men who through force of character or artistic sensibility suffer in isolation or alienation, outside the mainstream of society. This is typically continental fiction, not English — Conrad's vision remained Slavic. At the heart of all is an anarchy that repels and attracts, where one toys with the unimaginable and contemplates mysterious rites, where one defies the edicts of civilization and suffers secretly.

What makes this story so impressive is Conrad's ability to focus on the Kurtz-Marlow polarity as a definition of our times. European history as well as the history of individual men can be read more clearly in the light of Conrad's art; for he tells us that the most dutiful of men, a Marlow, can be led to the brink of savagery and brutality if the will to power touches him; that the most idealistic of men, Kurtz, can become a sadistic murderer; that the dirty work of this world is carried out by men whose reputations are preserved by lies. Conrad's moral tale becomes, in several respects, our story, the only way we can read history and each other. Hannah Arendt's definition of the "banality of evil," the nihilism of the average man, is fully relevant. It is a terrible story. Unlike Marlow, who possesses threads of heroism, we fail to confront it and prefer to acquiesce in our humiliation.

PSYCHOANALYTIC CRITICISM: A SELECTED BIBLIOGRAPHY

Some Short Introductions to Psychological and Psychoanalytic Criticism

Holland, Norman. "The 'Unconscious' of Literature." *Contemporary Criticism,* edited by Norman Bradbury and David Palmer. Stratford-upon-Avon Series, vol. 12. New York: St. Martin's Press, 1971.

Scott, Wilbur. *Five Approaches to Literary Criticism.* London: Collier-Macmillan, 1962. See the essays by Burke and Gorer as well as Scott's introduction to the section entitled "The Psychological Approach: Literature in the Light of Psychological Theory."

Wellek, René, and Austin Warren. *Theory of Literature.* New York: Harcourt, Brace and World, 1942. See the chapter "Literature and Psychology" in Part Three, "The Extrinsic Approach to the Study of Literature."

Wright, Elizabeth. "Modern Psychoanalytic Criticism." In *Modern Literary Theory: A Comparative Introduction,* edited by Ann Jefferson and David Robey. Totowa, N.J.: Barnes and Noble, 1982.

Freud and His Influence

Basler, Roy P. *Sex, Symbolism, and Psychology in Literature.* New York: Octagon Books, 1975. See especially pp. 13–19.

Freud, Sigmund. *The Standard Edition of the Complete Psychological Works*, edited by James Strachey. London: Hogarth Press, 1953–1974. Freud's best-known comments on art and neurosis are found in the twenty-third of the *Introductory Lectures on Psycho-Analysis* (vols. 15–16 of this edition). "The Uncanny" may be found in vol. 17, *An Infantile Neurosis and Other Works*.

Hoffman, Frederick J. *Freudianism and the Literary Mind*. Baton Rouge: Louisiana State University Press, 1945.

Kazin, Alfred. "Freud and His Consequences." In *Contemporaries*. Boston: Little, Brown, 1962.

Meisel, Perry, ed. *Freud: Twentieth Century Views*. Englewood Cliffs, N.J.: Prentice-Hall, 1981.

Porter, Laurence M. *The Interpretation of Dreams: Freud's Theories Revisited*. Twayne's Masterwork Studies Series. Boston: G. K. Hall, 1986.

Reppen, Joseph, and Maurice Charney. *The Psychoanalytic Study of Literature*. Hillsdale, N.J.: Analytic Press, 1985.

Trilling, Lionel. "Art and Neurosis." In *The Liberal Imagination*. New York: Scribners, 1950.

Psychological or Psychoanalytic Studies of Literature

Bettleheim, Bruno. *The Uses of Enchantment: The Meaning and Importance of Fairy Tales*. New York: Alfred A. Knopf, 1977. Although this book is about fairy tales instead of literary works written for publication, it offers model Freudian readings of well-known stories.

Crews, Frederick C. *Out of My System: Psychoanalysis, Ideology, and Critical Method*. New York: Oxford University Press, 1975.

———. *Relations of Literary Study*. New York: Modern Language Association of America, 1967. See the chapter entitled "Literature and Psychology."

Hallman, Ralph. *Psychology of Literature: A Study of Alienation and Tragedy*. New York: Philosophical Library, 1961.

Hartman, Geoffrey. *Psychoanalysis and the Question of the Text*. Baltimore: Johns Hopkins University Press, 1979. See especially the essays by Hartman, Johnson, Nelson, and Schwartz.

Hertz, Neil. *The End of the Line: Essays on Psychoanalysis and the Sublime*. New York: Columbia University Press, 1985.

Holland, Norman N. *Dynamics of Literary Response*. New York: Oxford University Press, 1968.

————. *Poems in Persons: An Introduction to the Psychoanalysis of Literature.* New York: W. W. Norton, 1973.

Kris, Ernest. *Psychoanalytic Explorations in Art.* New York: International Universities Press, 1952.

Lucas, F. L. *Literature and Psychology.* London: Cassell and Company, 1951.

Phillips, William, ed. *Art and Psychoanalysis.* New York: Columbia University Press, 1977.

Skura, Meredith. *The Literary Use of the Psychoanalytic Process.* New Haven, Conn.: Yale University Press, 1981.

Strelka, Joseph P. *Literary Criticism and Psychology.* University Park: Pennsylvania State University Press, 1976. See especially the essays by Lerner and Peckham.

Weiss, Daniel. *The Critic Agonistes: Psychology, Myth, and the Art of Fiction,* edited by Stephen Arkin and Eric Solomon. Seattle: University of Washington Press, 1985.

Psychoanalytic Approaches to Conrad

Crews, Frederick. "Conrad's Uneasiness — and Ours." In *Out of My System: Psychoanalysis, Ideology, and Critical Method.* New York: Oxford University Press. Mainly about *Heart of Darkness.*

Kartiganer, Donald M. "Freud's Reading Process: The Divided Protagonist Narrative and the Case of the Wolf-Man." In *The Psychoanalytic Study of Literature,* edited by Joseph Reppen and Maurice Charney. Hillsdale, N.J.: Analytic Press, 1985. Kartiganer relates the famous case history to Marlow's narrative in *Heart of Darkness.*

Kirschner, Paul. *Conrad: The Psychologist as Artist.* Edinburgh: Oliver and Boyd, 1968.

Meyer, Bernard C. *Joseph Conrad: A Psychoanalytic Biography.* Princeton, N.J.: Princeton University Press, 1967.

Rogers, Robert. *A Psychoanalytic Study of the Double in Literature.* Detroit: Wayne State University Press, 1970. Chapter 3 is devoted to "The Secret Sharer."

Reader-Response Criticism
and
Heart of Darkness

WHAT IS READER-RESPONSE CRITICISM?

Students are routinely asked in literature courses for their re-actions to texts they are reading. Sometimes there are so many differ-ent reactions that we may wonder whether everyone has read the same text. And some students respond so idiosyncratically to what they read that we say their responses are "totally off the wall."

Reader-response critics are interested in the variety of our re-sponses. Reader-response criticism raises theoretical questions about whether our responses to a work are the same as its meanings, whether a work can have as many meanings as we have responses to it, and whether some responses are more valid than, or superior to, oth-ers. It asks us to pose the following questions: What have we internal-ized that helps us determine what is — and what isn't — "off the wall"? What, in other words, is the wall, and what standards help us to define it?

Reader-response criticism also provides models that are useful in answering such questions. Adena Rosmarin suggests that a liter-ary work can be likened to an incomplete work of sculpture: to see it fully, we *must* complete it imaginatively, taking care to do so in a way that responsibly takes into account what is there. But there are other models, and other representatives of reader-response theory. Being fa-miliar with them will better allow you to "place" Rosmarin's version of reader-response theory and to see a variety of ways in which, as a reader-response critic, you could respond to *Heart of Darkness*.

Reader-response criticism, which emerged during the 1970s, focuses on what texts do to — or in — the mind of the reader, rather than looking at a text as something with properties exclusively its own. A "poem," Louise M. Rosenblatt wrote as early as 1969, "is what the reader lives through under the guidance of the text and experiences as relevant to the text." Rosenblatt knew her definition would be difficult for many to accept: "The idea that a *poem* presupposes a *reader* actively involved with a *text*," she wrote, "is particularly shocking to those seeking to emphasize the objectivity of their interpretations."[1]

Formalists — the old New Critics — are those readers who Rosenblatt expected would find the idea shocking. They preferred to discuss "the poem itself," the "concrete work of art," the "real poem." And they refused to describe what a work of literature makes a reader "live through." In fact, in *The Verbal Icon*, William K. Wimsatt and Monroe C. Beardsley defined as fallacious the very notion that a reader's response is part of the meaning of a literary work:

> The Affective Fallacy is a confusion between the poem and its *results* (what it *is* and what it *does*). . . . It begins by trying to derive the standards of criticism from the psychological effects of a poem and ends in impressionism and relativism. The outcome . . . is that the poem itself, as an object of specifically critical judgment, tends to disappear.[2]

Reader-response critics take issue with their formalist predecessors. Stanley Fish, who in 1970 published a highly influential article entitled "Literature in the Reader: Affective Stylistics," argues that any school of criticism that would see a work of literature as an object, that would claim to describe what it *is* and never what it *does*, is guilty of misconstruing what literature and reading really are. Literature exists when it is read, Fish suggests, and its force is an affective force. Furthermore, reading is a temporal process. Formalists pretend it is a spatial one as they step back and survey the literary work as if it were an object spread out before them. They may find elegant patterns of language in the texts they examine and reexamine, but they don't take into account the fact

---

[1]Louise M. Rosenblatt, "Towards a Transactional Theory of Reading," *Journal of Reading Behavior* 1 (1969), p. 3. Reprinted in *Influx: Essays on Literary Influence*, ed. Ronald Primeau (Port Washington, N. Y.: Kennikat Press, 1977), p. 127.

[2]William K. Wimsatt and Monroe C. Beardsley, *The Verbal Icon* (Lexington: University of Kentucky Press, 1954), p. 21.

that the work is something quite different to a reader turning pages, being moved by lines that appear and disappear as the reader reads.

In a discussion of the effect that a sentence by the seventeenth-century physician Thomas Browne has on a reader reading, Fish pauses to say this about his analysis — but also, by extension, about the overall critical strategy he has in large part developed: "Whatever is persuasive and illuminating about [it] . . . is the result of my sub-stituting for one question — what does this sentence mean? — another, more operational question — what does this sentence do?" He then quotes a line from John Milton's *Paradise Lost* that refers to Satan and the other fallen angels: "Nor did they not perceive their evil plight." Whereas more traditional critics might go on to say that the "meaning" of the line is, "They did perceive their evil plight," Fish de-scribes the uncertain movement of the reader's mind *to* that half-satisfying translation. Furthermore, he declares, "the reader's inability to tell whether or not 'they' do perceive and his involuntary question . . . are part of the line's *meaning*, even though they take place in the mind, not on the page."[3]

This stress on what pages *do* to minds is to be found in the writings of most, if not all, reader-response critics. Wolfgang Iser, author of *The Implied Reader* (1972) and *The Act of Reading: A Theory of Aesthetic Response* (1976), finds texts full of gaps, and these gaps, or "blanks," as he sometimes calls them, have a powerful effect on read-ers. They force the reader to explain them, to connect what the gaps separate, literally to create in the mind a poem or novel or play that isn't "there" in the text but that the text incites. Stephen Booth, who greatly influenced Fish by writing in the late 1960s what are now seen as reader-response papers and essays on Shakespeare, equally emphasizes what words, sentences, and passages "do." He stresses in his analyses the "reading *experience* that results" from a "multiplic-ity of organizations" in, say, a Shakespeare sonnet (italics added).[4] Sometimes these organizations don't make full sense, and sometimes they even seem curiously contradictory. But that is precisely what in-terests reader response critics, who, unlike formalists, are at least as interested in fragmentary, inconclusive, and even unfinished texts as

[3]Stanley E. Fish, "Literature in the Reader: Affective Stylistics," *New Literary History* 2 (1970), pp. 125–26. Reprinted in Primeau, *Influx,* p. 157, and in Stanley Fish's collection of essays, *Is There a Text in This Class? The Authority of Interpretive Communities* (Cambridge, Mass.: Harvard University Press, 1980), p. 26.

[4]Stephen Booth, *An Essay on Shakespeare's Sonnets* (New Haven, Conn.: Yale University Press, 1969), p. ix.

they are in polished, unified works. For it is the reader's struggle to *make sense* of a challenging work that reader-response critics seek to describe.

In *Self-Consuming Artifacts: The Experience of Seventeenth-Century Literature,* Fish reveals his preference for literature that makes readers work at making meaning. He contrasts two kinds of literary presentation — using the phrase "rhetorical presentation" to describe literature that reflects and reinforces opinions that readers already hold, and the phrase "dialectical presentation" to refer to works that prod and provoke. A dialectical text, rather than presenting an opinion as if it were truth, challenges readers to discover truths on their own. Such a text may not even have the kind of symmetry that formalist critics look for. Rather than offering a single, sustained argument, a dialectical text or self-consuming artifact may be "so arranged that to enter into the spirit and assumptions of any one of [its] . . . units is implicitly to reject the spirit and assumptions of the unit immediately preceding."[5] Such a text needs a reader-response critic to elucidate its workings. Another kind of critic is likely to try to explain why the units are unified and coherent, not contradicting and "consuming" their predecessors. The procedure of the reader-response critic is to describe the reader's way of dealing with the sudden twists and turns that characterize the dialectical text — that make the reader return to earlier passages and see them in an entirely new light.

"The value of such a procedure," Fish has written, "is predicated on the idea of meaning as *an event*," not as something "located (presumed to be imbedded) *in* the utterance" or "verbal object as a thing in itself."[6] By redefining meaning as an event, of course, the reader-response critic once again locates meaning in time: the reader's time. A text exists and signifies while it is being read, and what it signifies or means will depend, to no small extent, on *when* it is read. (*Paradise Lost* had some meanings for a seventeenth-century Puritan that it would not have for a twentieth-century atheist.)

With the redefinition of literature as something that only exists meaningfully in the reader — with the redefinition of the literary work as a catalyst of mental events — comes a concurrent redefinition of the reader. No longer is the reader the passive recipient of the ideas

[5]Stanley E. Fish, *Self-Consuming Artifacts: The Experience of Seventeenth-Century Literature* (Berkeley: University of California Press, 1972), p. 9.
[6]Fish, "Literature in the Reader," p. 128. Reprinted in Primeau, *Influx,* p. 159, and in Fish, *Is There a Text in This Class?,* p. 28.

that an author has planted in a text. "The reader is *active*,"[7] Rosenblatt insists, and Fish begins "Literature in the Reader" this way: "If at this moment someone were to ask, 'what are you doing,' you might reply, 'I am reading,' and thereby acknowledge that reading is . . . something *you do*."[8] In "How To Recognize a Poem When You See One," he is even more provocative: "Interpreters do not decode poems: they make them."[9] Iser, in focusing critical interest on the gaps in texts — on what is not said — similarly redefines the reader as an active maker. In an essay entitled "Interaction between Text and Reader," he argues that what is missing from a narrative causes the reader to fill in the blanks creatively.

Iser's title implies a cooperation between reader and text that is also implied in Rosenblatt's definition of a poem as "what the reader lives through under the guidance of the text." (She borrows the term "transactional" to describe the dynamics of the reading process, which in her view involves interdependent texts and readers interacting.) The view that texts and readers make poems together, though, is not shared by *all* interpreters that are generally thought of as reader-response critics. Steven Mailloux has divided reader-response critics into several general categories, three of the largest of which he labels "subjective," "transactive," and "social." Subjective critics like David Bleich (or Norman Holland after his conversion by Bleich) assume what Mailloux calls the "absolute priority of individual selves as creators of texts."[10] They do not, in other words, see the reader's response as a guided one but rather as one motivated by deep-seated, personal, psychological needs. What they find in texts is, in Holland's phrase, their own "identity theme." As readers, Holland has argued, we use "the literary work to symbolize and finally to replicate ourselves. We work out through the text our own characteristic patterns of desire."[11]

Subjective critics, as you may already have guessed, often find themselves confronted with the following question: if all interpretation is a function of private, psychological identity, then how is it that so

[7]Rosenblatt, "Towards a Transactional Theory of Reading," p. 3. Reprinted in Primeau, *Influx*, p. 123.
[8]Fish, "Literature in the Reader," p. 123. Reprinted in Primeau, *Influx*, p. 154, and in Fish, *Is There a Text in This Class?*, p. 22.
[9]Fish, *Is There a Text in This Class?*, p. 327.
[10]Steven Mailloux, *Interpretive Conventions: The Reader in the Study of American Fiction* (Ithaca, N.Y.: Cornell University Press, 1982), p. 31.
[11]Norman N. Holland, "UNITY IDENTITY TEXT SELF," *PMLA* 90 (1975), p. 816.

many readers have interpreted, say, Shakespeare's *Hamlet* in the same way? Subjective critics have answers to the question — Holland simply says that there are common identity themes, such as one involving an oedipal fantasy — but others have been dissatisfied by their responses to the question. Jonathan Culler cannot believe that individual readers, let alone whole groups of readers, are so uncomplicated that they see themselves in every book and express their personal identity in every act of reading.[12] Fish, who has himself had to explain why different readers interpret the same text similarly (and why the same reader reads different texts differently), has come up with perhaps a better answer than Holland's notion of shared fantasies. "Both the stability of interpretation among readers and the variety of interpretation in the career of a single reader . . . are functions of interpretive strategies." These strategies, which "exist prior to the act of reading and therefore determine the shape of what is read," are held in common by "interpretive communities."[13] Interpretive communities — such as the one including students reading *Heart of Darkness* in an American college or university — share and, gradually, change their reading strategies over the course of time.

As I have implicitly just suggested, reader-response criticism is not one monolithic school of thought, as is assumed by some detractors, who like to talk about the "School of Fish." As Mailloux points out in *Interpretive Conventions* (1982), the term "reader-response criticism" can refer to any number of critical approaches that focus on the process of reading. Some critics mentioned thus far have been one kind of reader-response critic at one time, another kind at another. Holland's growing subjectivism has already been hinted at, but Fish has undergone some radical shifts in his thinking as well. Having at first seen meaning as the cooperative production of readers and texts, Fish went on to become a subjectivist, and very nearly a "deconstructor" ready to suggest that all criticism is imaginative creation, fiction about literature, or *metafiction*. (In an essay entitled "Facts and Fictions: A Reply to Ralph Rader" (1975), Fish was by his own admission on the verge of giving up all claim to objectivity and of claiming, instead, merely that his own interpretations were "superior fictions.") With the development of

---

[12]Jonathan Culler, "Prolegomena to a Theory of Reading," in *The Reader in the Text,* ed. Susan Suleiman and Inge Crossman (Princeton, N.J.: Princeton University Press, 1980), p. 46.

[13]Stanley E. Fish, "Interpreting the *Variorum*," *Critical Inquiry* 2:3 (Spring 1976), pp. 481, 483. Reprinted in Fish, *Is There a Text in This Class?*, pp. 167, 171.

his notion of interpretive communities, however, Fish became more of a social, structuralist, reader-response critic; at present his project is to study reading communities and what Mailloux calls "interpretive conventions" in order to understand "the condition of a work's intelligibility."[14]

In spite of the gaps between reader-response critics and even between the assumptions that they have held at various stages of their respective careers, all tend to try to answer similar questions and to use similar strategies to describe the reader's response to a given text. One of the common questions that these critics tend to be asked has already been discussed: Why do individual readers come up with such similar interpretations if meaning is not embedded *in* the work itself? Other recurring, troubling questions are interrelated: Just who *is* the reader? (or, to place the emphasis differently, Just who is *the* reader?) Aren't you reader-response critics just talking about your own idiosyncratic responses when you describe what a line from *Paradise Lost* "does" in and to "the reader's" mind? What about my responses? What if they're different? Will you be willing to say that all responses are equally valid?

Fish describes what he means by "the reader" this way: "*the* reader is the *informed* reader." The informed reader is someone who is "sufficiently experienced as a reader to have internalized the properties of literary discourses, including everything from the most local of devices (figures of speech, etc.) to whole genres." And, of course, the informed reader is in full possession of the "semantic knowledge"[15] (knowledge of idioms, for instance) assumed by the text.

Other reader-response critics use terms other than "the *informed* reader" to define "*the* reader," and these other terms mean slightly different things. Wayne Booth uses the phrase "the implied reader" to mean the reader "created by the work." (Only "by agreeing to play the role of this created audience . . . can an actual reader correctly understand and appreciate the work."[16]) Gérard Genette and Gerald Prince prefer to speak of "the narratee, . . . the necessary counterpart of a given narrator, that is, the person or figure who receives a

[14]Stanley E. Fish, "Consequences," *Critical Inquiry* 11 (1985): p. 438. Reprinted in W. J. Mitchell, ed., *Against Theory: Literary Studies and the New Pragmatism* (Chicago: University of Chicago Press, 1985), p. 111.

[15]Fish, *Self-Consuming Artifacts*, p. 406.

[16]Susan R. Suleiman, Introduction to Suleiman and Crossman, *The Reader in the Text*, p. 8.

narrative."[17] Iser, like Booth, uses "the implied reader," but he also refers to "the educated reader" when he discusses what Fish calls the "informed" or "intended" reader. Thus, with different terms, each critic denies the claim that reader-response criticism will lead people to think that there are as many correct interpretations of a work as there are readers to read it.

As Mailloux has shown, reader-response critics share not only questions, answers, concepts, and terms for those concepts but also strategies of reading. Two of the basic "moves," as he calls them, are to show how a work gives readers something to do, and to describe what the reader does by way of response. There are more complex moves as well. For instance, a reader-response critic might typically (1) cite direct references to reading in the text, to justify the focus on reading and show how the inside of the text is continuous with what the reader is doing; (2) show how other, nonreading situations in the text nonetheless mirror the situation the reader is in ("Fish shows how in *Paradise Lost* Michael's teaching of Adam in Book XI resembles Milton's teaching of the reader throughout the poem"[18]); and (3) show, therefore, that the reader's response is, or is perfectly analogous to, the topic of the story. For Stephen Booth, *Hamlet* is the tragic story of "an audience that cannot make up its mind." In the view of Roger Easson, William Blake's *Jerusalem* "may be read as a poem about the experience of reading *Jerusalem*."[19]

In the essay that follows, Adena Rosmarin makes most if not all of the interpretive moves that have been discussed here. Beginning with a short history of the neglect of the reader, Rosmarin tells how traditional criticism has always assumed that both texts and readers were essentially passive: texts were construed as objects without worldly purpose, and readers were supposed to be disinterested. (Note that Rosmarin mentions Wimsatt and Beardsley's notion of the affective fallacy along with similar notions by more ancient critics and philosophers in order to attack it.) Having rejected

---

[17]Ibid., p. 13.

[18]Steven Mailloux, "Learning to Read: Interpretation and Reader-Response Criticism," *Studies in the Literary Imagination* 12 (1979), p. 103.

[19]Stephen Booth, "On the Value of *Hamlet*," in *Reinterpretations of Elizabethan Drama: Selected Papers from the English Institute,* ed. Norman Rabkin (New York: Columbia University Press, 1969), p. 152. Roger R. Easson, "William Blake and His Reader in *Jerusalem*," in *Blake's Sublime Allegory,* ed. Stuart Curran and Joseph A. Wittreich, Jr. (Madison: University of Wisconsin Press, 1973), p. 309.

several similar versions of the old account of readers and texts, Rosmarin then asks the one question that is central to the reader-response critic's enterprise: What is the experience of reading *Heart of Darkness* like?

One of the answers she gives was alluded to earlier. Reading *Heart of Darkness,* she suggests, is like looking at a broken torso, or an incomplete work of sculpture with pieces missing, that we must "figure out"; that is, finish in our imaginations by supplying poetic devices (figures) of our own. Calling *Heart of Darkness* an "inconclusive or fragmentary literary work," Rosmarin finds gaps even between sentences — gaps that make us go back and reread, thus enriching our experience of the text with a second (perhaps contradictory) experience. That experience, however, also becomes part of the developing event (meaning) that unfolds in our minds as we read. "The tale teaches the necessity and value of endless rereading," Rosmarin argues, thus employing one of the more complex strategies Mailloux lists (that of showing that "the reader's response is, or is perfectly analogous to, the topic of the story"). *Heart of Darkness,* Rosmarin provocatively suggests, can even be "usefully read as a text of reader-response theory."

Rosmarin prepares us for this claim by making other interpretive moves mentioned by Mailloux: she positions the reader in the text by finding, in the relationship between the storyteller Marlow and his audience (which includes our narrator, who is first a narratee), a "perfect replica" of the situation of the disinterested text and reader. Suddenly, though, the text warns us that passivity will do us no good; Marlow is not what he seems, and if we are to figure him out, we must be active readers of the first order.

That is what Rosmarin is: an active reader. Note how, whether her subject is Conrad's text or Plato's *Republic,* she always assumes that there is a purpose to what texts state, don't state, or misstate. And speaking of misstatements, Rosmarin's article contains a fascinating treatment of the lie Marlow tells to Kurtz's Intended. Stanley Fish once alluded to *Heart of Darkness,* saying that "if . . . there is a . . . debate over whether Marlow should or should not have lied, . . . I will interpret that debate as evidence of the difficulty readers experience when the novel asks them to render judgement."[20] That difficulty is what "Darkening the Reader" is all about.

[20]Stanley E. Fish, "Interpreting 'Interpreting the *Variorum,*'" *Critical Inquiry* 3:1 (Autumn 1976), p. 193. Reprinted in Fish, *Is There a Text in This Class?,* p. 177.

A READER-RESPONSE CRITIC AT WORK

ADENA ROSMARIN

Darkening the Reader:
Reader-Response Criticism and
Heart of Darkness

Neglecting the Reader for Two Millennia

Since the ancient Greeks, critics of literature have been primarily preoccupied with mimetic or didactic questions — with questions involving the imitation of reality and the instruction of the audience. Accordingly, there is a rich body of critical literature that wrestles with the difficulties of producing and judging representations of the world, however defined, and with the problem of deciding whether and how literature should teach as it pleases. This preoccupation with mimetic and didactic questions and with the value judgments that follow from such questions — this preoccupation in part accounts for criticism's conspicuous neglect of the reader of literature.

Another reason for the neglect suffered by the reader is the way literature has been defined and valued in modern times, which is to say since approximately 1800. *Good* literature, that is, has been defined as essentially *disinterested:* as lacking worldly purpose, as lacking not design but designs on its reader, as, in effect, lacking a reader at all. This critical program of disinterestedness — its scope gives it the force of a critical dogma — has recently come under heavy critique, particularly from Marxist and feminist critics. But the historical fact of its tenacious hold on the critical, aesthetic, and institutional imaginations of the last two centuries remains, an indisputable if perhaps unfortunate reason that talk about the reader and the reader's response to literature has been programmatically aborted before its conception.

To understand this last point and how it impinges on *Heart of Darkness,* it is helpful to recall three originating foci for the disinterestedness dogma: Kant's *Critique of Judgment* (1790), Shelley's *A Defence of Poetry* (written in 1821, published in 1840), and the essay published in 1949 by W. K. Wimsatt and Monroe C. Beardsley, "The Affective Fallacy." This essay codified disinterest in the reader, effectively prohibiting an entire critical generation from studying the reading experience.

For Kant it was "plain that the beautiful, the judging of which has at its basis a merely formal purposiveness; i.e., a purposiveness without purpose, is quite independent of the concept of the good, because the latter presupposes an objective purposiveness; i.e., the reference of the object to a definite purpose."[1] This severance of moral and aesthetic judgment may have been plain to Kant, as well as centrally important to his definition of literature, but to centuries of critics writing before Kant — as well as to many critics writing in the last two decades — this severance has seemed neither plain nor desirable. For feminists and Marxists in particular it has seemed not only not desirable but invidious.

Hostility towards this famous formulation is not without good reason, for an important question is here being finessed by Kant: Can any text, *even* a literary text, actually be this thoroughly cut off from the world from which it comes and to which it goes? Do not all texts, literary or not, bear the taint, if one wants to use that word (and a practitioner of the disinterestedness dogma would) of their worldly and purposeful origins? Common sense tells us how to answer this question, and any more rigorous or philosophical analysis only underscores the correctness, indeed the necessity, of our intuitive replies. The process of decontextualization — the severance of anything from its context — is always suspect, for, paradoxically, it is always done for a reason. Given that Kant was himself a philosopher and, to say the least, smart, we should assume that he knew what he was doing. We can infer his motive to have been this: setting up disinterestedness as the primary valuative criterion of literature was not done because literature really *is* disinterested but, rather, to privilege literature, to set it above and beyond other kinds of discourse, immersed as they obviously were — and are — in the world, occupied as they obviously were — and are — with working their effects on that world. Literature, in the Kantian view, is different and somehow purer than other kinds of discourse because, at its best, it is perfectly *self*-interested. Construed thus, however, disinterestedness becomes a dogma that not only is extremely effective but also is extremely *interested* — interested, that is, in promoting the worldly stature of literature, in arguing the case for its value above all other kinds of worldly discourse precisely because it can, far better than these other kinds, wear the cloak of otherworldliness with seductive and unarguable authority.

[1]Immanuel Kant, *Critique of Judgment,* in *Critical Theory Since Plato,* ed. Hazard Adams (New York: Harcourt Brace Jovanovich, 1970), p. 386.

Much of *Heart of Darkness* proceeds with startling directness from Kant's argument, in particular these important early lines, which introduce the tale's primary teller, the mood of his audience, and the landscape that, as in all Romantic and post-Romantic literature, images the minds of each:

> Marlow sat cross-legged right aft, leaning against the mizzen-mast. He had sunken cheeks, a yellow complexion, a straight back, an ascetic aspect, and, with his arms dropped, the palms of hands outwards, resembled an idol. . . . We exchanged a few words lazily. Afterwards there was silence on board the yacht. For some reason or other we did not begin that game of dominoes. We felt meditative, and fit for nothing but placid staring. The day was ending in a serenity of still and exquisite brilliance. The water shone pacifically; the sky, without a speck, was a benign immensity of unstained light. (p. 18)

The tale is told, in other words, by a figure conspicuous for his otherworldliness. And the world in which it is told itself seems otherworldly, an image not only of the perfectly disinterested mental states of teller and audience — "for some reason or other we did not begin that game of dominoes" — but also of the perfectly disinterested (and therefore perfect, from an aesthetic point of view) tale that we expect to hear. But the following lines, coming almost directly after the above, issue a warning: "Only the gloom to the west, brooding over the upper reaches, became more sombre every minute, as if angered by the approach of the sun" (p. 18). We are here warned, as we are throughout *Heart of Darkness,* not to be taken in by appearances, even as those appearances are given all possible poetic substance and seductive lure. This seduction-warning dialectic takes many forms: here political, there philosophical, here moral, there aesthetic. In the above passage we are being specifically warned that this tale will subscribe, or seem to subscribe, to the dogma of disinterestedness even as it mounts a devastating critique of that very dogma.

In the famous concluding line of *A Defence of Poetry,* Shelley declares poets to be "the unacknowledged legislators of the world."[2] In the no less famous concluding lines of "Ode to the West Wind," Shelley makes similarly explicit his deep preoccupation with the social and political power of literature. Still, despite such resounding

[2]Percy Bysshe Shelley, *A Defence of Poetry,* in Adams, *Critical Theory,* p. 513.

pronouncements, Shelley *also* wanted his literature seemingly unrhe-torical or, what is the same, seemingly disinterested. He solved his conflict by conceptualizing literature as something that is not heard but, rather, *over*heard: "A poet is a nightingale, who sits in darkness and sings to cheer its own solitude with sweet sounds; his auditors are as men entranced by the melody of an unseen musician, who feel that they are moved and softened, yet know not whence or why."[3] This renowned image of the relationship between poet and audience prefigures, with a precision that would be uncanny were it not also historical and pervasive, the relationship of Marlow and his immediate audience on the *Nellie*. The connection is so close that it seems a direct influence. But one need not argue the directness of Kant's or Shelley's influence on Conrad precisely because their influence was everywhere, saturating the literature and criticism of nineteenth-century England. And the fact of this saturation makes Conrad's turn on the disinter-estedness dogma in *Heart of Darkness* all the more interesting and significant.

Today's reader-response critic would find in Marlow a greater awareness of his audience than Shelley finds in his idealized nightingale. But our possession of an insightful methodology and some historical hindsight should not blind us to the significance of the repetition we have here before us. The fact that the world-weary narrative situation on the *Nellie* so closely replicates the otherworldly situation upon which Shelley bases his aesthetic theory argues the historical and theoretical potency of the nightingale image and, more generally, of the disinter-estedness dogma. This image, our most enduring statement of this dog-ma, has thus dominated not only our critical evaluation of literature and whether the reader and his response can in any way figure in that evalu-ation but also the very way in which literature that aspires to be great has been written.

Heart of Darkness, again taking our critical topic as our theo-retical example, is rather obviously trying to *do* something to its reader, to change him or his mind in some way. For one thing, as almost every critic has recognized, the work is obviously — if complexly — cri-tiquing late nineteenth-century imperialism. But *Heart of Darkness,* even as it mounts this explicit critique, also explicitly practices the dogma of disinterestedness, a paradoxical feat accomplished primarily by making Marlow's act of tale-telling adhere to Shelley's image: the

[3] Shelley, *Defence,* in Adams, *Critical Theory,* p. 502.

tale seems more like meditation than speech, and the audience seems less hearing than overhearing. There Marlow sits, almost invisible in the deepening darkness, simply thinking aloud. Or so it seems. The presence of his immediate audience seems almost if not entirely incidental, almost unnecessary to the telling of his tale.

A reader-response critic would observe that so many "seemings" should make us wary, suspicious of what we *seem* to be seeing. He might also observe that one of the tale's "actions" is not only the usual conflict of characters but also the less usual conflict of aesthetics and rhetoric here being discussed. Put otherwise, different definitions of literature are at war in *Heart of Darkness,* and the reader is being asked to sit in judgment on this agony as well as on that being narrated by Marlow, the most obvious instance of which is his struggle with Kurtz or, if you will, himself. The reader's judgment is uncertain on all scores. All that we can be certain of, given Conrad's superior artistry, in this work and in his others, is that each request for the reader's judgment is designed to prompt rethinking of his conventional or received ways of thinking about and valuing art — and of the "persons" it fabricates.

Finally, in our own century, Wimsatt and Beardsley argued that interest in the reader was not only unaesthetic but also fallacious: "The affective fallacy is a confusion between the poem and its *results* (what it *is* and what it *does*)."[4] The reader-response critic, of course, is interested in fostering precisely this confusion, in redefining the poem to be less like a thing and more like an event, an event that happens to its reader and that can be read and textualized as such.[5] Wimsatt and Beardsley are uniquely important for our purposes here because they make explicit and unequivocal not only criticism's traditional neglect of the reader but also the deepest reason for this neglect: hostility. If a stable object of study is to be had, the reader *must* be gotten rid of, and it is this reasoning that turns us to Plato and to the reasons behind history's most resonant expulsion: the exile of the Poet — of the Conrads and the Marlows — from that most famous if fictional State of Reason, Plato's *Republic.*

---

[4]W. K. Wimsatt and Monroe Beardsley, *The Affective Fallacy,* in Adams, *Critical Theory,* p. 1022.

[5]For elaborations of this point — that the poem is less like a thing and more like an event — see Stanley Fish's "Literature in the Reader: Affective Stylistics," *New Literary History* 2 (1970): 125; and Steven Mailloux's "Learning to Read: Interpretation and Reader-Response Criticism," *Studies in the Literary Imagination* 12 (1979), pp. 93–108.

Plato, the Passive Reader, and the Poet's Lie

When Plato threw the poet out of the Republic, he gave two reasons. The more famous of the two, the one that everyone immediately recalls, is that the poet lies. By this Plato meant not that the poet maliciously dissembles but that the very nature of his art forces him to stay at two removes from Reality. Plato had reasoned that there was an Ideal Realm, wherein dwelt all the Ideal Forms that, on earth, exist only in terms of their imperfect replicas. Every worldly bed, to take Plato's own example, is thus an imperfect copy of the Ideal Bed. And, by extension, every artistic representation of a worldly bed (or man, or action, or indeed anything on earth) is also an imperfect copy of an already imperfect copy. So the poet, by which term Plato meant not only poets but all artists, is doubly at fault. Or, more precisely, his art is.

It has become a commonplace of contemporary criticism, particularly as practiced and theorized by the deconstructionists, that every repetition repeats with a difference.[6] There are by definition no perfect representations: something is always added or emphasized, something always left out or deemphasized. All copies turn away from or *trope* (figure) their originals in some way. And, one should add, for some purpose. Thus beds, to continue with Plato's example, are three-dimensional in the world but are necessarily two-dimensional in a painting. Further, in the world they are made of, among other things, wood or metal. Never, however, are worldly beds made of words. Thus does the very act or medium of representation necessarily insert differences, no matter how realistic, how conforming to the object represented, the artist tries to be. It cannot be overemphasized that these differences or "faults" cannot be remedied: they not only reside in but in fact constitute the very nature of representation. Were it not for these differences, what we would have before us would be not a painting of a bed but the bed itself, not the tale of Marlow's experience, but the experience itself.

Similarly, the differences between Plato's worldly and Ideal beds cannot be remedied — except, *very* possibly, by the lifelong and arduous application of the process of reasoning, which, when focused on such matters, just might enable the reasoner to think his way back to an Image of the Original Bed or whatever. Plato recognized that the

[6]For a concise analysis and exemplification of this point, see the opening chapter, "Two Forms of Repetition," of J. Hillis Miller's *Fiction and Repetition: Seven English Novels* (Cambridge, Mass.: Harvard University Press, 1982), pp. 1–21.

chance of this happening, given man's tendency towards the irrational, was slight, but, since it was the only game in town, he went with it. His republic was accordingly organized to assist and encourage the process of reasoning in its citizenry: to remove all temptations to depart from the perfectly reasonable and to provide all possible opportunities to perfect the practice of reasoning. Clearly, since the poet added imperfections to the already imperfect, he was not wanted. One obstacle was more than enough.

But, turning now to the second reason for his expulsion, the poet also interfered with the development of reason in man by "feeding and watering the passions instead of drying them up."[7] Famous as these words are, this reason has taken second place to the poet's lying: the many defenses of poetry, all ultimately attempts to rebut Plato's opening move, concentrate on the crime of misrepresentation far more than on the arousal of the emotions. But, if the *Republic* is carefully read, this second reason will be found to have priority. We know this because the guardians of the state are allowed to lie for "the public good." Without dwelling on the philosophical and worldly difficulties that this exception creates, difficulties dramatically illustrated by leaders of our own time and in our own "republics," we can see that, for Plato, fear of lying, however great, pales before fear of passion. The state of reason, in both senses, rests on the premise of a citizen that behaves and thinks and even feels in terms of reason only. *Heart of Darkness* probes this premise by extension, characterizing in Kurtz, the accountant, the manager, and Marlow himself the myriad ways in which reason, when pushed to its logical conclusion, breaks down and, like the conspicuously symbolic hippo meat, goes bad.

But let us return to this business of the passions, overfed and overwatered. Why should Plato so fear that the experience of a play — and it is for Plato as it was for Aristotle the experience of Greek drama that was the typical literary experience — why should Plato so fear that this experience would devastate the reason of its audience? We do not, after all, experience the telling or the dramatization of an experience as we would the experience itself. To watch a man cry on the stage, to invoke another of Plato's examples, is not the same as crying. The difference is not only always present but also always enormous. Curiously, Plato's analysis of the poet's first fault, the imperfection of his

---

[7]Plato's exact words, from Book X of *The Republic,* the book that also contains the "bed" argument, are: "poetry . . . feeds and waters the passions instead of drying them up," in Adams, *Critical Theory,* p. 40.

representation, his "lie," was *based* upon recognition of this difference. But Plato's condemnation of the second fault *ignores* this difference, presuming instead the identity of artful and worldly experiences: the man in the audience *will* mirror the man on the stage. In sum, Plato's thinking on this point is not internally consistent. But if we remind ourselves that his thought, like all thinking that becomes discursive or written down for perusal by another, was in the service of a goal — in this case justifying the expulsion of the poet — then the fact that his two reasons are contradictory becomes evidence not of Plato's failure as a philosopher but evidence for the fact that even our most "disinterested" thinking is in fact always profoundly rhetorical and pragmatic, interested in any reason that works. This point should be kept in mind throughout our reading of Marlow's philosophic meditation, his dramatic simulation of Shelley's emblem of disinterestedness: "For a long time already he, sitting apart, had been no more to us than a voice" (p. 42).

Plato's fear of the audience's response, in other words, is based upon — depends upon — his conceptualization of the audience as *passive,* as composed of men who unthinkingly and, therefore, perfectly mirror what they see. Whereas the poet is condemned, in the first reason, for imperfectly mirroring what he represents, he is condemned in the second reason out of fear that his audience will perfectly mirror his representation.

The history of criticism, owing largely to this famous opening move, has continued until very recently to think of the reader of literature as unthinking, as a being passive to the point of stupidity, who brings to the work of reading neither developed moral judgment, nor interpretive finesse, nor literary sophistication, nor the ability to learn from his mistakes. While virtually every critic or theorist since Plato has in one way or another acknowledged the affective impact of literature (for what other reason would censors exist? for what other reason was the poet exiled?), the notion of the reader's passivity has died hard. This passivity had the further consequence of making the reader and his reading experience an apparently uninteresting, if not also fallacious, topic for critical inquiry. For it follows that if the reader is passive and simple of mind, so also is his experience. Hence, another reason for the long neglect.

Only with the advent of reader-response criticism has the reader been granted a mind. He has now "become" an active, necessary, and often self-conscious participant in the making of a text's meaning. That is, the reader-response critic conceptualizes a reader who, as he reads, is hard at work attempting to make good literary sense, however that may be defined, of the text being read. What makes reader-response criticism particularly intriguing, however, is its habit of taking these attempts to be most interesting and instructional when they fail, at least initially. The process of reading thus becomes one not only of continual thinking but of no less continual rethinking. And the reader, by virtue of this repeated process, becomes a better thinker and reader than he was when he began. The irony here should not go unnoticed: that by reconceptualizing the reader as an active if also emotional intelligence, the poet is implicitly also reconceptualized: no longer a block to the creation of thinking and, according to Platonic logic, therefore also moral men, he becomes perhaps our most powerful agent of this creation. Shelley defended the mental and moral force of poetry along just these lines: "Poetry strengthens the faculty which is the organ of the moral nature of man, in the same manner as exercise strengthens a limb."[8] Given the evidence of *Heart of Darkness* alone, we may infer Conrad also to have assumed and preferred a thinking reader, a reader empowered to value his thought-provoking art and artist, to whose "lie" we will eventually turn.

Marlow's Lie and the Reader's Response

What is the experience of reading *Heart of Darkness* like? This question is a particular version of the question that, whether asked explicitly or left implicit, begins all reader-response criticism: what is the experience of reading like? The reader-response critic's task is to answer this question, to undertake a simile hunt, to find or invent the "like" that will prove to *his* reader the most convincing, the most richly illuminating, the most powerful analogy for the text under examination. Reader-response criticism thus assumes as its typical structure a question-answer or problem-solution dialectic. It also, due to the simile or metaphor chosen by the critic as his fundamental sense-making tool, has a fundamentally metaphorical or figurative base. It is, in a very precise sense, a *figuring-out* of a problem or text.

Traditional literary criticism, like all nonfictional writing, has traditionally been most convincing when it has seemed to come up with *the* answer or *the* solution. When it has seemed, that is, not in the least figurative but perfectly straightforward or literal, and, moreover,

---

[8]Shelley, *Defence,* in Adams, *Critical Theory,* p. 503.

when it has reached what seems a perfect or permanent closure. The ideal critical reading — and here the Platonic tradition weighs very heavily — is not only a perfect wording or representation but also a last word. No more, ideally, needs be said. The topic — or text — is closed.

Recent criticism, however, perhaps taking its cue from the inconclusive or fragmentary literary works that have become its frequent topic — *Heart of Darkness* is such a work — recognizes not only the impossibility of the answer that needs no further questioning but also the undesirability of such an answer. Closure and perfection have acquired the taint of death, an acquisition recognized by the poets and novelists of the nineteenth and twentieth centuries long before it dawned on their critics.

Robert Browning repeatedly made these points, "arguing" in such dramatic monologues as "The Bishop Orders His Tomb" and "Cleon" the death-taint of closure: "I, I the feeling, thinking, acting man, / The man who loved his life so over-much, sleep in my urn" ("Cleon," ll. 321–23). "Urn" is not an innocent word here, for since Donne and Keats it has done double duty for the poem construed as object, as formally and perfectly finished, as ideally if forlornly bereft of its reader's interpretive activity. So the urn that Cleon anticipates is by this point in literary history not only a literal but also a poetic urn: it is the enclosure he fears but also the poem he speaks. In Browning's "Andrea del Sarto," the perfection of Andrea, who, as the reader in the poem's epigraph is warned, is "Called 'The Faultless Painter,' " is yet another form of self-entombment, of perfection run amuck, become a place altogether too final and private, as has Kurtz's. These dramatic monologues are meant to be undone by their readers, in much the way Marlow's tale is meant to be undone by its reader: questioned, and construed as problematic, even as the problem is left conspicuously and appropriately unsolved.

John Ruskin, the nineteenth-century art critic, wrote to Browning, complaining of the demands made by Browning's poetry on its readers. The exchange is worth quoting because it prefigures what we may posit to be the typical reader's response to *Heart of Darkness*:

Ruskin:

Your Ellipses are quite Unconscionable: before one can get through ten lines, one has to patch you up in twenty places, wrong or right, and if one hasn't much stuff of one's own to spare to patch with! You are worse than the worst Alpine Glacier I ever crossed. Bright, and deep enough truly, but so full of Clefts that half the journey has to be done with ladder and hatchet.[9]

Browning's reply:

I cannot begin writing poetry till my imaginary reader has conceded licences to me which you demur at altogether. I *know* that I don't make out my conception by my language, all poetry being a putting the infinite within the finite. You would have me paint it all plain out, which can't be. . . .[10]

A later critic, however, recognized that the source of Ruskin's complaint was coincident with the heart of Browning's art. Browning's "short poems have no completeness, no limpidity," wrote George Santayana. "They are little torsos made broken so as to stimulate the reader to the restoration of their missing legs and arms."[11]

So as to stimulate the reader to the restoration of their missing legs and arms. Reading *Heart of Darkness,* then, I posit to be *like* Ruskin's experience of trying to read Browning's poems. I also posit it to be *like* Santayana's description of the reader's attempts at restoration. Although both Ruskin and Santayana are in one sense saying the same thing about Browning's poetry, in another sense they are not: their attitudes, in sum, are perfectly opposed. For Ruskin, the passive or Platonic reader remained expected and ideal. For Santayana, writing several decades later, the active reader and the art that prompted that activity were not only suddenly possible but also most highly valued. The "broken" or inconclusive fiction (from Plato's point of view, the conspicuous "lie") and the active reader (from Plato's point of view, a reader dangerous precisely because he had a mind of his own and was using it, doubtless compounding the errors and passions represented by the poet) were the new standards of judgment. The juxtaposition of these two comments articulates a turning point in the history of criticism, a turning point at once emblemed by Conrad's tale and enacted within it — and by its reader as he reads it.

---

[9]John Ruskin's complaint — he had been reading Browning's *Men and Women* — is contained in a letter to Browning, the text of which is printed in David J. DeLaura, "Ruskin and the Brownings: Twenty-five Unpublished Letters," *Bulletin of the John Rylands Library,* 54 (1972), pp. 324–27.

[10]Browning's reply to Ruskin is quoted in *The Works of John Ruskin,* ed. E. T. Cook and Alexander Wedderburn, vol. 36 (London: George Allen, 1909), p. xxxiv.

[11]George Santayana, "The Poetry of Barbarism," in *Robert Browning: A Collection of Critical Essays,* ed. Philip Drew (Boston: Houghton Mifflin, 1966), p. 30.

It is of the utmost importance to keep the reader's *effort* in mind. He is *trying* to restore the missing legs and arms — limbs whose "missingness," not incidentally, is already the product of the reader's Platonic assumption, his assumption that there must *originally* have been not a broken torso but a perfect whole. With Conrad as with Browning, however, the limbs remain missing. The torso was *originally* a torso only, despite our mind's refusal — tutored by Plato — to accept that fact. *Heart of Darkness* represents, to be sure, a literal journey: a man Marlow goes to the Congo, where he has many and varied experiences, and returns to tell, in Ancient Mariner fashion, his story. But *Heart of Darkness* lets few if any of its readers remain content with such a reading. The work, in part by self-descriptions of its own inconclusiveness and profundity, in part by thickets of allusion to works and myths "outside" itself, insists throughout that its reader be unsatisfied with a literal or surface meaning. The demand is heavy on the reader: to *figure it out,* to find similes that will make sense of the hints of richness and depth that the tale parades before us. Yet, no matter how great our effort, our sense-making will remain inconclusive. We will be forever unable to repair the broken torso, to repair it to an original whole.

We are, of course, early on warned that our sense-making efforts will fail. Indeed, we are warned of virtually every interpretive and moral difficulty that this tale hands us, and this early warning system remains perhaps the least explored and most intriguing aspect of the tale's art. The frame narrator, who is our most obvious and reliable stand-in within the tale, who as listener is a near-replica of ourselves as a reader — who is simultaneously narrator and narratee — this narrator actually *tells* us how to think about the tale and our reading experience: "we knew we were fated, before the ebb began to run, to hear about *one* of Marlow's inconclusive experiences" (p. 21; emphasis mine). This warning is all important. It tells us not only that the inconclusiveness we will find in the tale is deliberate, not an error of our reading, but also that a good reading of this tale, contrary to what we expect good readings to be, will find not conclusions, whether aesthetic, as in the resolution of a plot conflict, or moral, as in the making of a judgment, but, rather, a conspicuous lack of them. We are warned, in sum, to be on the lookout for what is impossible to find.

And, lest we suspect that this "reader" in the tale is wrong to warn us thus, information vital to our trust of his judgment and our performance has been embedded in this warning. Again: "we knew we were fated . . . to hear about *one* of Marlow's inconclusive experiences." What the emphasis on "one" says is that Marlow's characteristic *genre* is the

tale of the "inconclusive experience," that he has accordingly produced
many tales in this genre, that he is accordingly a practiced and deliberate
designer of such experiences, meaning both his own and the reader's.
The emphasis on "one" also tells us that the remarks of our reader-
surrogate — reticent, infrequent, yet always attention-getting — are
to be trusted throughout. We are to treat them as if they were our
own. He is a *practiced* "reader" of Marlow's tales and, as the quotation below suggests, of the tales of seamen more generally. He has
heard many such tales, both the uncommon sort told by Marlow and
the more common sort told by others. His basis for contrast is firm.
He is familiar with the unfamiliarity of the tale we are about to read
even as its unfamiliarity is not lost on him. He is, in sum, the perfect
guide to Marlow's textual jungle.

So perfect, in fact, that he is able to make us metaphors for
our passage, thereby initiating the uninitiated reader before-the-fact.
The following passage has justly captured the imaginations of even the
most professional readers of Marlow's tale precisely because it gives us
a way of making sense of this most strange experience:

> The yarns of seamen have a direct simplicity, the whole meaning
> of which lies within the shell of a cracked nut. But Marlow was
> not typical (if his propensity to spin yarns be excepted), and to him
> the meaning of an episode was not inside like a kernel but outside,
> enveloping the tale which brought it out only as a glow brings out
> a haze, in the likeness of one of these misty halos that sometimes
> are made visible by the spectral illumination of moonshine. (pp.
> 19–20)

This immensely suggestive and, for that very reason, conspicuously unclear image — it is, one might say, the image of imaged obscurity — suggests that meanings in *Heart of Darkness* are not easily approached, that, if approached, they show themselves to be multiple, and
that this multiplicity refuses to be layered into any of the oppositions
that, as readers of texts or interpreters of the world, we conventionally use as instruments of sense-making. Kernel/cloud, appearance/real-
ity, surface/ground, inside/outside, shallow/profound, literal/figurative,
clear/obscure, truth-telling/lie-making, light/dark, good/bad — all such
oppositions are themselves opposed in this tale, repeatedly shown to be
inadequate to the task of making sense.

For example: color. The associations of white and black in Western
society closely parallel both those of light and dark — a primarily intellectual, indeed Platonic, opposition — and those of good and bad, the

most fundamental moral opposition. When Marlow describes his city of departure as a "whited sepulchre" (p. 24), white is immediately problematized for the reader. The color acquires not only sepulchral connotations but also moral dubiousness, Marlow's description recalling the Biblical phrase for the hypocrite, the man of inner darkness whitewashed by outer manner and conventional deed. Further into the tale and up the river, white grows yet more problematic, yet less enlightening: "When the sun rose there was a white fog, very warm and clammy, and more blinding than the night" (p. 54). The reversal of the intellectual metaphor — that light signifies knowledge and darkness ignorance — could hardly be more startling, more sensually phrased, or more total.

On the other hand, darkness does not, by virtue of this reversal, turn into its opposite, into a perverse sort of whiteness that can now be relied upon. While it is true that dark men in this tale tend to behave in ways more moral *and* more civilized than do white men — virtually every critic notes, for example, that the near-starving cannibals on board keep their hungry eyes off their masters — darkness remains the place and mode of Marlow's terminal struggle with Kurtz. It also remains the term Marlow uses to phrase his most probing and, of course, permanently unanswered question about Kurtz and himself: "The thing was to know what he belonged to, how many powers of darkness claimed him for their own" (p. 64). Further: "His was an impenetrable darkness. I looked at him as you peer down at a man who is lying at the bottom of a precipice where the sun never shines" (p. 85). But, on the other hand, Marlow also tells us this: "I know that the sunlight can be made to lie, too" (p. 89). Finding ourselves in deeply unfamiliar territory, we are left to negotiate darkness on our own.

Repeated reversal of our conventional color/moral code, while only one of the myriad confusions dealt the reader of *Heart of Darkness,* is nevertheless the most explicit confusion. Its resolution, insofar as there is one, thus warrants our attention: it is what one might call "off-color," meaning color that cannot quite or ever be pinned down or worded. "Ivory," however, comes close. Construed as a thing, ivory is the corrupt currency that fuels the whole African venture, the economics upon which the heart of darkness rests. The reader is told repeatedly that its worth is "unspeakable," that its cost is measured in terms of souls as well as of lives. Made to read in terms of the metaphor of ivory, the reader learns that the economics and ethics of this darkness are inextricable, each equally "off-white," each equally dependent upon the other for definition. The fact that ivory is the color of Kurtz's face presses this point home: the color bespeaks contamination, a mutual transference between the spheres of morality and vision, between the self one is and the self one seems to be. "Ivory" is a way of saying that the mask and the masked are one. It is also a way of stating the work's implicit morality, being a white that, having made the acquaintance of its opposite, now dwells in perpetual shadow, the sphere of moral dubiety. Ivory also, particularly when dead or fossilized, turns yellow. And yellow is the color of the place on the map into which Marlow goes, the text of landscape and mindscape that Marlow's journey "reads." Yellow is also the color of Marlow's face, a face that fuses the text of his self with the text he has so excruciatingly "read." It is this kind of inquiry into the work's oppositional structure and its breakdown that allows the reader to rescue some sense from the tale's apparent non-sense, to answer, if only in part, the tale's radical questioning of his "normal" life in a world of tidy oppositions.

The color of Marlow's face, however, warrants yet more attention. He, after all, is our surrogate voyager into the unknown, our guide to the "heart of darkness" that at once titles the tale and is left to the reader to define. Marlow, as he himself emphasizes, pulls back at the last moment from Kurtz's fate: "True, he had made that last stride, he had stepped over the edge, while I had been permitted to draw back my hesitating foot. And perhaps in this is the whole difference . . ." (p. 87). Perhaps. Marlow reads this difference as salvational for him, but it is worth recalling that Plato's complaint about the poet and about the world resides in just such a difference, in just this failure to repeat exactly. Yet, repeated exactly, Marlow implies that *he* would have become Kurtz, and, repeated exactly, that his tale of that experience would have *us* become Marlow. As it is, Marlow has, it seems, been deeply enough changed by his voyage, as was the Ancient Mariner, or Dante, or Virgil, or any of the other myriad literary and mythological voyagers into the myriad kinds of darkness man had imagined or found. No one, apparently, returns intact, and, in this tale, yellow seems the primary sign of the moral contamination acquired at one remove.

Similarly, greyness or twilight, another off-color, is the primary sign of the death struggle experienced at one remove or, put otherwise, experienced but survived:

I have wrestled with death. It is the most unexciting contest you can imagine. It takes place in an impalpable greyness, with nothing underfoot, with nothing around, without spectators, without clamour, without glory. . . . If such is the form of ultimate wisdom, then life is a greater riddle than some of us think it to be. I was within a hair's-breadth of the last opportunity for pronouncement, and I found with humiliation that probably I would have nothing to say. (p. 86)

The fact that Marlow, at this supposedly climactic moment, has nothing to say cannot be overemphasized. Like the Ancient Mariner — and like his creator, Coleridge — the inability to speak, the having nothing to say, is the soul's rock bottom. *Heart of Darkness* does its own turn on this Romantic tradition, for here rock bottom is a paradoxical place: where there is nothing underfoot, where there is not only nothing to say but no one to hear or to watch, where, in all senses, there is only enough light to see that there is none.

What, then, is the reader meant to make of this "off" world? Of this "off" text? Most obviously, he is meant to learn that the assumptions, of all kinds, that he brings to this tale are not to be trusted, that his conventional code for reading either the world or its texts is at best insufficient, always misleading, and at worst invidious. Color is the most obvious code-system that this tale undoes, but the reader's "mistakes" are everywhere waiting to be made. At times, the reader is straight-out *told* what to think or, more precisely, how to unthink, and rethink. As in the kernel metaphor. Or, as here: "And this *stillness* of life did not in the least resemble a *peace*" (p. 49) (emphasis mine).

More frequently, however, the reader is left to stumble, often immediately, sometimes long after the initial step. Consider how Marlow relates his response to Kurtz's face: "Oh, I wasn't touched. I was fascinated" (p. 85). Consider as well how he inverts the initial blandness of the following comment: " 'They adored him,' he said. The tone of these words was so extraordinary that I looked at him searchingly" (p. 71). In the former example Marlow corrects his response to emphasize his fascination, and the reader follows him in both correction and emphasis. We are asked to misread in order to read better. In the latter example, Marlow presents the words spoken and *then* tells us about the tone in which they were spoken. The order, as is always the case in reader-response criticism, is close to all-important. "They adored him": the sentence, as the reader first reads it, is unexceptional, the reverse of notable. But Marlow's subsequent statement of the sentence's tonality turns our response around, makes us strive to image a tonality that will convert these all-too-ordinary words into something extraordinary. Yet our imagination, here as elsewhere, gets no further help. There are no more clues. There is no basis for judging the worth of our reading performance. Whether we have imagined and reimagined successfully is left for us to decide. Having been shown the gap, we are left to our own devices, to fill it as best we can. But our "devices," not insignificantly, improve significantly as our reading of this tale progresses.

The most spectacular mistake that Marlow and the reader make is the error of "reading" the heads on the supposed fenceposts. Our first sight of the shrunken heads is a quick glance, through Marlow's glass: "There was no enclosure or fence of any kind; but there had been one apparently, for near the house half a dozen slim posts remained in a row, roughly trimmed, and with their upper ends ornamented with round carved balls. The rails, or whatever there had been between, had disappeared" (pp. 67–68). Here Marlow, and the reader along with him, reason backwards from what appears to be a broken torso to a (Platonic) original, replacing the rails, constructing a fence that must have been. Some several pages later Marlow lets us know that we have read much too quickly, that we, as he had been, have been taken in by appearances, that we have adroitly made the very error that the art of his tale-telling wanted us to make:

> And then I made a brusque movement, and one of the re-
> maining posts of that vanished fence leaped up in the field of
> my glass. You remember I told you I had been struck at the
> distance by certain attempts at ornamentation, rather remarkable
> in the ruinous aspect of the place. Now I had suddenly a nearer
> view, and its first result was to make me throw my head back
> as if before a blow. Then I went carefully from post to post
> with my glass, and I saw my mistake. These round knobs were
> not ornamental but symbolic; they were expressive and puzzling,
> striking and disturbing — food for thought and also for vul-
> tures if there had been any looking down from the sky; but
> at all events for such ants as were industrious enough to as-
> cend the pole. They would have been even more impressive,
> those heads on the stakes, if their faces had not been turned to
> the house. Only one, the first I had made out, was facing my way.
> (p. 73)

Note how long the reader of this passage is kept in suspense. Not until the next-to-last sentence is our gradually accruing suspicion confirmed: the ornaments are in fact heads, human heads, grotesquely turned, as if on the lathe of Kurtz's diseased imagination, into or-naments. Marlow here plays with the reader, keeping him guessing as long as possible, building suspicion within this passage in much the way suspense, our anticipation of his encounter with Kurtz, is built within the tale as a whole. To exaggerate and complicate the delay, we are misled, lied to in one of the many local lies that emblem the larger "lie" that is his tale itself: "These round knobs were not ornamental but symbolic." Symbolic indeed. They may be symbolic, but they are first and foremost heads. What these altered heads are symbols of we are never told — as usual. And, just to unkink this "lie" completely, the heads *are* ornaments, however bizarre. More precisely, they are being *used* as ornaments, and this use is what makes them bizarre.

By the tale's end, the reader is thus well tutored — or should be — in the experience of finding himself left hanging, of having to reread repeatedly, of anticipating what never comes or, if it does come, comes not in the expected way. Thus does the reader of *Heart of Darkness* learn to expect the unexpected without ever learning enough to guess what that unexpected might be. The long-awaited struggle with Kurtz proves a massive and murky disappointment, largely and lamely summed up in what must be the least inspired language in this linguistically extravagant tale: "I've been telling you what we said — repeating the phrases we pronounced — but what's the good? They were common everyday words — the familiar, vague sounds exchanged on every waking day of life. But what of that? They had behind them, to my mind, the terrific suggestiveness of words heard in dreams, of phrases spoken in nightmares" (p. 82).

Hardly anything could be more annoying and less impressive than to hear about a "terrific suggestiveness" that we never hear. The climax, in sum, amounts to not much — a fact confirmed by Marlow's conspicuous neglect, both in his experience and in his tale, of Kurtz's demise. The reader does not *see* his death — an absence itself important — and, following the fractured phrase made famous by T. S. Eliot's use of it as an epigraph for "The Hollow Men" (1925) — "Mistah Kurtz — he dead" — Marlow tells us that he continued on with his dinner, although he was "of course aware that the next day the pilgrims buried something in a muddy hole" (p. 86). The epitaph with which Marlow honors Kurtz and his experience of Kurtz could hardly be more stunning in its insouciance, and the reader cannot help but be taken aback. Asked to switch gears so quickly, to transform Kurtz from a long-awaited god to a quickly disposed of "something," the reader cannot help but feel had.

By the time the reader and Marlow have to negotiate his encounter with the Intended, we have been made into very good and very wary readers. Even so, we remain, along with Marlow, not quite up for this last and truly climactic loss of our readerly and moral balance:

> "And you admired him," she said. "It was impossible to know him and not to admire him. Was it?"
> "He was a remarkable man," I said unsteadily. Then before the appealing fixity of her gaze, that seemed to watch for more words on my lips, I went on. "It was impossible not to — "
> "Love him," she finished eagerly, silencing me into an appalled dumbness. "How true! how true! But when you think that no one knew him so well as I! I had all his noble confidence. I knew him best."
> "You knew him best," I repeated. And perhaps she did. But with every word spoken the room was growing darker, and only her forehead, smooth and white, remained illumined by the unextinguishable light of belief and love. (p. 91)

Well, if the reader can read this without a stumble or stall, he can read the entire tale thus. But the art of *Heart of Darkness* — and within that art the art, the lie-making powers, of the poet Marlow — works fiercely against such smoothness of reading. Our stumbles, stalls, and multiple kinds of readerly stammering are the very heart of our reading experience. The room grows darker as he lies — if that is what he is doing, and, whatever it is that he is doing, he does it again, more famously, as he repeats "the horror" as "your name" — yet, through it all, "her forehead, smooth and white, remained illumined by the unextinguishable light of belief and love."

Where, finally, to land: that is the question that plagues the reader not only here, at the end, but throughout *Heart of Darkness*. And the question is no easier to answer at the end than it has been at any point along the way. The balance that the tale teaches us to hold is a kind of permanent off-balance, its enlightenment a kind of permanent twilight, its color, however construed, permanently off. Put in terms of reading, the tale teaches the necessity and value of endless rereading. Put in terms of morals, it teaches the virtue of not being able to — or even trying to — answer in any permanent way such questions as are posed by Marlow's various "lies." The tale teaches what one might call the moral wisdom of dwelling in the land of "perhaps": " 'You knew him best,' I repeated. And perhaps she did." Or, put in Santayana's terms, we learn to appreciate the simultaneously aesthetic and moral art of the "broken torso." Recalling but also turning against Plato's terms, we have learned both the reasons for and the dangers of inferring its "missing legs and arms."

Reader-Response Criticism:
Heart of Darkness as a Text of Theory

If methodologies are instruments for reading literary texts, so also are literary texts instruments for reading methodologies. Thus did Keats's "Ode on a Grecian Urn" function as a favorite topic-text for the New Critics: it enabled them to state, in brilliant words no less, their basic assumptions about making sense and value of poetry even as they invoked those assumptions to read the poem. Similarly, *Wuthering Heights,* with its startling array of orphans, unreliable narrators, densely figured surfaces, and its veerings towards absence — thus has this novel proven a happy hunting ground for the deconstructionist methodology. *Heart of Darkness* shares many of these characteristics and thus seems another "natural" for that methodology.

Yet, as I began by saying, there are no "natural" fits between literary texts and critical methodologies. There are only more or less useful fits. That is, the question of fit should be taken as a pragmatic rather than a philosophical question, a question of which literary text will work best, best reveal the characteristic dynamics of a particular methodology. While *Heart of Darkness* may be read in terms of many methodologies, and, as this essay argues, is particularly well read in terms of the dynamics, assumptions, and problems of reader-response criticism, the fact that this work can textualize the dynamics of more than one methodology in itself breaks down the notion of a natural or philosophical fit. Ultimately, we can ask any question of any text. The answers may not in all cases be of equal interest or of equal use — it would, indeed, be astounding if they were — but whether or not they are is, emphatically, a pragmatic question.

Heart of Darkness, primarily due to the representation within the work of a poet-figure telling a tale to an audience, may not only be more than usually well read by the methodology of reader-response criticism but may also, more than most literary texts, function as an instrument for reading reader-response criticism. It can well be read, that is, as a text of theory, specifically of reader-response theory: raising questions about and exposing the dynamics of the critical practice of reading the reader's response as if it were itself a text. *Heart of Darkness* is also usefully read as a text of reader-response theory because it is primarily about the problems of making sense, whether worldly or readerly. Further, it emphasizes the fact that meaning, in addition to being characteristically problematic, is also characteristically more like an event than like an object.

What, then, does reading *Heart of Darkness* tell us — or, more precisely, has reading *Heart of Darkness* told us — about the critical practice of reading in terms of the reader reading? It has told us that the reader-response critic is interested in the *process* of reading as well as in the sense the reader finally makes — or doesn't make. The text, as we have seen, refuses to conclude in the larger sense, but it also is restless on the sentence level, frequently refusing the reader the luxury of a quick, stable, or one-time read. It makes us interested in our mistakes and misjudgments as well as in our "takes" and judgments. The text teaches its readers and its critics — they are often the same — that what is of greatest interest and value is the effort and the process, not any particular and seemingly final sense any particular reader may feel satisfied with.

More than most texts, *Heart of Darkness* thus raises and is comfortable with the question of multiple readings and multiple readers. This means not merely that the same reader goes back to the text and repeats his original reading. There is always a difference with each repetition, a difference that this text teaches us to construe, not as Plato would, as error, but, rather, as a uniquely valuable richness. And, "multiple readers" means not simply that the text has many readers — so much is obvious — and that, because they are reading the same text, they are all having the same reading experience, but, rather, that readers of this text, being different persons, reading in different times and places, are bound to have different experiences. This particular text welcomes the problem of this difference — if it be a problem — as an extension of the many problems it represents within itself.

Further, the reader need not and perhaps should not be conceptualized as a *person*. I have repeatedly referred to the reader's experience as being like a text for the reader-response critic: that is his primary explanatory metaphor. I have here been using *Heart of Darkness* as an instrumental text, as a text that can be read to make sense of things and texts other than itself. So also can the reader's experience be used. And, when conceptualized thus, it can be seen that this reader is himself most appropriately construed as a kind of critical instrument, as a way for the critic to make a particular kind of sense. All of which does not mean that this construct, being made in a particular time and place by a particular person, is not itself historical or, in a profound sense, real. The question of the lie, the fabrication by Marlow of his tale, and, within that tale, what he tells the Intended, can be rephrased as a question of self, of the reader's self as well as of the tale-teller's self. *Heart of Darkness* raises the one question explicitly, the other by implication. For this second question it suggests as many answers as it does for the first. And it leaves them no less permanently suggestive, permanently open-ended, permanently ready for new readings, new readers, and new theories of readings and readers.

READER-RESPONSE CRITICISM: A SELECTED BIBLIOGRAPHY

Some Introductions to Reader-Response Criticism

Fish, Stanley E. "Literature in the Reader: Affective Stylistics." *New Literary History* 2 (1970): 123–61. Collected in *Is There a Text in This Class? The Authority of Interpretive Communities,* edited by Stanley Eugene Fish. Cambridge, Mass.: Harvard University Press, 1980. Also collected in *Influx: Essays on Literary Influence,* edited by Ronald Primeau. Port Washington, N.Y.: Kennikat Press, 1977.

Mailloux, Steven. "Learning to Read: Interpretation and Reader-Response Criticism." *Studies in the Literary Imagination* 12 (1979): 93–108.

————. "Reader-Response Criticism?" *Genre* 10 (1977): 413–31.

Rosenblatt, Louise M. "Towards a Transactional Theory of Reading." *Journal of Reading Behavior* 1 (1969): 31–47. Collected in Primeau, *Influx: Essays on Literary Influence,* cited above.

Sulieman, Susan R. "Introduction: Varieties of Audience-Oriented Criticism." In *The Reader in the Text: Essays on Audience and Interpretation,* edited by Susan R. Sulieman and Inge Crossman. Princeton, N.J.: Princeton University Press, 1980.

Tompkins, Jane P. "An Introduction to Reader-Response Criticism." In *Reader-Response Criticism: From Formalism to Post-Structuralism,* edited by Jane P. Tompkins. Baltimore, Md.: Johns Hopkins University Press, 1980.

Reader-Response Criticism in Anthologies and Collections

Fish, Stanley Eugene. *Is There a Text in this Class? The Authority of Interpretive Communities.* Cambridge, Mass.: Harvard University Press, 1980. In this volume are collected most of Fish's most influential essays, including "Literature in the Reader," "What It's Like to Read *L'Allegro* and *Il Penseroso,*" "Interpreting the

Variorum," "Is There a Text in This Class?" "How to Recognize a Poem When You See One," and "What Makes an Interpretation Acceptable?"

Garvin, Harry R., ed. *Theories of Reading, Looking, and Listening*. Lewisburg, Pa.: Bucknell University Press, 1981. See the essays by Cain and Rosenblatt.

Primeau, Ronald, ed. *Influx: Essays on Literary Influence*. Port Washington, N.Y.: Kennikat Press, 1977. See the essays by Fish, Holland, and Rosenblatt.

Tompkins, Jane, ed. *Reader-Response Criticism: From Formalism to Post-Structuralism*. Baltimore, Md.: Johns Hopkins University Press, 1980. See especially the essays by Bleich, Fish, Holland, Prince, and Tompkins.

Sulieman, Susan R., and Inge Crossman, eds. *The Reader in the Text: Essays on Audience and Interpretation*. Princeton, N.J.: Princeton University Press, 1980. See especially the essays by Culler, Iser, and Todorov.

Reader-Response Criticism: Some Major Works

Bleich, David. *Subjective Criticism*. Baltimore, Md.: Johns Hopkins University Press, 1978.

Booth, Stephen. *An Essay on Shakespeare's Sonnets*. New Haven, Conn.: Yale University Press, 1969.

Eco, Umberto. *The Role of the Reader*. Bloomington: Indiana University Press, 1979.

Fish, Stanley Eugene. *Self-Consuming Artifacts: The Experience of Seventeenth-Century Literature*. Berkeley: University of California Press, 1972.

————. *Surprised by Sin: The Reader in Paradise Lost*. 2nd ed. Berkeley: University of California Press, 1971.

Holland, Norman N. *5 Readers Reading*. New Haven, Conn.: Yale University Press, 1975.

Iser, Wolfgang. *The Implied Reader: Patterns of Communication in Prose Fiction from Bunyan to Beckett*. Baltimore, Md.: Johns Hopkins University Press, 1974.

Jauss, Hans Robert. *Toward an Aesthetic of Reception*. Translated by Timothy Bahti. Introduction by Paul de Man. Brighton, Eng.: Harvester Press, 1982.

Mailloux, Steven. *Interpretive Conventions: The Reader in the Study of American Fiction*. Ithaca, N.Y.: Cornell University Press, 1982.

Prince, Gerald. *Narratology*. New York: Mouton, 1982.

Exemplary Short Readings of Major Texts

Anderson, Howard. "*Tristram Shandy* and the Reader's Imagination." *PMLA* 86 (1971): 966–73.

Berger, Carole. "The Rake and the Reader in Jane Austen's Novels." *Studies in English Literature, 1500–1900* 15 (1975): 531–44.

Booth, Stephen. "On the Value of Hamlet." *Reinterpretations of English Drama: Selected Papers from the English Institute,* edited by Norman Rabkin. New York: Columbia University Press, 1969.

Easson, Robert R. "William Blake and His Reader in *Jerusalem*." In *Blake's Sublime Allegory,* edited by Stuart Curran and Joseph A. Wittreich. Madison: University of Wisconsin Press, 1973.

Kirk, Carey H. "*Moby Dick*: The Challenge of Response." *Papers on Language and Literature* 13 (1977): 383–90.

Feminist Criticism
and
Heart of Darkness

WHAT IS FEMINIST CRITICISM?

"It's queer how out of touch with truth women are," the teller of the tale at the heart of *Heart of Darkness* says to the all-male audience sitting before him on a boat. "They live in a world of their own," he continues, "and there has never been anything like it, and never can be":

> It is too beautiful altogether, and if they were to set it up it would go to pieces before the first sunset. Some confounded fact we men have been living contentedly with ever since the day of creation would start up and knock the whole thing over. (p. 27)

In the story Marlow goes on to tell, women are conspicuous by their absence, and even when they are present they seem, as Marlow might say, "out of it." Can such a story — can a novel framing such a story — even survive, let alone be enriched by, feminist analysis?

A more important question leaps to mind: what would feminist criticism have to gain from an encounter with *Heart of Darkness*? Conrad's novel seems too easy a target; a novel by Jane Austen or Virginia Woolf, even Nathaniel Hawthorne or Thomas Hardy, would seem to offer better rewards all around — to the author, to the text, to the reader, and to the feminist project.

But feminist criticism comes in many forms, and feminist critics have a variety of goals. One group of feminist critics, for instance, revisits books by male authors and looks at them from a woman's point of view to see how they both reflect and shape the attitudes that have held women back. The following survey of several feminist approaches and goals indicates why a feminist critic might want to write about *Heart of Darkness*. More important, it suggests what feminist criticism can show us about our language, culture, and selves even as it shows us *Heart of Darkness* in a new light.

During the past twenty years, three strains of feminist criticism have emerged: strains which can be categorized as French, American, and British. These categories should not be allowed to obscure either the global implications of the women's movement or the fact that interests and ideas have been shared by feminists from France, Great Britain, and the United States. British and American feminists have examined similar problems while writing about many of the same writers and works, and American feminists have recently become much more receptive to French theories about femininity and writing. Still, historically speaking, French and American and British feminists have examined similar problems from different perspectives.

French feminists have tended to focus their attention on language, analyzing the ways in which meaning is produced. They have concluded that language as we commonly think of it is a decidedly male realm. Drawing upon the ideas of the psychoanalytic philosopher Jacques Lacan, French feminists remind us that language is a realm of public discourses. A child enters the linguistic realm just as it comes to grasp its separateness from its mother, just about the time boys — but not girls — identify with their father, the family representative of culture. The language learned reflects a binary logic that opposes such terms as active/passive, masculine/feminine, sun/moon, father/mother, head/heart, son/daughter, intelligent/sensitive, brother/sister, form/matter, phallus/vagina, reason/emotion. Because this logic tends to group with masculinity such qualities as light, thought, and activity, French feminists have said that the structure of language is phallocentric: it privileges the phallus and, more generally, masculinity by associating them with the things and values that are more appreciated by the (masculine-dominated) culture. Moreover, French feminists believe, "masculine desire dominates speech and posits woman as an idealized fantasy-fulfillment for the incurable emotional lack caused by separation from the mother."[1]

Thus, in the view of French feminists, language is associated with separation from the mother, is characterized by distinctions that represent the world from the male point of view, and is a system that seems to give women one of two choices. Either they can imagine and represent themselves as men imagine and represent them (in which case they may speak, but will speak as men) or they can remain a "gap" in the world that masculine logic would describe, in which case they choose silence, becoming in the process "the invisible and unheard sex."[2]

But language only *seems* to give women such a narrow range of choices, some influential French feminists have argued. Another possibility is that women can develop a *feminine* language. In various ways, pioneering French feminists such as Annie Leclerc, Xavière Gauthier, and Marguerite Duras have suggested that there is something that may be called *l'écriture feminine:* women's writing. Fairly recently, Julia Kristeva has said that feminine language is semiotic, not symbolic. Rather than rigidly opposing and ranking elements of reality, rather than symbolizing one thing but not another in terms of a third, feminine language is rhythmic and unifying. (If from the male perspective it seems fluid to the point of being chaotic, that is a fault of the male perspective.)

Feminine language derives, according to Kristeva, from the pre-oedipal period of fusion between mother and child. Because it is associated with the maternal, feminine language is not only threatening to culture, which is patriarchal, but is also a medium through which women may be creative in new ways. But Kristeva has paired her central, liberating claim — that truly feminist innovation in all fields requires an understanding of the relation between maternity and feminine creation — with a warning. A feminist language that refuses to participate in masculine discourse, that rests its future entirely in a feminine, semiotic discourse, risks being politically marginalized by men. That is to say, it risks being relegated to the outskirts (pun intended) of what is considered socially and politically significant.

Kristeva, who associates feminine writing with the female body, is joined in her views by other leading French feminists. Hélène Cixous, for instance, also posits an essential connection between the woman's

---

[1]Ann Rosalind Jones, "Inscribing Femininity: French Theories of the Feminine," in *Making a Difference: Feminist Literary Criticism,* ed. Gayle Greene and Coppélia Kahn (London: Methuen, 1985), p. 83.
[2]Ibid.

body, whose sexual pleasure has been repressed and denied expression, and women's writing. "Write your self. Your body must be heard,"[3] Cixous urges; once they learn to "write their bodies," women will not only realize their sexuality but enter history and move toward a future based on a "feminine" economy of giving rather than the masculine economy of hoarding. For Luce Irigaray, women's sexual pleasure (*jouissance*) cannot be expressed by the dominant, ordered, "logical," masculine language. She explores the connection between women's sexuality and women's language through the following analogy: as women's *jouissance* is more multiple than men's unitary, phallic pleasure ("woman has sex organs just about everywhere"), so "feminine" language is more diffusive than its "masculine" counterpart. ("That is undoubtedly the reason . . . her language . . . goes off in all directions and . . . he is unable to discern the coherence," Irigaray writes.[4])

Cixous's and Irigaray's emphasis on feminine writing as an expression of the female body has drawn criticism from other French feminists. Many argue, for instance, that an emphasis on the body either reduces "the feminine" to a biological essence or elevates it in a way that shifts the valuation of masculine and feminine but retains the binary categories. For Christine Fauré, Irigaray's celebration of women's difference fails to address the issue of masculine dominance, and a Marxist-feminist, Catherine Clement, has warned that "poetic" descriptions of what constitutes the feminine will not challenge that dominance in the realm of production. The boys will still make the toys, and decide who gets to use them. In her effort to redefine women as political rather than as sexual beings, Monique Wittig has called for the abolition of sexual categories that Cixous and Irigaray retain and revalue as they celebrate women's writing.

American feminist critics have shared with French critics both an interest in and a cautious distrust of the concept of feminine writing. Annette Kolodny, for instance, worries that the "richness and variety of women's writing" will be missed if we see in it only its "feminine mode" or "style."[5] And yet Kolodny herself goes on in the same essay to point

[3]Hélène Cixous, "The Laugh of the Medusa," in *New French Feminisms,* ed. Elaine Marks and Isabelle de Courtivron (Amherst: University of Massachusetts Press, 1980), p. 250.

[4]Luce Irigaray, *This Sex Which Is Not One,* trans. Catherine Porter (Ithaca, N.Y.: Cornell University Press, 1985), pp. 101–03.

[5]Annette Kolodny, "Some Notes on Defining a 'Feminist Literary Criticism,' " *Critical Inquiry* 2 (1975), p. 78.

out that women *have* had their own style, which includes reflexive constructions ("she found herself crying") and particular recurring themes
(clothing and self-fashioning are two that Kolodny mentions — other
American feminists have focused on madness, disease, and the demonic).

Interested as they have become in the French subject of feminine
style, American feminist critics began by analyzing literary texts rather
than by philosophizing abstractly about language. Many reviewed the
great works by male writers, embarking on a revisionist rereading of literary tradition. Looking at, among other things, the portrayals of women
characters, these critics exposed the patriarchal ideology implicit in
such works, showing how clearly this tradition of systematic masculine
dominance is inscribed in our literary tradition. Kate Millett, Carolyn
Heilbrun, and Judith Fetterley, among many others, created this model
for American feminist criticism, a model that Elaine Showalter came
to call the "feminist critique" of "male-constructed literary history."[6]
Meanwhile another group of critics including Sandra Gilbert, Susan
Gubar, Patricia Meyer Spacks, and Showalter herself created a somewhat different model, one that Showalter has termed "gynocriticism."

Whereas the feminist critique has analyzed works by men, practitioners of gynocriticism have studied the writings of those women
who, against all odds, produced what Showalter calls "a literature of
their own." In *The Female Imagination,* Spacks has looked into the
female literary tradition to find out how great women writers have
felt, perceived themselves, and imagined reality across the ages. Gilbert
and Gubar, in *The Madwoman in the Attic,* concern themselves with
well-known women writers of the nineteenth century, but they too find
that general concerns, images, and themes recur, because the authors
they treat write "in a culture whose fundamental definitions of literary
authority are both overtly and covertly patriarchal."[7]

If one of the purposes of gynocriticism is to restudy well-known
women authors, another goal is to rediscover women's history and
culture, particularly women's communities that have nurtured female
creativity. Still another, related purpose is to discover neglected or
forgotten women writers and thus to forge an alternative literary tradition, a canon that better represents the female perspective by better

---

[6]Elaine Showalter, "Towards a Feminist Poetics," in *Women Writing and Writing
about Women,* ed. Mary Jacobus (New York: Barnes and Noble, 1979), p. 25.

[7]Sandra M. Gilbert and Susan Gubar, *The Madwoman in the Attic: The Woman Writer
and the Nineteenth-Century Literary Imagination* (New Haven, Conn.: Yale University
Press, 1979), p. 45.

representing the literary works that have been written by women. Showalter, in *A Literature of Their Own,* admirably began to fulfill this purpose, providing as she did a remarkably thorough overview of women's writing through three of its phases. She defines these as the "Feminine, Feminist, and Female" phases, phases during which women first imitated a masculine tradition (1840–1880), then protested against its standards and values (1880–1920), and finally advocated their own autonomous, female perspective (1920 to the present).

With the recovery of a body of women's texts, attention has returned to a question raised a decade ago by Lillian Robinson: doesn't American feminist criticism need to formulate a theory of its own practice? Won't reliance on theoretical assumptions, categories, and strategies developed by men and associated with other, nonfeminist, schools of thought prevent feminism from being accepted as equivalent to these other critical discourses? Not all American feminists believe that a special or unifying theory of feminist practice is urgently needed; Showalter's historical approach to women's culture allows a feminist critic to utilize theories based on nonfeminist disciplines. Kolodny has advocated a "playful pluralism" encompassing a variety of critical schools and methods. But Jane Marcus and others have responded that if feminists adopt too wide a variety of approaches, they may relax the tensions between feminists and the educational establishment, tensions that are necessary for political activism. Thus, many continue to call for a distinct, feminist theory.

The question of whether feminism weakens or fortifies itself by emphasizing its separateness — and by developing, through separateness, unity — is one of several areas of debate within American feminism. Another area of disagreement touched upon earlier, between feminists who stress universal feminine attributes (the feminine imagination, feminine writing) and those who focus on the political conditions experienced by particular groups of women during specified periods in history, parallels a larger distinction between American feminist critics and their British counterparts. While it has been customary to refer to an Anglo-American tradition of feminist criticism, British feminists tend to distinguish themselves from what they see as an American overemphasis on texts linking women across boundaries and decades and an underemphasis on popular art and culture.

British feminists regard their own critical practice as more political than that of American feminists, whom they have often faulted for being uninterested in historical detail. (Thus, they would join such American critics as Myra Jehlen to suggest that a continuing preoccupation with women writers would create the danger of placing women's texts outside the history that conditions them.) In their view, the American opposition to male stereotypes that denigrate women has often led to counterstereotypes of feminine virtue that ignore real differences of race, class, and culture among women. In addition, they argue, American celebrations of individual heroines falsely suggest that powerful individuals may be immune to repressive conditions — and may even imply that *any* individual can go through life unconditioned by the culture and ideology in which he or she lives. Similarly, the American endeavor to recover women's history — for example, by emphasizing that women developed their own strategies to gain power within their sphere — is seen by British feminists like Judith Newton and Deborah Rosenfelt as unfortunate, a project that "mystifies" male oppression, that is, disguises it as something that has ended up creating, for women, a special world of opportunities. More important from the British standpoint, the universalizing and "essentializing" tendencies in both American practice and French theory disguise women's oppression by highlighting sexual difference, implicitly suggesting that a dominant system is impervious to political change. British feminist theory, by contrast, emphasizes engagement with historical process to promote social change.

An interpretation on the British feminist model is materialist and ideological, as well as feminist. It is materialist because it emphasizes that an understanding of the material conditions of men's and women's lives is central to an understanding of culture, and that both literature and criticism are cultural products. It is ideological in its concern with the production of ideology by a culture, and in its concern with the way that ideology determines cultural practice and social change.

The essay on *Heart of Darkness* that follows, by the American feminist Johanna M. Smith, may at first seem to exemplify that form of criticism developed by the British school of feminism. Approaching Marlow's narrative as the product of a moment both in the history of imperialism and in the history of patriarchy, Smith exposes the presence of patriarchal and imperialist ideologies throughout Marlow's (and Conrad's) narrative. She shows how these guide the creation of the novel's (minor) women characters, causing the characters either to remain silent (for if they spoke, they would surely condemn their oppressors, calling them what they are) or causing them to speak the myths men would have them speak.

But Smith is not entirely British in her orientation; like many feminists in Britain, France, and America, she shares the interests and interpretive strategies of feminists on both sides of the Atlantic. In her attention to silent women and to women who speak but speak as men, as well as in her suggestion that feminist readers may hear Conrad's silent women speaking their mind through "gaps" in the discourse of Marlow's story, Smith shows an awareness of French feminist issues. And an awareness of the American, gynocritical position is evident in the opening sentence of "Too Beautiful Altogether," the one in which she admits that a man's novel about manly adventure may not *seem* to be important to the feminist enterprise. Finally, what Smith gives us is a revealing feminist critique — of Marlow, his story, *Heart of Darkness,* its author. " 'Storytellers' in western culture . . . as often legitimatize the dominant culture as challenge it," Gayle Greene and Coppélia Kahn have written. What the feminist critique shows, they assert, is that "the dominant ideology . . . marginalizes women."[8] Smith effectively demonstrates as much through her close analysis of the words of Marlow, one of the great storytellers of a patriarchal literary tradition.

A FEMINIST CRITIC AT WORK

JOHANNA M. SMITH

"Too Beautiful Altogether":
Patriarchal Ideology in *Heart of Darkness*

> . . . *What [men] have said so far, for the most part, stems from the opposition activity/passivity, from the power relation between a fantasized obligatory virility meant to invade, to colonize, and the consequential phantasm of woman as a "dark continent" to penetrate and to "pacify."*
>
> –HÉLÈNE CIXOUS, "The Laugh of the Medusa"

A story about manly adventure narrated and written by a man, *Heart of Darkness* might seem an unpropitious subject for feminist criticism. As my epigraph suggests, however, a feminist approach to

[8]Gayle Greene and Coppélia Kahn, Introduction to Greene and Kahn, *Making a Difference,* pp. 21–22.

Conrad's story of colonizing can interrogate its complex interrelation of patriarchal and imperialist ideologies. By examining the women in Marlow's narrative, we can identify the patriarchal-imperialist blend that requires the kinds of women he creates. To do so is to engage in a feminist critique of ideology, for, as Myra Jehlen puts it, "Feminist thinking is really *re*thinking, an examination of the way certain assumptions about women and the female character enter into the fundamental assumptions that organize all our thinking."[1] Such rethinking about *Heart of Darkness* reveals the collusion of imperialism and patriarchy: Marlow's narrative aims to "colonize" and "pacify" both savage darkness and women. Silencing the native laundress and symbolizing the equally silent savage woman and the Company women, Marlow protects himself from his experience of the darkness they stand for. The two speaking women he creates, his aunt and the Intended, perform a similar function. As we will see later, Marlow, by restricting unsatisfactory versions of imperialist ideology to them, is able to create his own version, a belief to keep the darkness at bay.

I use "ideology" here in two senses, to mean not only a conscious system of belief, either imposed on or willingly adopted by the believer, but also the unconscious grounding of individual experience, what Catherine Belsey calls "the very condition of our experience of the world."[2] In the first sense, ideology works to impose unified, consensus meaning on disparate experiences and perceptions, to mystify or disguise difference as deviation. Most characteristically, ideology fulfills this function by disguising customary social systems as natural relations; cultural systems in which one nation or gender has power over another, for instance, are presented as the natural order. It is through this guise of the natural that the second sense of "ideology" becomes operative: we take for granted what is natural, and hence ideology becomes the unexamined ground of our

[1]Myra Jehlen, "Archimedes and the Paradox of Feminist Criticism," in *Feminist Theory: A Critique of Ideology*, ed. Nannerl O. Keohane, Michelle Z. Rosaldo, and Barbara C. Gelpi (Chicago: University of Chicago Press, 1972), p. 189.
[2]Catherine Belsey, *Critical Practice* (London: Methuen, 1980), p. 5. Here and in what follows I have also drawn on Terry Eagleton's *Marxism and Literary Criticism* (Berkeley: University of California Press, 1976), pp. 1–36, and Michèle Barrett's "Ideology and the Cultural Production of Gender," in *Feminist Criticism and Social Change: Sex, Class and Race in the Production of Culture*, ed. Judith Newton and Deborah Rosenfelt (New York: Methuen, 1985), pp. 65–85. This collection addresses the complex problem of defining ideology, the debate over the problem, and the relevance of that debate for feminist criticism.

experience. Thus internalized, ideology becomes cultural practice, the way we live. Because it *is* practice, however, it cannot remain static; as our experiences and formulations of what is natural shift, ideology "has continually to be renewed, recreated, defended, and modified."[3]

Subject to change in this way, ideology may fail to sufficiently repress the contradictions not only of experience but of language. This failing becomes evident in the language that ideology attempts to co-opt. Here lies the connection between ideology and literature.[4] It is impossible to write a value-free literary work, for its language and techniques are permeated with ideology; a realist work, for instance, necessarily presents a certain view of what constitutes the realistic, a view which suppresses alternatives. But language itself remains fluid, its several meanings denying the stasis that ideology attempts to impose. Once an author fixes it in a specific literary work, the language may appear to function in the service of an ideology, yet its inherent fluidity will reveal a gap between the work and the ideological project imposed on it. Despite the author's project in support of an ideology, then, this gap enables the reader to interpret that ideology as not natural but imposed, as not fixed but fluid and contradictory. If we approach such a gap with what Adrienne Rich calls feminist "re-vision" — the act of "entering an old text from a new critical direction"[5] — we can recover the contradictions that the language of ideology intends to efface.

Revealing the contradictions within two central statements of ideology in *Heart of Darkness* — Kurtz on imperialism and Marlow on Kurtz, who represents that same imperialism — will serve as a paradigm for my subsequent readings of the women in the novel.

The gap within Kurtz's imperialist report well illustrates the problem of ideology in *Heart of Darkness*. In his report to the International Society for the Suppression of Savage Customs, imperialism ideologically disguises its desire for conquest as a humanitarian impulse. "By the simple exercise of our will," Kurtz writes, "we can exert a power for good practically unbounded" (p. 65). If power

[3]Raymond Williams, *Marxism and Literature* (Oxford: Oxford University Press, 1978), p. 112.

[4]On this connection see Catherine Belsey, "Constructing the Subject: Deconstructing the Text," in Newton and Rosenfelt, *Feminist Criticism and Social Change*, pp. 43–64.

[5]Adrienne Rich, "When We Dead Awaken: Writing as Re-Vision," in *On Lies, Secrets, and Silence: Selected Prose, 1966–1978* (New York: Norton, 1979), p. 35.

over the other is perceived ideologically "as a power for good," then this perception legitimates "the simple exercise of our will": it becomes "natural" to use this power to suppress savage customs. Yet, as I have suggested, even dominant ideologies are not as monolithic or stable as Kurtz's statement would like to imply. Under stress, as both imperialism and patriarchy were at the end of the nineteenth century, what was hitherto seen as "natural" might be demystified; brought out of the realm of the natural or unexamined, it becomes visible and visibly artificial. This stress splits Kurtz's report, so that a gap appears between his early advocacy of the imperialist power for good and the end of the text, "evidently scrawled much later": "Exterminate all the brutes!" (pp. 65–66). The gap between initial altruism and these concluding words reveals the contradiction in imperialism between the ideological disguise of power and its exercise.

A similar contradiction within Marlow informs his narrative. While the full Chinese-box complexity of Marlow's narrative technique is beyond the scope of my essay,[6] one characteristic passage of vacillation will reveal this contradiction. Although he admits that he "tingle[d] with enthusiasm" for the altruism conveyed in Kurtz's "unbounded power of eloquence" (p. 65), he then suggests that Kurtz's memory belongs in "the dust-bin of progress" among "the dead cats of civilisation" (p. 66). Like this shift in tone, Marlow's portraits of the native laundress, the savage woman, and the Company women are intended to conceal his seduction by Kurtz's eloquence, his investment in the imperialist project of which he was a part. The nature of Marlow's investment — his need for belief in the imperialist ideology that patriarchy undergirds — is most fully demonstrated in his portrayals of his aunt and the Intended. To see the force of this need for belief, we must first examine the three representations of women through which Marlow disguises his complicity in the Company's imperialism.

Several disguises are evident in the early vignette of the native laundress and the accountant: the latter's sartorial spruceness masks the Company's imperialist-patriarchal brutality, while Marlow's irony at his expense masks his own collusion in the Company's project. As the accountant explains the origin of his miraculous linen, it

6On this aspect of the story see Peter Brooks, *Reading for the Plot* (New York: Alfred A. Knopf, 1984), pp. 238–63.

becomes clear that he has forced a native woman to become his laundress. "I've been teaching one of the native women," he tells Marlow; "It was difficult. She had a distaste for the work" (p. 32). These few dry sentences disguise the accountant's conjoined use of imperialist and patriarchal oppression, and Marlow's response performs a similar function. Although he mocks the accountant for looking like "a hairdresser's dummy," he also expresses a grudging admiration: the accountant's shirts are "achievements of character" which display his "backbone," and he concludes that "thus this man had verily accomplished something" (p. 32). Through ironic juxtaposition Marlow derides the accountant's accomplishment, but irony functions here, as throughout his narrative, to protect him from recurring horror at his own complicity in such achievements. Prior to this episode Marlow had airily admitted that "I also was a part of the great cause"; a moment later, however, he was "appalled" to recognize it as "a flabby, pretending, weak-eyed devil" (p. 30). His ironic judgment now allows him to replace the appalling "flabby devil" of imperialism with the comic "backbone" of the accountant.

In order to do so, of course, Marlow must silence the laundress who provides the backbone's starch, and this silencing evinces his concurrence in the imperialism of patriarchy. Both ideologies operate in this vignette of successful oppression, but only one is mocked; hence a gap opens between the imperialism visible to Marlow and the patriarchal attitude which remains unseen by him because it seems natural. Within this gap the laundress is made vividly present by virtue of her absence; here she, rather than Marlow or the accountant, might speak of her "distaste" for the latter's oppression. The reader comes to recognize that power as patriarchal imperialism — a hitherto hidden version of the evident ideology Marlow deplores when it sends native *men* to the grove of death.

Here the reader also begins to recognize the meaning of Marlow's power, as the masculine narrator of his story, to conceal not only the laundress's story but those of the other women in *Heart of Darkness*. Like Kurtz's eloquence in support of imperialism, Marlow's narrative is a mystification of power relations, specifically those between men and women. If we turn from the silent laundress to the other silent women in the story, the savage woman and the Company women, we can see the purposes this silencing serves. As Hélène Cixous puts it, "[men] want to keep woman in the place of mystery, consign her to mystery, as they say 'keep her in her place, keep her at a distance.' "⁷ As Marlow creates these women to symbolize the enigma of the jungle, his ideological project is to distance and control both mysteries.

The savage woman who appears as Kurtz is being carried onto the ship is a symbol Marlow creates in order to control the threatening wilderness.⁸ "A wild and gorgeous apparition of a woman" (p. 76), she is less a woman than an otherworldly vision. Marlow's adjectives describe not her but the impression she makes on him as a being "savage and superb, wild-eyed and magnificent," "ominous and stately" (p. 76). Most importantly, of course, he uses her to symbolize the mystery of the jungle:

> the immense wilderness, the colossal body of the fecund and mysterious life seemed to look at her, pensive, as though it had been looking at the image of its own tenebrous and passionate soul. (p. 76)

The distancing language of this passage shows Marlow separating the woman herself from the material reality she represents for him: the "body" of the jungle, outside her, looks not at her body or at its own "soul" but at the "*image*" of its soul in her. Here Marlow symbolizes the woman and personifies the jungle, thereby confounding them and containing both. A complex of potentially threatening forces is thus brought under control; stylized, it becomes "pensive," nonthreatening.

Once the savage woman moves, she is no longer stylized in Marlow's picture and becomes a sexual and emotional threat; to defuse this threat, Marlow assigns meanings to her behavior. As she approaches the ship, "looking at us . . . like the wilderness itself" and "brooding over an inscrutable purpose" (p. 77), it appears that the jungle, reunited with its soul, is menacing the intruders. Hence Marlow interprets the woman's behavior as he had earlier symbolized her appearance.

---

⁷Hélène Cixous, "Castration or Decapitation?" *French Feminist Theory,* a special issue of *Signs* 7 (1981), p. 49.

⁸In criticism as well as literature, as Lillian S. Robinson says in *Sex, Class, and Culture* (New York: Methuen, 1978), such symbolizing is "particularly sinister" for women; Jungian "liturgical pronouncements about The Masculine and The Feminine," for instance, tend to perpetuate "specious generalizations" about both male and female psyches (p. 7). Although her reading of the story is Jungian, Zohreh T. Sullivan points to the ideological uses of such generalizations by noting that the savage woman, like the Intended, is "recognized, suppressed and rejected" in the service of masculine and imperialist autonomy. See Sullivan's article, "Enclosure, Darkness, and the Body: Conrad's Landscape," *The Centennial Review* 25 (1981), pp. 59–79.

> Suddenly she opened her bared arms and threw them up rigid
> above her head, as though in an uncontrollable desire to touch
> the sky, and at the same time the swift shadows darted out on
> the earth, swept around on the river, gathering the steamer in a
> shadowy embrace. (p. 77)

Assigning the woman's gesture a meaning ("as though . . . "), Marlow
displaces the hint of sexuality in her "desire" onto the jungle's "shadowy
embrace." His reason for doing so emerges when we recall that he has
earlier described the jungle's absorption of Kurtz as sexual cannibalism:
"it had taken him, loved him, embraced him, got into his veins, consumed his flesh" (p. 64). If this sexuality were to move from the jungle
back into the savage woman's body, then her earlier look of "inscrutable
purpose" might be a direct, nonsymbolic sexual threat; hence Marlow
reconceals her sexuality by carefully investing her with desire not for him
but "to touch the sky." Even if the content of her gesture is the "wild
sorrow" and "dumb pain" he sees in her face, this too is a threat, for
Marlow has already (over)responded to experience with savage sorrow.
When he had earlier feared that Kurtz was dead, he admits, his "sorrow
had a startling extravagance of emotion, even such as I had noticed in
the howling sorrow of these savages" (p. 63). As Henry Staten notes,
Marlow's back-pedaling from emotion in this earlier scene has indicated
his masculine view that "unrestrained grief should be left to the natives
and the women."[9] Faced in the savage woman with not only the threat
of sexuality but the allure of grief, Marlow must contain both with a
stylized picture of a woman reaching for the unattainable.

Two additional elements in Marlow's description of the savage
woman provide a final example of his ideological reading of her. I have
said that Marlow does his best to ignore her body; he does, however,
detail her "barbarous ornaments," concluding that "She must have had
the value of several elephant tusks on her" (p. 76). The woman's body is
here commodified, becoming the thing on which value is displayed; in
addition, the tusks connect her with the victimized jungle being invaded
in the Company's quest for ivory. Marlow does note that her hair is
"done in the shape of a helmet" and that she wears gauntlets, but he
dismisses these martial decorations as charms which have meaning only
as proto-ivory. Similarly, he relays the Russian's report that the woman
can not only speak but talk "like a fury" (p. 77), but he downplays this
information by appending it to his own image of her.

---

[9]Henry Staten, "Conrad's Mortal Word," *Critical Inquiry* 12 (1986), p. 723.

As Marlow turns the savage woman's body into an image of the jungle, this process works in the service of both patriarchal and imperialist ideology. It is an effort to defuse and hence control the power and sexuality both of the woman who "tread[s] the earth proudly" and of that "fecund" earth itself (p. 76). As the patriarchal ideology intends with its power of image-making to distance and hence conquer the woman's body, so the imperialist ideology intends with its power for good to distance and conquer the mysterious life of the jungle. And both the savage woman and the jungle are momentarily silenced by Marlow's images of them. As these images interrupt the movement of his narrative, however, they create gaps by which the reader can see the impossibility of such ideological containment. During Marlow's later visit to the Intended, the jungle's life recurs in a voice which dramatizes imperialism's failure to suppress it. In contrast, the savage woman is here denied direct speech, yet her appearance culminates in "a *formidable* silence" (p. 77; emphasis added).

Like the laundress's, the savage woman's silence provides a space in the text which reveals what Belsey calls "the truth about ideology": "the truth which ideology represses, its own existence as ideology itself."[10] It is possible, for instance, to recover from Marlow's description hints of the woman's power rather than her victimization. If we reverse his emphasis and concentrate on the woman's military ornaments and her vehement speech, they indicate that she might not be invested in Kurtz's departure in any of the ways that suggest themselves. That is, I have been rereading Marlow's interpretation of the woman as a feminist, to reveal his denial of her sexuality and her grief; but to reinstate these qualities means that I continue to read her, as Marlow does, ideologically: she remains conventionally feminine (sexually and emotionally dependent on Kurtz) and conventionally native (economically dependent on him as an ivory-trader). But what if she is neither? What if she is a woman warrior whose gestures and speech remained unreadable, giving her the power that "a formidable silence" indicates? Her silence opens a gap in which our readings, even as they seek to counter Marlow's, are shown to be as grounded in ideology as his.

In the two women Marlow encounters at the Company's Brussels office, we find his third attempt to evade his collusion in imperialism by symbolizing women. Marlow loads the knitters with images from classical and Christian mythology. Although there are only two of them,

---

[10]Belsey, "Constructing the Subject," in Newton and Rosenfelt, *Feminist Criticism and Social Change*, p. 63.

for instance, his insistence on their knitting serves to link them with the three Fates of Greek and Roman myth, who control human destiny by spinning, measuring, and snipping the thread of life. Furthermore, when Marlow describes two young men being "piloted over" (p. 25) from civilization into the jungle by the elder knitter, the verb connects her with Charon, the pilot who ferries the dead across the Styx into Hades. Finally, Marlow's last view of "these two, guarding the door of Darkness" (p. 25) suggests the dual figure of Sin in *Paradise Lost:* half woman and half serpent, she is "the portress of hell gate."[11] These images, like the irony directed at the Company's accountant, are narrative retrospection, a technique intended to protect Marlow from the realization his narrative revives: that in this office, by contracting himself to the Company, he had joined its "conspiracy" (p. 25). The responsibility for this decision is displaced onto the younger woman, "introducing, introducing continuously [young men] to the unknown" (p. 25), and the elder, "uncanny and fateful" in her "unconcerned wisdom." Through these women, whom he silences by figuring them as fates or demonic forces accountable for his actions, Marlow silences his own doubts. The boundary between the self and the other, between individual adventure and Company conspiracy, is crossed once Marlow steps through the office door; hence he attempts to distance the troubling aspects of his decision behind the apparently solid boundary of gender difference.

Yet this maneuver is only momentarily successful: the elder woman returns into Marlow's narrative. As he begins his journey into the jungle to retrieve Kurtz, who has escaped from the ship, this woman "obtrude[s] herself upon my memory" (p. 80), that is, breaches the boundary of the displacing mind. Her reappearance serves as a double signal that Marlow's effort to distance the "other" — women and the troubling realities associated with their image — was bound to fail. First, this search for Kurtz itself initiates a crossing of boundaries. As he penetrates the jungle, Marlow is penetrated by it: "I confounded the beat of the drum with the beating of my heart" (p. 81). Hitherto distanced by being symbolized in the savage woman, the jungle can no longer be thus controlled; the gender boundary is not impermeable, the jungle is not a place where men are men and women are symbols. The second signal of Marlow's failed displacements is the form in which the elder Fate returns. Intruding as "the knitting old woman with the cat," the uneasiness Marlow displaced onto the Company women now

[11]John Milton, *Paradise Lost,* ed. Alastair Fowler (New York: Longman, 1971) 2:746.

returns with greater strength for its suppression. This silent figure of civilized domesticity only seems incongruous in the jungle; her reappearance dramatizes the futility of Marlow's attempt to separate the domestic and the larger world, the woman's sphere and the man's.

This failure of ideology becomes most evident in Marlow's portrayals of his aunt and the Intended, for they arise from the contradiction between experience and ideology. His helplessness before this contradiction places Marlow in what Karen Klein calls the feminine predicament, a situation defined by a sense of physical and/or social powerlessness.[12] This loss of control over circumstances is epitomized in Marlow's experience of Kurtz. On the one hand, as we have seen, he is overpowered by Kurtz's "unbounded eloquence" in the service of imperialism's ideology; on the other hand, he is equally drawn to Kurtz's final summation, "The horror! The horror!" because it is equally "the expression of some sort of belief" (p. 86). The core of Marlow's feminine predicament, the contradiction between beliefs that he feels powerless to reconcile, results in the portraits of his aunt and the Intended. Both portraits involve attempts by Marlow to extricate himself from his feminine predicament. Through them he creates a feminine sphere of belief that can stand alongside the masculine sphere of Kurtz's final, horrible belief; located in separate domains, these contradictory ideologies need not confront each other.

The belief that will later be grounded in the aunt and the Intended first emerges in the preface to Marlow's story. Like his irony, Marlow's belief in the idea behind imperialism is a retrospective attempt to mask his complicity in the Company's imperialism. He admits that

> The conquest of the earth, which mostly means the taking it away from those who have a different complexion or slightly flatter noses than ourselves, is not a pretty thing when you look into it too much. What redeems it is the idea only . . . not a sentimental pretence but an idea; and an unselfish belief in the idea — something you can set up, and bow down before, and offer a sacrifice to. . . . (p. 21)

Although this statement precedes Marlow's story, it is important to remember that he has already "looked into" what he is about to tell. Resolving this predicament requires an ideological belief that an ugly

---

[12]Karen Klein, "The Feminine Predicament in Conrad's *Nostromo*," in *Brandeis Essays in Literature,* ed. John Hazel Smith (Waltham, Mass.: Brandeis English and American Literature Department, 1983), pp. 101–16.

exercise of power ("Exterminate all the brutes!") can be redeemed by an idea. But Marlow's credo displays all the contradictions he intends it to suppress: between the reality and the idea, between an idea and a "sentimental pretence" (how would one tell the difference?), between an unselfish belief and (implicitly) a selfish one. When he "br[eaks] off" (p. 21) these framing sentences and then begins his story, the resultant gap reveals the contradiction between his need for imperialist belief and his experience of the horror, a divergence resolved through the world of his aunt and the Intended.

Marlow's feminine predicament explains not only why he creates his aunt and the Intended but also why, unlike the women we have examined, these two are not silenced. He needs them for their speech: by mocking the lack of worldly experience which their words convey, he can recuperate that experience as a manly encounter with truth. By having them feebly echo the case Kurtz has made for imperialism, he can reverse the powerlessness evinced in his response to Kurtz's eloquence.

Marlow begins his story by creating in his aunt a woman whose lack of experience and debased imperialist rhetoric can be ridiculed; she exemplifies the "sentimental pretence" which must be distinguished from "an idea" and then rejected. Through the Intended, whose voice is "the echo of [Kurtz's] magnificent eloquence" (p. 87), Marlow fulfills two aims. He contains Kurtzian imperialism within the feminine sphere so that, when the Intended comes to embody "unselfish belief" in the "idea" of imperialism, she provides a locus for his own belief in this idea. At the same time, by lying to her about the horror, he maintains his belief in the truth of horrible experience. Marlow's creation of these women thus further undercuts his already damaged narrative authority: the whole of his story is seen to be a manful effort to shore up imperialism through patriarchy, through the nineteenth-century ideology of separate spheres.

Marlow's introduction of his aunt, by mocking her intercession with the Company on his behalf, reflects the patriarchal ideology excluding women from the man's sphere. Although Marlow prides himself on going "on my own legs" (p. 22), his desire for a position with the Company forces a new approach: "would you believe it? — I tried the women. I, Charlie Marlow, set the women to work — to get a job. Heavens!" (p. 23). Despite what is implied here — that no woman could have influence in such male matters — Marlow's aunt does get him the job he wants. To conceal the consequent implication, his own powerlessness, Marlow mocks his aunt's efforts: that it is *she* who was "determined to make no end of fuss" (p. 23) disguises the failure of his own eagerness. In this way he maintains his view that the world of experience is and should be a man's world.

This stance is developed in Marlow's farewell visit to his aunt. Like her room, which "most soothingly looked just as you would expect a lady's drawing-room to look" (p. 26), her "emissary of light" (p. 26) school of imperialism is predictably feminine; hence her ideas invite Marlow's mockery. In their defense she quotes Scripture "brightly" (that is, she is devout but flighty). She is "carried off her feet" by "rot" and "humbug" (unlike Marlow, she cannot recognize falsity). Her view of his job — " 'weaning those ignorant millions from their horrid ways' " — is adjectivally idealistic, hence feminine, while his — "the Company was run for profit" — is starkly realistic, hence masculine (p. 27).

But his aunt's belief in "weaning those ignorant millions" is not unambiguously feminine: it is a variant of the masculine imperialism in Kurtz's "we can exert a power for good practically unbounded." Why, then, do these words from Kurtz have "the unbounded power of eloquence" for Marlow, at least initially, while his aunt's similar vision is dismissed out of hand? To answer this question, we must examine a central passage in which Marlow equates truth with sensible masculine acceptance of fact. Commenting on one of his aunt's "bright" remarks, Marlow says:

> It's queer how out of touch with truth women are. They live in a world of their own, and there had never been anything like it, and never can be. It is too beautiful altogether, and if they were to set it up it would go to pieces before the first sunset. Some confounded fact we men have been living contentedly with ever since the day of creation would start up and knock the whole thing over. (p. 27)

Here it is assumed ("It's queer" — that is, strange but true) that all women (extrapolating from one woman) are out of touch with truth, which is identified with masculine fact. It follows that the "world of their own" which women inhabit is nonfactual and therefore "too beautiful altogether": "there has never been anything like it, and never can be." Hence the product of this sphere, his aunt's "sentimental pretence" of redemption, can be denied because it is not validated by experience.

The experience of truth, like its recognition, is a male province. Marlow's view that the horrid ways of savages reveal truth, and that only a man can experience it, emerges as he describes the native rites he responded to. Again we must remember Marlow's retrospective technique: this experience precedes his narrative and thus informs its patriarchal condescension to his aunt's inexperience. The native rites display "truth stripped of its cloak of time"; "if you were man enough," Marlow tells his male audience, you would admit your response to it, as he did; in fact, to "meet that truth with his own true stuff" one must be "as much of a man" as the savages (p. 51). While Marlow's aunt is not "man enough" to experience savagery in a way that will result in truth, both Kurtz and Marlow are. Hence Kurtz's imperialistic eloquence is for Marlow merely "too high-strung, I think" (p. 65), while the aunt's can be dismissed as sentimental pretence.

As Marlow elaborates his explanation of manly experience, he equates belief and truth as masculine provinces. A man's "true stuff" is his "own inborn strength" (p. 51); having distinguished this inner strength from principles — mere "acquisitions, clothes, pretty rags" — Marlow concludes that "you want a deliberate belief." This explanation is intended to establish that belief is inherently masculine. Equating "a man's true stuff" with both his "inborn strength" and a "deliberate belief," it proposes that stuff/strength/belief is inborn in men, natural to them; even though belief is acquired ("deliberate"), it is made to seem different in kind from principles, an "acquisition" with a whiff of the feminine ("pretty rags"). Belief, then, becomes a fully masculine activity: it inheres naturally in men and comes to the surface through manly experience.

Through this process of mystification, Marlow's explanation becomes an ideological defense of masculine belief. Filtered through his manly experience, belief in the imperialist "idea" can now be used to redeem a reality which is "not pretty." Like his response to the savage rites, then, Marlow's narrative of his experience of Kurtz is put to this use: it recuperates the Kurtzian ideology, validates what might otherwise seem "too beautiful." For this project to be successful, however, Marlow must cope with one of the "confounded facts" inimical to the woman's world: that Kurtz's own final expression of belief contradicts the "idea" which redeems conquest. The difficulty here is suggested by the fact that, while Marlow can dismiss Kurtz as "very little more than a voice," he seems constrained to add that "the memory of that time lingers" in "voices, voices — even the girl herself — now — " (p. 63).

This first mention of the Intended is the prelude to the feminine sphere she will inhabit: belief in her will balance Kurtz's final expression of belief only in the "horror." The necessity of this alternative for Marlow becomes clear when we look at an instance in which he silences Kurtz. What exactly does Kurtz say, after he has crawled into the jungle, to dissuade Marlow from carrying him back to the ship? Marlow conceals this speech, saying only that "No eloquence could have been so withering to one's belief in mankind as his final burst of sincerity" (p. 82). Here the contradiction between the eloquence of power and the brutality of its exercise, which Marlow has already noted in Kurtz's report, enters his own experience directly. Kurtz's earlier eloquence now stands in stark contrast to his sincerity, and this sincerity threatens to wither the belief in mankind that underpins imperialism. If this new voice drowns out Kurtz's earlier eloquence, then belief in the idea is impossible and Marlow's experience is indeed what he fears it to be: "one immense jabber . . . without any kind of sense" (p. 63). Fear of this possibility halts Marlow's narrative "for a long time" (p. 63); this gap between his fear of the jabber and his production of the denying patriarchal ideology reveals that Marlow must order the cacophony of "voices, voices" — Kurtz's eloquence, his sincerity, and the Intended's voice — by setting her speech off against the others.

When Marlow resumes his narrative, then, he does so with his triumph over Kurtz: "I laid the ghost of his gifts at last with a lie" (p. 63). This foreshadowing of his lie to the Intended is appropriately followed by a statement of the "deliberate belief" he has now invested in her:

> Oh, she is out of it — completely. They — the women I mean — are out of it — should be out of it. We must help them to stay in that beautiful world of their own, lest ours gets worse. Oh, she had to be out of it. (p. 63)

Where Marlow had earlier dismissed this world as "too beautiful altogether," its beauty is now essential: carefully kept "out of it," separated from "our" world of experience, the woman's world will keep the masculine world from deteriorating. The patriarchal ideology of separate spheres which underpins the imperialist ideology could hardly be better formulated. This juxtaposition of lie and idea reveals that the former is in the service of the latter: by lying to the Intended, Marlow lodges her in the so-called "world of her own" created out of his own need to defend against what he has "looked into too much."

Marlow's visit to the Intended dramatizes the consequent necessity that she, like all the women in this story, exist as his creation. As he had earlier commodified the savage woman, he now reduces the Intended to a "pure brow," a "forehead, smooth and white" which offers "the unextinguishable light of belief and love" (pp. 90, 91). He locates in her a "beautiful generosity" (p. 92) and "a mature capacity for fidelity, for belief, for suffering" (p. 90) — in short, the "unselfish belief" he requires. Most important, her faith in the power of Kurtzian eloquence enables Marlow to contain and transform that eloquence. "Bowing [his] head before the faith that was in her, before that great and saving illusion" (p. 92), Marlow first privileges the Intended's belief in Kurtz; in other words, what in Marlow would seem a simple illusion is now elevated to become her "great and saving illusion." By doing so, Marlow removes the threat of eloquence from the realm of his own experience and translates it into her "out of it" world. In order to partake in the "saving illusion" that is ideological belief, Marlow must distance it from the man's sphere where it contradicted Kurtz's final, harsh expression of belief. In this way he orders the "jabber" which would have destroyed his own belief in the idea; he believes now not in Kurtzian eloquence but in her belief. As Marlow bows in spirit before her faith, then, we see fulfilled his ideological project of creating the redeeming idea — "something you can set up, and bow down before, and offer a sacrifice to" (p. 21). While he appears to be bowing down before *her* faith, in reality he is idolizing his own "idea" — the "something" he has "set up" in her.

To complete the posture of belief, however, a sacrifice is required, and who better than the Intended, with her Marlow-imposed "capacity for suffering"? Hence the final lie: saying that Kurtz's last words were the Intended's name, Marlow conceals that they were actually "The horror! The horror!" (p. 85). It is true that Marlow feels he has sacrificed himself: although he "hate[s], detest[s], and can't bear a lie" (p. 91), he has told this one to the Intended, he says, out of his desire to save her soul and out of his "infinite pity" for her suffering (p. 93). But surely the particular lie he chooses is meant to punish her, to satisfy his "dull anger" with her naiveté and her insistence that he give her "something . . . to live with" (p. 93). He and his audience (and the reader) know that by substituting the Intended's name for "The horror! The horror!" he equates the two; keeping her ignorant of this equation is a mode of humiliating her. The intimations of punishing assault are carried through by the setting; in that "place of cruel and absurd mysteries" (p. 91), the lie sacrifices her, appearing to penetrate her like a ritual sword. This suggestion of sexual violation is strengthened by Marlow's description of her response: his lie elicits from the Intended, he says, "an exulting and terrible cry" (p. 93). It is the man who caused it who interprets the cry in this ameliorating way: in his version the "unspeakable pain" (p. 93) he intended to inflict is validated (like the rape victim, she asked for it) by the accompanying "inconceivable triumph" (and she liked it).[13] Marlow can both bow down before a belief he needs but scorns and, through the lie, punish the Intended for his own need.

This contradiction, that Marlow can both honor the Intended's faith and simultaneously assault her with his lie, demonstrates his continuing commitment to Kurtz. During his visit to the Intended, Marlow brings the "conquering darkness" with him into her house (p. 89), a darkness which includes Kurtz's dying cry, "The horror! The horror!" Because Marlow's loyalty is finally dual — to "a power for good" and to "The horror! The horror!" — his lie has a dual purpose. It sacrifices the Intended not only to maintain in her the echo of Kurtz's eloquence but also to produce a second echo, the "exulting and terrible" cry which reaffirms Kurtz's final cry. Marlow has it both ways: the lie protects the Intended from the "jabber" and hence allows his structure of belief, the woman's "beautiful world," to stand; because Marlow knows it is a lie, however, the world in which men can experience the truth of horror also continues to stand.

Here we see not only the ideology of separate spheres but also why it is produced. The motive is ideological disguise: by creating an alternative woman's sphere "lest ours gets worse," men can continue to confront their "own true stuff" in their world while masking the threat represented by Kurtz, who has so fully confronted his "stuff" that he has "kicked the very earth to pieces" (p. 82). A lie such as Marlow's must be told by a man to a woman, so as to deny her the masculine truth, to confine her to "that beautiful world" he has constructed as a counter to the masculine world. Marlow withholds Kurtz's view of the world as horror because, he says, telling the Intended the truth would have been "too dark altogether" (p. 94). This shift from his earlier "too beautiful altogether" reverberates with the defensive rationale for his ideological separation of man's and woman's worlds. These words, the last of Marlow's narrative, also provide an ironic echo of Kurtz's last words: while Marlow concludes by denying Kurtz's cry, those words have produced his, for both conclusions are "the expression of some sort of belief."

Of the similar ironies which conclude *Nostromo,* Klein says that "The ironic vision is used as an evasion; it functions here in literature as

---

[13]Staten argues that Marlow functions as Kurtz's emissary, thereby fulfilling the latter's sadistic project of forcing the Intended into the total mourning that will confirm his existence. While Staten is the only critic to my knowledge who gives full value to the Intended's cry, his reading nonetheless seems to share Marlow's commodifying treatment of her: his tendency to reduce her to a cry is not unlike Marlow's tendency to use her as a function of himself.

it does in life as a form of detachment." It is clear that Marlow uses irony in this way; it allows him to mask his ambivalence about the imperialism of the Company which employs him, to disguise his dependence on women, and to tell, as if he were detached from its purpose, a story which both affirms and denies the beliefs through which his culture operates. The concluding ironies of *Nostromo,* Klein suggests, perform a like function for readers and for Conrad, so that "We, just like the author, can remove ourselves from disturbing feelings."[14] To rest in ironies in this way, to distance ourselves as critics from the expression of patriarchy in *Heart of Darkness,* would be to participate in Marlow's detachment. My intent has been to show that feminist criticism is a method of avoiding his detachment, of making ourselves aware of the patriarchal ideology in which he and perhaps we too unwittingly participate.

FEMINIST CRITICISM: A SELECTED BIBLIOGRAPHY

French Feminist Theory

Beauvoir, Simone de. *The Second Sex.* 1949. Edited and translated by H. M. Parshley. New York: Modern Library, 1952.

Cixous, Hélène. "The Laugh of the Medusa." Translated by Keith Cohen and Paula Cohen. *Signs* 1 (1976): 875–94.

French Feminist Theory. Special issue, *Signs* 7 (1981). Essays by Cixous, Fauré, Irigaray, Kristeva.

Gelfand, Elissa D., and Virginia Thorndike Hules. *French Feminist Criticism: Women, Language, and Literature. An Annotated Bibliography.* New York: Garland, 1984.

Irigaray, Luce. *This Sex Which Is Not One.* Translated by Catherine Porter. Ithaca, N.Y.: Cornell University Press, 1985.

Kristeva, Julia. *Desire in Language: A Semiotic Approach to Literature and Art,* edited by Leon S. Roudiez. Translated by Thomas Gora, Alice Jardine, and Leon S. Roudiez. New York: Columbia University Press, 1980.

Marks, Elaine, and Isabelle de Courtivron, eds. *New French Feminisms: An Anthology.* Amherst: University of Massachusetts Press, 1980.

Moi, Toril. *Sexual/Textual Politics: Feminist Literary Theory.* London: Methuen, 1985.

---

[14]Klein, "The Feminine Predicament," in *Brandeis Essays,* p. 115.

Wittig, Monique. *Les Guérillères*. Translated by David Le Vay. New York: Avon, 1973.

British and American Feminist Theory

Greer, Germaine. *The Female Eunuch*. New York: McGraw-Hill, 1971.

Heilbrun, Carolyn. *Toward a Recognition of Androgyny*. New York: Alfred A. Knopf, 1973.

Kolodny, Annette. "Some Notes on Defining a 'Feminist Literary Criticism.' " *Critical Inquiry* 2 (1975): 75–92.

Millett, Kate. *Sexual Politics*. Garden City, N.Y.: Doubleday, 1970.

Woolf, Virginia. *A Room of One's Own*. New York: Harcourt, 1929.

The Feminist Critique

Ellmann, Mary. *Thinking About Women*. London: Macmillan, 1968.

Fetterly, Judith. *The Resisting Reader: A Feminist Approach to American Fiction*. Bloomington: Indiana University Press, 1978.

Kolodny, Annette. *The Lay of the Land: Metaphor as Experience in American Life and Letters*. Chapel Hill: University of North Carolina Press, 1975.

See also Beauvoir, Greer, Heilbrun, and Millett, cited above.

Gynocriticism: Women's Writing and Creativity

Auerbach, Nina. *Communities of Women: An Idea in Fiction*. Cambridge, Mass.: Harvard University Press, 1978.

Gilbert, Sandra M., and Susan Gubar. *The Madwoman in the Attic: The Woman Writer and the Nineteenth-Century Literary Imagination*. New Haven, Conn.: Yale University Press, 1979.

Jacobus, Mary, ed. *Women Writing and Writing about Women*. New York: Barnes and Noble, 1979.

Miller, Nancy K., ed. *The Poetics of Gender*. New York: Columbia University Press, 1986.

Poovey, Mary. *The Proper Lady and the Woman Writer: Ideology as Style in the Works of Mary Wollstonecraft, Mary Shelley, and Jane Austen*. Chicago: University of Chicago Press, 1984.

Showalter, Elaine. *A Literature of Their Own: British Women Novelists from Brontë to Lessing*. Princeton, N.J.: Princeton University Press, 1977.

————. *The New Feminist Criticism: Essays on Women, Literature, and Theory.* New York: Pantheon, 1985.

Spacks, Patricia Meyer. *The Female Imagination.* New York: Alfred A. Knopf, 1975.

Marxist and Class Analysis

Barrett, Michèle. *Women's Oppression Today: Problems in Marxist Feminist Analysis.* London: Verso, 1980.

Delany, Sheila. *Writing Woman: Women Writers and Women in Literature, Medieval to Modern.* New York: Schocken, 1983.

Keohane, Nannerl O., Michelle Z. Rosaldo, and Barbara C. Gelpi, eds. *Feminist Theory: A Critique of Ideology.* Chicago: University of Chicago Press, 1982. See especially the essays by Elshtain, Jehlen, Kristeva, MacKinnon, and Marcus.

Mitchell, Juliet. *Woman's Estate.* New York: Pantheon, 1971.

Moteith, Moira, ed. *Women's Writing: A Challenge to Theory.* Brighton, Eng.: Harvester, 1986. See especially the essays by Monteith and Humm.

Newton, Judith Lowder. *Women, Power and Subversion: Social Strategies in British Fiction, 1778–1860.* Athens: University of Georgia Press, 1981.

Newton, Judith, and Deborah Rosenfelt, eds. *Feminist Criticism and Social Change: Sex, Class and Race in Literature and Culture.* New York: Methuen, 1985. See especially the essays by Jones and Smith.

Robinson, Lillian. *Sex, Class, and Culture.* New York: Methuen, 1986.

Women's History/Women's Studies

Bell, Roseann P., et al., eds. *Sturdy Black Bridges: Visions of Black Women in Literature.* New York: Anchor, 1979.

Bridenthal, Renata, and Claudia Koonz, eds. *Becoming Visible: Women in European History.* Boston: Houghton Mifflin, 1977.

Cott, Nancy F., and Elizabeth H. Pleck, eds. *A Heritage of Her Own: Toward a New Social History of American Women.* New York: Simon and Schuster, Touchstone, 1977.

Faderman, Lillian. *Surpassing the Love of Men: Romantic Friendship and Love Between Women from the Renaissance to the Present.* New York: Morrow, 1981.

The Lesbian Issue. Special issue, *Signs* 9 (1984).

Newton, Judith L., Mary P. Ryan, and Judith R. Walkowitz, eds. *Sex and Class in Women's History*. London: Routledge and Kegan Paul, 1983.

Schipper, Mineke, ed. *Unheard Words: Women and Literature in Africa, the Arab World, Asia, the Caribbean, and Latin America*. London: Allison and Busby, 1979.

Feminism and Other Critical Approaches

Armstrong, Nancy, ed. *Literature as Women's History I*. A special issue of *Genre* 19–20 (1986–87) containing feminist and new historicist analyses.

Feminist Studies 14 (1988). A special issue devoted to feminism and deconstruction. See especially Mary Poovey's "Feminism and Deconstruction."

Feminist Conrad Criticism

Brydon, Diana. " 'The Thematic Ancestor': Joseph Conrad, Patrick White, and Margaret Atwood." *World Literature Written in English* 24 (1984): 386–97.

Klein, Karen. "The Feminine Predicament in Conrad's *Nostromo*." In *Brandeis Essays in Literature,* edited by John Hazel Smith. Waltham, Mass.: Brandeis English and American Literature Department, 1983, 101–16.

Sullivan, Zohreh T. "Enclosure, Darkness, and the Body: Conrad's Landscape." *The Centennial Review* 25 (1981): 59–79.

Deconstruction
and
Heart of Darkness

WHAT IS DECONSTRUCTION?

Deconstruction has a reputation for being the most complex and forbidding of contemporary critical approaches to literature, but in fact almost all of us have, at one time, either deconstructed a text or badly wanted to deconstruct one. Sometimes when we hear a lecturer effectively marshal evidence to show that a book means primarily one thing, we long to interrupt and ask what he or she would make of other, conveniently overlooked passages, passages that seem to contradict the lecturer's thesis. Sometimes, after reading a provocative critical article that *almost* convinces us that a familiar work means the opposite of what we assumed it meant, we may wish to make an equally convincing case for our old way of reading the text. It isn't that we think that the poem or novel in question better supports our interpretation; it's that we think the text can be used to support *both* readings. And sometimes we simply want to make that point: that texts can be used to support seemingly irreconcilable positions.

To want to make that point is to feel the deconstructive itch. J. Hillis Miller, the preeminent American deconstructor, puts it this way: "Deconstruction is not a dismantling of the structure of a text, but a demonstration that it has already dismantled itself. Its apparently solid

ground is no rock but thin air."[1] To deconstruct a text isn't to show
that all the high old themes aren't there to be found in it. It is, rather, to
show that a text — not unlike DNA with its double helix — can have
intertwined, opposite "discourses" — strands of narrative, threads of
meaning.

Ultimately, of course, deconstruction refers to something larger
and more complex than the practice of showing that a text means
contradictory things. For one thing, the term refers to a way of reading
texts practiced by critics who have been influenced by the writings
of the French philosopher Jacques Derrida. It is important to gain
some understanding of Derrida's project and of the historical backgrounds of his work before reading Miller's deconstruction of Conrad,
let alone attempting to deconstruct a text. But it is important, too,
to approach deconstruction with anything but a scholar's sober and almost worshipful respect for knowledge and truth. Deconstruction
offers a playful alternative to traditional scholarship: a confidently
adversarial alternative. It deserves to be approached in the spirit that
animates it.

Derrida, a philosopher of language who coined the term "deconstruction," argues that we tend to think and express our thoughts in
terms of opposites. Something is black but not white, masculine and
therefore not feminine, a cause rather than an effect, and so forth.
These mutually exclusive pairs or dichotomies are too numerous to
list but would include, for example, beginning/end, conscious/uncon-
scious, presence/absence, speech/writing, and construction/destruction
(the opposition that Derrida's word deconstruction tries to contain and
subvert). If we think hard about these dichotomies, Derrida suggests,
we will realize that they are not simply oppositions; they are also
little hierarchies. In other words, they contain one term that our
culture views as being superior and one term viewed as negative or
inferior. Sometimes the superior or positive term seems only subtly
positive ("speech," "masculine," "cause"), whereas sometimes we know
immediately which term is culturally preferable ("presence" and "beginning" and "consciousness" are easy choices). But always the hierarchy
exists.

Of particular interest to Derrida, perhaps because it involves the

---

[1] J. Hillis Miller, "Stevens' Rock and Criticism as Cure, II," *The Georgia Review*
30 (1976), p. 341.

language in which all the other dichotomies are expressed, is the hierarchical opposition "speech/writing." Derrida argues that the "privileging" of speech — that is, the tendency to think of speech in positive terms, writing in negative terms — cannot be disentangled from the privileging of presence. (Postcards are written by absent friends; we read Plato because he cannot speak from beyond the grave.) Furthermore, the tendency to privilege both speech and presence is, according to Derrida, part of the Western tradition of *logocentrism,* the belief that in some ideal, perfect beginning were creative *spoken* words, words such as "Let there be light," spoken by an ideal, perfect, *present* God. According to logocentric tradition, these words can now only be represented in unoriginal speech or writing (such as the written phrase in quotation marks above). Derrida doesn't seek to reverse the hierarchized opposition between speech and writing, or presence and absence, or early and late, for to do so would be to fall into a trap and perpetuate the same forms of thought and expression that he seeks to deconstruct. Rather, he seeks to erase the dividing line or boundary between oppositions such as that between speech and writing, and to do so in such a way as to throw the order and values implied by the opposition into question.

Going back to the theories of Ferdinand de Saussure, who invented the modern science of linguistics, Derrida reminds us that the association of speech with present and obvious and ideal meaning and writing with absent, merely pictured, and therefore less reliable meaning is suspect to say the least. As Saussure demonstrated, words are *not* the things they name and, indeed, they are only arbitrarily associated with those things. Neither spoken nor written words have present, positive, identifiable attributes themselves; they have meaning only by virtue of their difference from other words (red, read, reed). In a sense, meanings emerge from the gaps or spaces between them. Take "read" as an example. To know whether it is the present or past tense form of the verb — whether it rhymes with "red" or "reed" — we need to see it in relation to some other word (e.g., "yesterday").

Because the meanings of words lie in the differences between them and in the differences between them and the things they name, Derrida suggests that all language is constituted by *différance,* a word he has coined that puns on two French words meaning to differ and defer: words are the deferred presences of the things they mean, and their meaning is grounded in difference. (Derrida, by the way, changes the *e* in the French word *différence* to an *a* in his neologism *différance;*

the change, which can be seen in writing but cannot be heard in spoken French, is itself a playful, witty challenge to the notion that writing is inferior or "fallen" speech.)

In *De la grammatologie* [*Of Grammatology*] (1967) and *Dissemination* (1972), Derrida begins to redefine writing by deconstructing some old definitions. In *Dissemination* he traces logocentrism back to Plato, who in the *Phaedrus* has Socrates condemn writing and who, in all the great dialogues, powerfully postulates that metaphysical longing for origins and ideals that permeates Western thought. "What Derrida does in his reading of Plato," Barbara Johnson points out, "is to unfold dimensions of Plato's *text* that work against the grain of (Plato's own) Platonism."[2] That, remember, is what deconstruction always does according to Miller: it shows a text dismantling itself.

In *Of Grammatology,* Derrida turns to the *Confessions* of Jean-Jacques Rousseau and exposes a grain running against the grain. Rousseau, another great Western idealist and believer in innocent, noble origins, on one hand condemns writing as mere representation, a corruption of the more natural, childlike, direct, and therefore undevious speech. On the other hand, Derrida notes, Rousseau admits his own tendency to lose self-presence and blurt out exactly the wrong thing in public. He confesses that, by writing at a distance from his audience, he can often get his thoughts out better. ("If I were present, one would never know what I was worth," Rousseau admits.[3]) Thus, writing is a *supplement* to speech that is at the same time *necessary*. Barbara Johnson, sounding like Derrida, puts it this way: "Recourse to writing is necessary to recapture a presence whose lack has never been preceded by any fullness." Thus, Derrida shows, one strand of Rousseau's discourse makes writing seem a secondary, even treacherous supplement, while another makes it seem necessary to communication.

Have Derrida's deconstructions of *Confessions* and the *Phaedrus* explained these texts, interpreted them, opened them up and shown us what they mean? Not in any traditional sense, for Derrida would say that anyone attempting to find a single, correct meaning in a text is simply imprisoned by that structure of thought that would oppose two readings and declare one to be right and not wrong, correct rather than incorrect. Whereas in fact any work of literature

---

[2]Barbara Johnson, Translator's Introduction to Jacques Derrida, *Dissemination* (Chicago: University of Chicago Press, 1981), p. xxiv.

[3]Jean-Jacques Rousseau, *Confessions,* as translated by Gayatri Spivak in Jacques Derrida, *Of Grammatology,* trans. Gayatri Spivak (Baltimore: Johns Hopkins University Press, 1974), p. 142.

that we interpret defies the laws of Western logic, the laws of opposition and noncontradiction. Texts don't say "A and not B," in the views of post-structuralist critics. They say "A and not-A," and so do texts written by literary critics, who are also involved in producing creative writing. But it is the very incompatibility of discourses within literary texts that makes literature mysterious, problematic, worthy of attention. Such incompatibilities will not be found by a reader who believes that construction and destruction are utterly opposed and that the critic must construct an argument showing that a text means one and not the other.

Although its ultimate aim may be to critique Western idealism and logic, deconstruction began as a response to structuralism and to formalism, another structure-oriented theory of reading. (Deconstruction, which is really only one kind of post-structuralist criticism, is sometimes referred to as post-structuralist criticism, or even as post-structuralism.)

Structuralism, Robert Scholes tells us, may now be seen as a reaction to " 'modernist' alienation and despair."[4] Using Saussure's theory as Derrida was to do later, European structuralists attempted to create a *semiology,* or science of signs, one that would give humankind at once a scientific and holistic way of studying the world and its human inhabitants. Roland Barthes, a structuralist who later shifted toward post-structuralism, hoped to recover literary language from the isolation in which it had been studied and to show that the laws that govern it govern all signs, from road signs to articles of clothing. Claude Lévi-Strauss, a structural anthropologist who studied everything from village structure to the structure of myths, looked in the latter for what he called "mythemes": building blocks such as very basic plot elements. By showing that the same mythemes recur in the similar myths of different cultures, he suggested that all myths may be elements of one great myth being written by the collective human mind.

Derrida could not accept the notion that structuralist thought might someday explain the laws governing human signification and thus provide the key to understanding the form and meaning of everything from an African village to a Greek myth to Rousseau's *Confessions.* In his view, the scientific search for what unifies humankind by a structural anthropologist like Claude Lévi-Strauss amounts to a new version of the old search for the lost ideal, whether it be

---

[4]Robert Scholes, *Structuralism in Literature: An Introduction* (New Haven, Conn.: Yale University Press, 1974), p. 3.

Plato's bright realm of the Idea or the pure Paradise of Genesis or Rousseau's unspoiled Nature. As for the structuralist belief that texts have "centers" of meaning, that derives, in Derrida's view, from the logocentric belief that there is a reading of the text that accords with "the book as seen by God."[5] Jonathan Culler, in *Structuralist Poetics,* explains what Derrida objects to in structuralist literary criticism by saying that when

> one speaks of the structure of a literary work, one does so from a certain vantage point: one starts with notions of the meaning or effects of a poem and tries to identify the structures responsible for those effects. Possible configurations or patterns that make no contribution are rejected as irrelevant. That is to say, an intuitive understanding of the poem functions as the 'centre.'. . . : it is both a starting point and a limiting principle.

For these reasons, Derrida and his post-structuralist followers reject the very notion of linguistic competence introduced by Noam Chomsky, a structural linguist. The idea that there is a competent reading, Culler explains, "gives a privileged status to a particular set of rules of reading, . . . granting pre-eminence to certain conventions and excluding from the realm of language all the truly creative and productive violations of those rules."[6]

Post-structuralism calls into question assumptions made about literature by formalist, as well as by structuralist, critics. Formalism, or the New Criticism as it was once more usually called, assumes a work of literature to be a free-standing, self-contained object, its meanings lying in the complex network of relations that can be found between its constituent parts (images, sounds, rhythms, allusions, etc.). Deconstruction is, to be sure, somewhat like formalism in several ways. For one thing, both the formalist and the deconstructor focus on the literary text; neither is likely to read a poem or novel by relating it to events in the author's life, letters, historical period, or even culture. For another thing, formalists, long before deconstructors, discovered counter-patterns of meaning in the same text. Formalists find ambiguity and irony; deconstructors find contradiction and undecidability.

Here, though, the two groups part ways. Whereas the formalist believes a complete understanding of a literary work to be possible

---

[5]Jacques Derrida, *L'écriture et la différence.* I am quoting a passage translated by Jonathan Culler in Culler's *Structuralist Poetics* (Ithaca, N.Y.: Cornell University Press, 1975), p. 242.

[6]Culler, *Structuralist Poetics,* pp. 244, 241.

— an understanding in which even the ambiguities will be seen to have a definite, meaningful function — post-structuralists celebrate the apparently limitless possibilities for the production of meaning that come about when the language of the critic enters the language of the text. Such a view directly opposes the formalist view that a work of literary art has organic unity (and therefore, structuralists would say, a "center"), if only we could find it.

Post-structuralists break with formalists, too, over an issue they have debated structuralists on. The issue involves metaphor and metonymy, two terms for different kinds of rhetorical "tropes" or figures of speech. *Metonymy* refers to a figure that is chosen to stand for something that it is commonly associated with, or with which it happens to be contiguous or juxtaposed. "I'll have the cold plate today," when said to a waitress, is a metonymic figure of speech for "I'll eat the cold food you're serving today." We refer to the food we want as a plate simply because plates are what food happens to be served on — and because everyone understands that by "plate" we mean food. A *metaphor,* on the other hand, is a figure of speech that supposedly involves a special, intrinsic, nonarbitrary relationship with what it stands for. To refer to your car as wheels is, arguably, to make a kind of metaphor. If you believe, when you say you are blue, that there is some intrinsic, timeless likeness between that color and melancholy feeling — a likeness that just doesn't exist between sadness and yellow — then you are using "blue" metaphorically.

Whereas both formalists and structuralists make much of the opposition between metaphor and metonymy, Derrida, Miller, and the late Paul de Man have contended with the distinction deconstructively. They have questioned not only the distinction but also, and perhaps especially, the privilege we grant to metaphor, which we tend to view as the positive and superior figure of speech. De Man, in *Allegories of Reading,* analyzes a passage from Marcel Proust's *Swann's Way* and shows that it is about the nondistinction between metaphor and metonymy — and that it makes its claim metonymically. Miller, in *Fiction and Repetition: Seven English Novels,* connects the belief in metaphorical correspondences with other metaphysical beliefs, such as those in origins, endings, transcendence, and underlying truths. Isn't it likely, deconstructors keep implicitly asking, that every metaphor was once a metonym, but that we have simply forgotten what arbitrary juxtaposition or contiguity gave rise to the association that now seems mysteriously special?

The hypothesis that what we call metaphors are really old metonyms may perhaps be made clearer by the following example. We used the word "Watergate" as a metonym to refer to a political scandal that happened to begin in the Watergate building complex. Recently, we have used part of the building's name ("gate") to refer to other scandals ("Irangate"). But already, some people who use and "understand" these terms are unaware that Watergate is the name of a building. In five hundred years, isn't it possible that "gate," which began as part of a simple metonym, will seem like the perfect metaphor for scandal — a word that suggests corruption and wrongdoing with a strange and inexplicable rightness?

This is how deconstruction works: by showing that what was prior and privileged in the old hierarchy (metaphor or speech) can just as easily seem secondary, the deconstructor causes the formerly privileged term to exchange properties with the formerly devalued one. Causes become effects and (d)evolutions become origins, but the result is not the destruction of the old order or hierarchy and the construction of a new one. It is, rather, *deconstruction*. Robert Scholes explains it this way: "If either cause or effect can occupy the position of an origin, then origin is no longer originary; it loses its metaphorical privilege."[7]

Once deconstructed, "literal" and "figurative" can exchange properties, so that the prioritizing boundary between them is erased: all words, even "dog" and "cat," are understood to be figures; it's just that we have used some of them so long that we have forgotten how arbitrary, how metonymic, they are. And, just as literal and figurative can exchange properties, criticism can exchange properties with literature, in the process coming to be seen not as a mere supplement — the second, negative, and inferior term in the binary opposition creative writing / literary criticism — but rather as an equally creative form of work. Would we write if there were not already in existence critics — intelligent readers motivated and able to make sense of what is written? Who, then, depends upon whom?

"It is not difficult to see the attractions" of deconstructive reading, Jonathan Culler has commented. "Given that there is no ultimate or absolute justification for any system or for the interpretations from it," the critic is free to value "the activity of interpretation itself, . . . rather than any results which might be obtained."[8] Not everyone, however, has so

[7]Scholes, *Structuralism in Literature*, p. 88.
[8]Culler, *Structuralist Poetics*, p. 248.

readily seen the attractions of deconstruction. Two eminent critics, M. H. Abrams and Wayne C. Booth, have observed that a deconstructive reading "is plainly and simply parasitical" on what Abrams calls "the obvious or univocal meaning."[9] They are suggesting, in other words, that there would be no deconstructors if there were not already in existence critics able to see and show that — and how — texts have central and definite meanings. Miller responded in an essay entitled "The Critic as Host," in which he not only deconstructed the oppositional hierarchy (host/parasite) but also the two terms themselves, showing each to be too multiple in meaning to be part of a simple dichotomy. "Host" means hospitable welcomer and military horde, and "parasite" originally had a positive connotation: in Greek, *parasitos* meant "beside the grain" and referred to a friendly guest. Finally, Miller suggests, the words "parasite" and "host" are inseparable, depending upon one another for their meaning much as do authors and critics, structuralists and post-structuralists.

The purpose of deconstruction, Miller has written, is to show "the existence in literature of structures of language which contradict the law of non-contradiction." Why find the grain that runs against the grain? To restore what Miller has called "the strangeness of literature," to reveal the "capacity of each work to surprise the reader," to demonstrate that "literature continually exceeds any formula or theory with which the critic is prepared to encompass it."[10]

In the essay that follows, Miller does all these things, including admitting that his own reading is "exceeded" by *Heart of Darkness*. In the last paragraph of his essay, he confesses his own complicity as a demystifying commentator: "I have attempted," he writes, "to perform an act of generic classification, with all the covert violence and unreason of that act, since no work is wholly commensurate with the boundaries of any genre."

The generic classification Miller refers to is his attempt to classify *Heart of Darkness* as an apocalypse and the apocalypse as an extended parable. (Whereas a parable is a little allegorical story designed to reveal some moral truth, an apocalypse is a highly figurative book of

[9]M. H. Abrams, "Rationality and the Imagination in Cultural History," *Critical Inquiry* 2 (1976), pp. 457–58.
[10]J. Hillis Miller, *Fiction and Repetition: Seven English Novels* (Cambridge, Mass.: Harvard University Press, 1982), p. 5.

revelation or prophecy.) Of course, as a post-structuralist writing in opposition to the tradition of Western metaphysics, Miller classifies parables and apocalypses as genres that only *seem* to reveal spectral truths, be they the Bright Ideal or the Heart of Darkness. Miller deconstructs Jesus' parable of the sower to show how it is against itself; what its words reveal, Miller contends, is that if you need them then you cannot understand them. Miller also deconstructs Conrad's parable about the two kinds of stories, the parable of the "nut and the moonlit haze." (You will recall the contrast made between the "yarns of seamen . . . , the whole meaning of which" lies inside like a nut in a shell, and Marlow's stories, the meaning of which is said to lie "outside, enveloping the tale," which brings "it out only as a glow brings out a haze" [p. 19].) The narrator's distinction begins to unravel, the more Miller discusses it — and the more he discusses the story Marlow actually tells.

What Miller is really unravelling, of course, is a set of hierarchized, binary oppositions between kinds of texts. By questioning the privileged status of apocalypses, parables, and Marlow's stories, he is erasing numerous boundaries: between the Bible and literature, high forms of narrative and low, and, ultimately, between literature and criticism. (He sets himself and us in the same line of "guilty witnesses" that includes the narrator, whose witness of Marlow perpetuates what Marlow witnessed, and Marlow himself.) And, of course, Miller is deconstructing the metaphor/metonymy opposition. Parables, apocalypses, and allegories are shown to be like metaphors; in strange ways, they can supposedly highlight invisible things with which they are, supposedly, fundamentally and inevitably involved. They supposedly allow us to experience, in the present, such things as Timeless Truth, the End, or the Beginning. In fact, Miller's reading contends, parables and apocalypses cannot reveal metaphysical secrets because, like all signs, they are metonyms, no more intrinsically involved with ultimate truths than the cold plate we order is with the plate, than the mist around the moon is with the sun's reflected light.

Conrad's distinctions, Miller shows, are "made in terms of figures," and even these figures, by an "unavoidable necessity," have to have other, different, supplemental figures to explain them. (Marlow's tales bring out meaning *as* a glow brings out a haze, *in the likeness* of one of those misty halos. . . .) To highlight the figurative nature of language, as Miller does throughout his reading of *Heart of Darkness,* is a typical post-structuralist move. Equally typical, though, is Miller's wondering whether all these figures of figures, supplements to supplements, necessarily carry us further away from Marlow's experience and its meaning. Like the fellows on the *Nellie*, who are said by Marlow to "see more than I could," for "you see me," figures "see" — and show — us more than a sailor like Marlow could possibly have experienced (p. 42).

Implicit in all of Miller's critical procedures, of course, is the post-structuralist assumption that *Heart of Darkness* defies the logic of noncontradiction. Like anything written — and the "apocalypse is after all a written not an oral genre" — *Heart of Darkness* says both "A" and "not-A." Its figures both illuminate their own workings and undermine them; it promises to reveal something and then shows us that that something (pure darkness) is what cannot be seen or shown, except as an absence. An ironic text, it is founded, Miller says, on unreason and is "indeterminate or undecidable in meaning."

The unfolding of indeterminacies requires an unusual style, one which Miller deploys adeptly in "*Heart of Darkness* Revisited." "I begin with three questions," Miller begins. (Are there three? Are they answered or even answerable?) "I shall approach an answer . . . by a roundabout way." To write is to defer, just as to read the book of Revelation is to know what has not yet entered human experience. Miller's argument defers many central questions while drawing us close, in the process, to the workings of Conrad's text.

A DECONSTRUCTIVE CRITIC AT WORK

J. HILLIS MILLER

Heart of Darkness Revisited

I begin with three questions: Is it a senseless accident, a result of the crude misinterpretation or gross transformation of the mass media that the cinematic version of *Heart of Darkness* is called *Apocalypse Now*, or is there already something apocalyptic about Conrad's novel in itself? What are the distinctive features of an apocalyptic text? How would we know when we had one in hand?[0]

I shall approach an answer to these questions by the somewhat roundabout way of an assertion that if *Heart of Darkness* is perhaps

only problematically apocalyptic, there can be no doubt that it is parabolic. The distinctive feature of a parable, whether sacred or secular, is
the use of a realistic story, a story in one way or another based firmly
on what Marx calls man's "real conditions of life, and his relations with
his kind,"[1] to express another reality or truth not otherwise expressible.
When the disciples ask Jesus why he speaks to the multitudes in parables, he answers, "Therefore speak I to them in parables: because they
seeing see not; and hearing they hear not, neither do they understand"
(Matthew 13:13). A little later Matthew tells the reader that "without
a parable spake he not unto them: That it might be fulfilled which was
spoken by the prophet, saying, I will open my mouth in parables; I will
utter things which have been kept secret from the foundation of the
world" (Matthew 13:34–35). Those things which have been kept
secret from the foundation of the world will not be revealed until they
have been spoken in parable, that is, in terms which the multitude
who lack spiritual seeing and hearing nevertheless see and hear, namely, the everyday details of their lives of fishing, farming, and domestic
economy.

Conrad's story is a parable, in part, because it is grounded firmly
in the details of real experience. Biographers such as Ian Watt, Frederick
Karl, and Norman Sherry tell us all that is likely to be learned of Conrad's actual experience in the Congo, as well as of the historical originals
of Kurtz, the particolored harlequin-garbed Russian, and other characters in the novel. If parables are characteristically grounded in representations of realistic or historical truth, *Heart of Darkness* admirably
fulfills this requirement of parable. But it fills another requirement, too.
Conrad's novel is a parable because, although it is based on what Marx
called "real conditions," its narrator attempts through his tale to reveal
some as-yet-unseen reality.

Unlike allegory, which tries to shed light on the past or even
on our origins, parable tends to be oriented toward the future, toward
last things, toward the mysteries of the kingdom of heaven and how to
get there. Parable tends to express what Paul at the end of Romans, in
echo of Matthew, calls "the revelation of the mystery, which was kept
secret since the world began, but now is made manifest" (Romans
16:25–26). Parable, as we can now see, has at least one thing in
common with apocalypse: it too is an act of unveiling that which
has never been seen or known before. Apocalypse *means* unveiling;

---

[1]Karl Marx, "Manifesto of the Communist Party," in *The Marx-Engels Reader,*
2nd ed., ed. Robert C. Tucker (New York: W. W. Norton, 1978), p. 476.

an apocalypse is a narrative unveiling or revelation. The last book of the Bible is the paradigmatic example of apocalypse in our tradition, though it is by no means the only example. The book of Revelation seeks to unveil a mystery of the future, namely, what will happen at time's ending.

My contention, than, is that *Heart of Darkness* fits, in its own way, the definitions of both parable and apocalypse, and that much illumination is shed on it by interpreting it in the light of the generic classifications. As Marlow says of his experience in the heart of darkness: "It was somber enough, too — . . .not very clear either. No, not very clear. And yet it seemed to throw a kind of light" (p. 21). A narrative that sheds light, that penetrates drkness, that clarifies and illuminates — this is one definition of that mode of discourse called parabolic or apocalyptic, but it might also serve to define the work of criticism or interpretation. All criticism claims to be enlightenment or *Aufklärung*.

How, though, does a story enlighten or clarify: in what ways may narratives illuminate or unveil? Conrad's narrator distinguishes between two different ways in which a narrative may be related to its meaning:

> The yarns of seamen have a direct simplicity, the whole meaning of which lies within the shell of a cracked nut. But Marlow was not typical (if his propensity to spin yarns be excepted), and to him the meaning of an episode was not inside like a kernel but outside [Ms: outside in the unseen], enveloping the tale which brought it out only as a glow brings out a haze, in the likeness of one of these misty halos that sometimes are made visible by the spectral illumination of moonshine. (pp. 19–20)

The narrator here employs two figures to describe two kinds of stories: simple tales and parables. Through the two figures, moreover, Conrad attempts to present the different ways in which these two kinds of narration relate to their meanings.

The meanings of the stories of most seamen, says the narrator, are inside the narration like the kernel of a cracked nut. I take it the narrator means the meanings of such stories are easily expressed, detachable from the stories and open to paraphrase in other terms, as when one draws an obvious moral: "Crime doesn't pay," or "Honesty is the best policy," or "The truth will out," or "Love conquers all." The figure of the cracked nut suggests that the story itself, its characters and narrative details, are the inedible shell which must be removed and discarded so the meaning of the story may be assimilated. This relation of the story to its meaning is a particular version of the relation of container to thing contained. The substitution of contained for container, in this case meaning for story, is one version of that figure called in classical rhetoric *synecdoche,* but this is a metonymic rather than a metaphorical synecdoche.[2] The meaning is adjacent to the story, contained within it as nut within shell, but the meaning has no intrinsic similarity or kinship to the story. Its relation to the story that contains it is purely contingent. The one happens to touch the other, as shell surrounds nut, as bottle its liquid contents, or as shrine-case its iconic image.

It is far otherwise with Marlow's stories. Their meaning — like the meaning of a parable — is outside, not in. It envelops the tale rather than being enveloped by it. The relation of container and thing contained is reversed. The meaning now contains the tale. Moreover, perhaps because of that enveloping containment, or perhaps for more obscure reasons, the relation of the tale to its meaning is no longer that of dissimilarity and contingency. The tale is the necessary agency of the bringing into the open or revelation of that particular meaning. It is not so much that the meaning is like the tale. It is not. But the tale is in preordained correspondence to or in resonance with the meaning. The tale magically brings the "unseen" meaning out and makes it visible.

Conrad has the narrator express this subtle concept of parabolic narration according to the parabolic "likeness" of a certain atmospheric phenomenon. "Likeness" is a homonym of the German *Gleichnis,* which is itself a term for parable. The meaning of a parable appears in the "spectral" likeness of the story that reveals it, or rather, it appears in the likeness of an exterior light surrounding the story, just as the narrator's theory of parable appears not as such but in the "likeness" of the figure he proposes. Thus, the figure does double duty, both as a figure for the way Marlow's stories express their meaning and as a figure for itself, so to speak; that is, as a figure for its own mode of working. This is according to a mind-twisting torsion of the figure back on itself that is a regular feature of such figures of figuration, parables of parable, or stories about storytelling. The figure both illuminates its

---

[2]In metaphorical synecdoche a part of something is used to signify the whole: "I see a sail" means "I see a ship." A metonymic synecdoche is one in which the signifying part is really only something contiguous with the thing signified, not intrinsic to it; "the bottle" is a metonymic synecdoche for liquor, since glass cannot really be part of liquor in the way a sail is part of a ship.

own workings and at the same time obscures or undermines it, since a figure of a figure is an absurdity, or, as Wallace Stevens puts it, there is no such thing as a metaphor of a metaphor. What was the figurative vehicle of the first metaphor automatically becomes the literal tenor of the second metaphor.[3]

Let us look more closely at the exact terms of the metaphor Conrad's narrator proposes. To Marlow, the narrator says, "the meaning of an episode was not inside like a kernel but outside, enveloping the tale which brought it out only as a glow brings out a haze, in the likeness of one of these spectral illuminations of moonshine." The first simile here ("as a glow") is doubled by a second, similitude of a similitude ("in the likeness of . . ."). The "haze" is there all around on a dark night, but, like the meaning of one of Marlow's tales, it is invisible, inaudible, intangible in itself, like the darkness, or like that "something great and invincible" Marlow is aware of in the African wilderness, something "like evil or truth, waiting patiently for the passing away of this fantastic invasion" (p. 37–38). The haze, too, is like the climactic name for that truth, the enveloping meaning of the tale: "the horror," those last words of Kurtz that seem all around in the gathering darkness when Marlow makes his visit to Kurtz's Intended and tells his lie. "The dusk," Marlow says, "was repeating them in a persistent whisper all around us, in a whisper that seemed to swell menacingly like the first whisper of a rising wind. 'The horror! The horror!' " (p. 93).

The working of Conrad's figure is much more complex than perhaps it at first appears, both in itself and in the context of the fine grain of the texture of language in *Heart of Darkness* as a whole, as well as in the context of the traditional complex of figures, narrative motifs, and concepts to which it somewhat obscurely alludes. The atmospheric phenomenon that Conrad uses as the vehicle of his parabolic metaphor is a perfectly real one, universally experienced. It is as referential and as widely known as the facts of farming Jesus uses in the parable of the sower. If you sow your seed on stony ground it will not be likely to sprout. An otherwise invisible mist or haze at night will show up as a halo around the moon. As in the case of Jesus' parable of the sower,

[3]The "vehicle" of a figurative expression is the term used to refer to something else; the "tenor" is the person, thing, or concept referred to by the vehicle. In the metaphorical synecdoche used as an example in footnote 2 on p. 212, "sail" is the vehicle, "ship" the tenor; in the metonymic synecdoche, "bottle" is the vehicle, "liquor" the tenor. If you say you feel blue to mean you feel sad, "blue" is the vehicle, "sadness" the tenor.

Conrad uses his realistic and almost universally known facts as the means of expressing indirectly another truth less visible and less widely known, just as the narrative of *Heart of Darkness* as a whole is based on the facts of history and on the facts of Conrad's life but uses these to express something transhistorical and transpersonal, the evasive and elusive "truth" underlying both historical and personal experience.

Both Jesus' parable of the sower and Conrad's parable of the moonshine in the mist, curiously enough, have to do with their own efficacy — that is, with the efficacy of parable. Both are posited on their own necessary failure. Jesus' parable of the sower will give more only to those who already have and will take away from those who have not even what they have. If you can understand the parable you do not need it. If you need it you cannot possibly understand it. You are stony ground on which the seed of the word falls unavailing. Your eyes and ears are closed, even though the function of parables is to open the eyes and ears of the multitude to the mysteries of the kingdom of heaven. In the same way, Conrad, in a famous passage in the preface to *The Nigger of the "Narcissus,"* tells his readers, "My task which I am trying to achieve is, by the power of the written word, to make you hear, to make you feel — it is, before all, to make you *see*." No reader of Conrad can doubt that he means to make the reader see not only the vivid facts of the story he tells but the evasive truth behind them, of which they are the obscure revelation, what Conrad calls, a bit beyond the famous phrase from the preface just quoted, "that glimpse of truth for which you have forgotten to ask." To see the facts, out there in the sunlight, is also to see the dark truth that lies behind them. All Conrad's work turns on this double paradox: first the paradox of the two senses of seeing, seeing as physical vision and seeing as seeing through, as penetrating to or unveiling the hidden invisible truth, and second the paradox of seeing the darkness in terms of the light. Nor can the careful reader of Conrad doubt that in Conrad's case too, as in the case of the Jesus of the parable of the sower, the goal of tearing the veil of familiarity from the world and making us *see* cannot be accomplished. If we see the darkness already, we do not need *Heart of Darkness*. If we do not see it, reading *Heart of Darkness* or even hearing Marlow tell it will not help us. We shall remain among those who "seeing see not; and hearing they hear not, neither do they understand." Marlow makes this clear in an extraordinary passage in *Heart of Darkness,* one of those places in which the reader is returned to the primary scene of narration on board the *Nellie*. Marlow is explaining the first lie he told for Kurtz, his prevarication misleading the bricklayer at the Central Station into believing he (Marlow) has great power back home:

> "I became in an instant as much of a pretence as the rest of the bewitched pilgrims. This simply because I had a notion it somehow would be of help to that Kurtz whom at the time I did not see — you understand. He was just a word for me. I did not see the man in the name any more than you do. Do you see him? Do you see the story? Do you see anything? It seems to me I am trying to tell you a dream — making a vain attempt, because no relation of a dream can convey the dream-sensation, that commingling of absurdity, surprise, and bewilderment in a tremor of struggling revolt, that notion of being captured by the incredible which is of the very essence of dreams. . . ."
>
> He was silent for a while.
>
> ". . . No, it is impossible; it is impossible to convey the life-sensation of any given epoch of one's existence — that which makes its truth, its meaning — its subtle and penetrating essence. It is impossible. We live, as we dream — alone. . . ."
>
> He paused again as if reflecting, then added:
>
> "Of course in this you fellows see more than I could then. You see me, whom you know. . . ."
>
> It had become so pitch dark that we listeners could hardly see one another. For a long time already he, sitting apart, had been no more to us than a voice. There was not a word from anybody. The others might have been asleep, but I was awake. I listened, I listened on the watch for the sentence, for the word, that would give me the clue to the faint un-easiness inspired by this narrative that seemed to shape itself without human lips in the heavy night-air of the river. (p. 42)

The denial of the possibility of making the reader see by means of literature is made here through a series of moves, each one ironically going beyond and undermining the one before. When this passage is set against the one about the moonshine, the two together bring out into the open, like a halo in the mist, the way *Heart of Darkness* is posited on the impossibility of achieving its goal of revelation, or, to put this another way, the way it is a revelation of the impossibility of revelation.

In Conrad's parable of the moonshine, the moon shines already with reflected and secondary light. Its light is reflected from the primary light of that sun which is almost never mentioned as such in *Heart of Darkness*. The sun is only present in the glitter of its reflection from this or that object, for example, the surface of that river which, like the white place of the unexplored Congo on the map, fascinates Marlow like a snake. In one passage it is moonlight, already reflected light, which is reflected again from the river: "The moon had spread over everything a thin layer of silver — over the rank grass, over the mud, upon the wall of matted vegetation standing higher than the wall of a temple, over the great river I could see through a sombre gap glittering, glittering, as it flowed broadly by without a murmur" (p. 41). In the case of the parable of the moonshine too that halo brought out in the mist is twice-reflected light. The story, according to Conrad's analogy, the facts that may be named and seen, is the moonlight, while the halo brought out around the moon by the reflection of the moonlight from the diffused, otherwise invisible droplets of the mist, is the meaning of the tale, or rather, the meaning of the tale is the darkness which is made visible by that halo of twice-reflected light. But of course the halo does nothing of the sort. It only makes visible more light. What can be seen is only what can be seen. In the end this is always only more light, direct or reflected. The darkness is in principle invisible and remains invisible. All that can be said is that the halo gives the spectator indirect knowledge that the darkness is there. The glow brings out the haze, the story brings out its meaning, by magically generating knowledge that something is there, the haze in one case, the meaning of the story, inarticulate and impossible to be articulated, in any direct way at least, in the other. The expression of the meaning of the story is never the plain statement of that meaning but is always no more than a parabolic "likeness" of the meaning, as the haze is brought out "in the likeness of one of those misty halos that sometimes are made visible by the spectral illumination of moonshine."

In the passage in which Marlow makes explicit his sense of the impossibility of his enterprise, he says to his auditors on the *Nellie* first that he did not see Kurtz in his name any more than they do. The auditors of any story are forced to see everything of the story "in its name," since a story is made of nothing but names and their adjacent words. There is nothing to see literally in any story except the words on the page, the movement of the lips of the teller. Unlike Marlow, his listeners never have a chance to see or experience directly the man behind the name. The reader, if he happens at this moment to think of it (and the passage is clearly an invitation to such thinking, an invocation of it), is in exactly the same situation as that of Marlow's auditors, only worse. When Marlow appeals to his auditors, Conrad is by a kind of ventriloquism appealing to his readers: "Do you see him? Do you see the story? Do you see anything? It seems to me I am trying to tell you a dream — making a vain attempt." Conrad speaks through Marlow to us. The reader too can reach the truth behind the story only through names, never through any direct perception or experience. In the reader's case it is not even names proffered by a living man before him, only names coldly and impersonally printed on the pages of the book he holds in his hand. Even if the reader goes behind the fiction to the historical reality on which it is based, as Ian Watt and others have done, he or she will only confront more words on more pages — Conrad's letters or the historical records of the conquest and exploitation of the Congo. The situation of the auditors even of a living speaker, Marlow says, is scarcely better, since what a story must convey through names and other words is not the fact but the "life-sensation" behind the fact "which makes its truth, its meaning — its subtle and penetrating essence." This is once more the halo around the moon, the meaning enveloping the tale. This meaning is as impossible to convey by way of the life-facts that may be named as the "dream-sensation" is able to be conveyed through a relation of the bare facts of the dream. Anyone knows this who has ever tried to tell another person his dream and has found how lame and flat, or how laughable, it sounds, since "no relation of a dream can convey the dream-sensation." According to Marlow's metaphor or proportional analogy: as the facts of a dream are to the dream-sensation, so the facts of a life are to the life-sensation. Conrad makes an absolute distinction between experience and the interpretation of written or spoken signs. The sensation may only be experienced directly and may by no means, oral or written, be communicated to another: "We live, as we dream, alone."

Nevertheless, Marlow tells his auditors, they have one direct or experimental access to the truth enveloping the story: "You fellows see more than I could then. You see me, whom you know." There is a double irony in this. To see the man who has had the experience is to have an avenue to the experience for which the man speaks, to which he bears witness. Marlow's auditors see more than he could then — that is, before his actual encounter with Kurtz. Ironically, the witness cannot bear witness for himself. He cannot see himself or cannot see through himself or by means of himself, in spite of, or in contradiction of, Conrad's (or Marlow's) assertion a few paragraphs later that work is "the chance to find yourself. Your own reality — for yourself, not for others — what no other man can ever know. They can only see the mere show, and never can tell what it really means" (p. 44). Though each man can only experience his own reality, his own truth, the paradox involved here seems to run, he can only experience it through another or by means of another as witness to a truth deeper in, behind the other. Marlow's auditors can only learn indirectly, through Marlow, whom they see. They therefore know more than he did. Marlow could only learn through Kurtz, when he finally encountered him face to face. The reader of *Heart of Darkness* learns through the relation of the primary narrator, who learned through Marlow, who learned through Kurtz. This proliferating relay of witnesses, one behind another, each revealing another truth further in which turns out to be only another witness corresponds to the narrative form of *Heart of Darkness*. The novel is a sequence of episodes, each structured according to the model of appearances, signs, which are also obstacles or veils. Each veil must be lifted to reveal a truth behind which always turns out to be another episode, another witness, another veil to be lifted in its turn. Each such episode is a "fact dazzling, to be seen, like the foam on the depths of the sea, like a ripple on an unfathomable enigma" (p. 57), the fact for example that though the cannibal Africans on Marlow's steamer were starving, they did not eat the white men. But behind each enigmatic fact is only another fact. The relay of witness behind witness behind witness, voice behind voice behind voice, each speaking in ventriloquism through the one next farther out, is a characteristic of the genre of the apocalypse. In the book of Revelation, God speaks through Jesus, who speaks through a messenger angel, who speaks through John of Patmos, who speaks to us.

There is another reason beyond the necessities of revelation for this structure. The truth behind the last witness, behind Kurtz for example in *Heart of Darkness,* is, no one can doubt it, death, "the horror"; or, to put this another way, "death" is another name for what Kurtz names "the horror." No man can confront that truth face to face and survive. Death or the horror can only be experienced indirectly, by way of the face and voice of another. The relay of witnesses both reveals death and, luckily, hides it. As Marlow says, "the inner truth is hidden — luckily, luckily" (p. 49). This is another regular feature of the genre of the apocalypse. The word "apocalypse" means "unveiling," "revelation," but what the apocalypse unveils is not the truth of the end of the world which it announces, but the act of unveiling. The unveiling unveils unveiling. It leaves its readers, auditors, witnesses, as far as ever from the always "not quite yet" of the imminent revelation — luckily. Marlow says it was not his own near-death on the way home down the river, "not my own extremity I remember best," but Kurtz's "extremity that I seem to have lived through." Then he adds, "True, he had made that last stride, he had stepped over the edge, while I had been permitted to draw back my hesitating foot. And perhaps in this is the whole difference; perhaps all the wisdom, and all truth, and all sincerity, are just compressed into that inappreciable moment of time in which we step over the threshold of the invisible. Perhaps!" (p. 87). Marlow, like Orpheus returning without Eurydice from the land of the dead, comes back to civilization with nothing, nothing to bear witness to, nothing to reveal but the process of unveiling that makes up the whole of the narration of *Heart of Darkness*. Marlow did not go far enough into the darkness, but if he had, like Kurtz he could not have come back. All the reader gets is Marlow's report of Kurtz's last words, that and a description of the look on Kurtz's face: "It was as though a veil had been rent. I saw on that ivory face the expression of sombre pride, of ruthless power, of craven terror — of an intense and hopeless despair" (p. 85).

I have suggested that there are two ironies in what Marlow says when he breaks his narration to address his auditors directly. The first irony is the fact that the auditors see more than Marlow did because they see Marlow, whom they know; the second is that we readers of the novel see no living witness. (By Marlow's own account that is not enough. Seeing only happens by direct experience, and no act of reading is direct experience. The book's claim to give the reader access to the dark truth behind appearance is withdrawn by the terms in which it is proffered.) But there is, in fact, a third irony in this relay of ironies behind ironies in that Marlow's auditors of course do not see Marlow either. It is too dark. They hear only his disembodied voice. "It had become so pitch dark," says the narrator, "that we listeners could hardly see one another. For a long time already he, sitting apart, had been no more to us than a voice." Marlow's narrative does not seem to be spoken by a living incarnate witness, there before his auditors in the flesh. It is a "narrative that seemed to shape itself without human lips in the heavy night-air of the river." This voice can be linked to no individual speaker or writer as the ultimate source of its messages, not to Marlow, nor to Kurtz, nor to the first narrator, nor even to Conrad himself. The voice is spoken by no one to no one. It always comes from another, from the other of any identifiable speaker or writer. It traverses all these voices as what speaks through them. It gives them authority and at the same time dispossesses them, deprives them of authority, since they only speak with the delegated authority of another. As Marlow says of the voice of Kurtz and of all the other voices, they are what remain as a dying unanimous and anonymous drone or clang that exceeds any single identifiable voice and in the end is spoken by no one: "A voice. He was very little more than a voice. And I heard — him — it — this voice — other voices — all of them were so little more than voices — and the memory of that time itself lingers around me, impalpable, like a dying vibration of one immense jabber, silly, atrocious, sordid, savage, or simply mean, without any kind of sense. Voices, voices — . . ." (p. 63).

For the reader, too, *Heart of Darkness* lingers in the mind or memory chiefly as a cacophony of dissonant voices. It is as though the story were spoken or written not by an identifiable narrator but directly by the darkness itself, just as Kurtz's last words seem whispered by the circumambient dusky air when Marlow makes his visit to Kurtz's Intended, and just as Kurtz himself presents himself to Marlow as a voice, a voice which exceeds Kurtz and seems to speak from beyond him: "Kurtz discoursed. A voice! a voice! It rang deep to the very last. It survived his strength to hide in the magnificent folds of eloquence the barren darkness of his heart" (p. 84). Kurtz has "the gift of expression, the bewildering, the illuminating, the most exalted and the most contemptible, the pulsating stream of light, or the deceitful flow from the heart of an impenetrable darkness" (p. 62). Kurtz has intended to use his eloquence as a means of "wringing the heart of the wilderness," but "the wilderness had found him out early, and had taken on him a terrible vengeance for the fantastic invasion" (p. 73). The direction of the flow of language reverses. It flows from the darkness instead of toward it. Kurtz is "hollow at the core" (p. 73), and so the wilderness can speak through him, use him so to speak as a ventriloquist's dummy through which its terrible messages may be broadcast to the world: "Exterminate all the brutes!" "The horror!" (pp. 66, 85). The speaker to is spoken through. Kurtz's disembodied voice, or the voice behind voice behind voice of the narrators, or that "roaring chorus of articulated, rapid, breathless utterance" (p. 83) shouted by the natives on the bank, when Kurtz is taken on board the steamer — these are in the end no more direct a testimony of the truth than the words on the page as Conrad wrote them. The absence of a visible speaker of Marlow's words and the emphasis on the way Kurtz is a disembodied voice function as indirect expressions of the fact that *Heart of Darkness* itself is words without person, words which cannot be traced back to any single personality. This is once more confirmation of my claim that *Heart of Darkness* belongs to the genre of the parabolic apocalypse. The apocalypse is after all a written not an oral genre, and, as Jacques Derrida has pointed out, one characteristic of an apocalypse is that it turns on the invitation or "Come" spoken or written always by someone other than the one who seems to utter or write it.[4]

A full exploration of the way *Heart of Darkness* is an apocalypse would need to be put under the multiple aegis of the converging figures of irony, antithesis, catachresis, synecdoche, aletheia, and personification. Irony is a name for the pervasive tone of Marlow's narration, which undercuts as it affirms. Antithesis identifies the division of what is presented in the story in terms of seemingly firm oppositions that always ultimately break down. Catachresis is the proper name for a parabolic revelation of the darkness by means of visible figures that do not substitute for any possible literal expression of that darkness. Synecdoche is the name for the questionable relation of similarity between the visible sign, the skin of the surface, the foam on the sea, and what lies behind it, the pulsating heart of darkness, the black depths of the sea. Unveiling or *aletheia* labels that endless process of apocalyptic revelation that never quite comes off. The revelation is always future. Personification, finally, is a name for the consistent presentation of the darkness as some kind of living creature with a heart, ultimately as a woman who unmans all those male questors who try to dominate her. This pervasive personification is most dramatically embodied in the native woman, Kurtz's mistress: "the immense wilderness, the colossal body of the fecund and mysterious life seemed to look at her, pensive, as though it had been looking at the image of its own tenebrous and passionate soul" (p. 76).

Heart of Darkness is perhaps most explicitly apocalyptic in announcing the end, the end of Western civilization, or of Western imperialism, the reversal of idealism into savagery. As is always the case with apocalypses, the end is announced as something always imminent, never quite yet. Apocalypse is never now. The novel sets women, who are out of it, against men, who can live with the facts and have a belief to protect them against the darkness. Men can breathe dead hippo and not be contaminated. Male practicality and idealism reverse, however. They turn into their opposites because they are hollow at the core. They are vulnerable to the horror. They *are* the horror.

---

[4]See Jacques Derrida, "D'un ton apocalyptique adopté naguère en philosophie," in *Les Fins de l'homme,* ed. Phillippe Lacoue-Labarthe and Jean-Luc Nancy (Paris: Flammarion, 1981), pp. 445–79, especially p. 468ff. The essay has recently been translated by John P. Leavey, Jr., and published in the 1982 number of *Semeia* (pp. 62–97).

The idealistic suppression of savage customs becomes, "Exterminate all the brutes!" Male idealism is the same thing as the extermination of the brutes. The suppression of savage customs is the extermination of the brutes. This is not just word play but actual fact, as the history of the white man's conquest of the world has abundantly demonstrated. This conquest means the end of the brutes, but it means also, in Conrad's view of history, the end of Western civilization, with its ideals of progress, enlightenment, and reason, its goal of carrying the torch of civilization into the wilderness and wringing the heart of the darkness. Or it is the imminence of that end which has never quite come as long as there is someone to speak or write of it.

I claim to have demonstrated that *Heart of Darkness* is not only parabolic but also apocalyptic. It fits that strange genre of the apocalyptic text, the sort of text that promises an ultimate revelation without giving it, and says always "Come" and "Wait." But there is an extra twist given to the paradigmatic form of the apocalypse in *Heart of Darkness*. The *Aufklärung* or enlightenment in this case is of the fact that the darkness can never be enlightened. The darkness enters into every gesture of enlightenment to enfeeble it, to hollow it out, to corrupt it and thereby to turn its reason into unreason, its pretense of shedding light into more darkness. Marlow as narrator is in complicity with this reversal in the act of identifying it in others. He too claims, like the characteristic writer of an apocalypse, to know something no one else knows and to be qualified on that basis to judge and enlighten them. "I found myself back in the sepulchral city," says Marlow of his return from the Congo,

> resenting the sight of people hurrying through the streets to filch a little money from each other, to devour their infamous cookery, to gulp their unwholesome beer, to dream their insignificant and silly dreams. They trespassed upon my thoughts. They were intruders whose knowledge of life was to me an irritating pretense, because I felt so sure they could not possibly know the things I knew.
> (p. 87)

The consistent tone of Marlow's narration is ironical. Irony is truth-telling or a means of truth-telling, of unveiling. At the same time it is a defense against the truth. This doubleness makes it, though it seems so coolly reasonable, another mode of unreason, the unreason of a fundamental undecidability. If irony is a defense, it is also inadvertently a means of participation. Though Marlow says, "I have a voice

too, and for good or evil mine is the speech that cannot be silenced"
(p. 51), as though his speaking were a cloak against the darkness, he
too, in speaking ironically, becomes, like Kurtz, one of those speaking
tubes or relay stations through whom the darkness speaks. As theorists of irony from Friedrich Schlegel and Soren Kierkegaard to Paul
de Man have argued, irony is the one trope that cannot be mastered
or used as an instrument of mastery. An ironic statement is essentially
indeterminate or undecidable in meaning. The man who attempts to
say one thing while clearly meaning another ends up by saying the
first thing too, in spite of himself. One irony leads to another. The
ironies proliferate into a great crowd of little conflicting ironies. It
is impossible to know in just what tone of voice one should read
one of Marlow's sardonic ironies. Each is uttered simultaneously in
innumerable conflicting tones going all the way from the lightest
and most comical to the darkest, most somber and tragic. It is impossible to decide exactly which quality of voice should be allowed
to predominate over the others. Try reading aloud the passage cited
above and you will see this. Marlow's tone and meaning are indeterminate; his description of the clamor of native voices on the shore or
of the murmur of all those voices he remembers from that time in his
life also functions as an appropriate displaced description of his own
discourse. Marlow's irony makes his speech in its own way another
version of that multiple cacophonous and deceitful voice flowing from
the heart of darkness, "a complaining clamour, modulated in savage
discords," or a "tumultuous and mournful uproar," another version
of that "one immense jabber, silly, atrocious, sordid, savage, or simply mean, without any kind of sense," not a voice, but voices (pp.
54, 63). In this inextricable tangle of voices and voices speaking
within voices, Marlow's narration fulfills, no doubt without deliberate
intent on Conrad's part, one of the primary laws of the genre of the
apocalypse.

The final fold in this folding in of complicities in these ambiguous
acts of unveiling is my own complicity as demystifying commentator.
Behind or before Marlow is Conrad, and before or behind him stands
the reader or critic. My commentary unveils a lack of decisive unveiling
in *Heart of Darkness*. I have attempted to perform an act of generic
classification, with all the covert violence and unreason of that act, since
no work is wholly commensurate with the boundaries of any genre. By
unveiling the lack of unveiling in *Heart of Darkness,* I have become
another witness in my turn, as much guilty as any other in the line of
witnesses of covering over while claiming to illuminate. My *Aufklärung*

too has been of the continuing impenetrability of Conrad's *Heart of Darkness*.

DECONSTRUCTION: A SELECTED BIBLIOGRAPHY

Deconstruction, Post-Structuralism, and Structuralism: Introductions, Guides, and Surveys

Arac, Jonathan, Wlad Godzich, and Wallace Martin, eds. *The Yale Critics: Deconstruction in America*. Minneapolis: University of Minnesota Press, 1983. See especially essays by Bové, Godzich, Pease, and Corngold.

Cain, William E. "Deconstruction in America: The Recent Literary Criticism of J. Hillis Miller." *College English* 41 (1979): 367–82.

Culler, Jonathan. *On Deconstruction: Theory and Criticism After Structuralism*. Ithaca, N.Y.: Cornell University Press, 1982.

——— . *Structuralist Poetics: Structuralism, Linguistics and the Study of Literature*. Ithaca, N.Y.: Cornell University Press, 1975. See especially Chapter 10.

Jefferson, Ann. "Structuralism and Post-Structuralism." *Modern Literary Theory: A Comparative Introduction*. Totowa, N.J.: Barnes and Noble, 1982.

Leitch, Vincent B. *Deconstructive Criticism: An Advanced Introduction*. New York: Columbia University Press, 1983.

Norris, Christopher. *Deconstructive Theory and Practice*. London: Methuen, 1982.

Raval, Suresh. *Metacriticism*. Athens: University of Georgia Press, 1981.

Scholes, Robert. *Structuralism in Literature: An Introduction*. New Haven, Conn.: Yale University Press, 1974.

Selected Works by Jacques Derrida

Derrida, Jacques. *Dissemination*. Translated by Barbara Johnson. Chicago: University of Chicago Press, 1981. See especially the concise, incisive Translator's Introduction; it provides a useful point of entry into this work and others by Derrida.

——— . *Of Grammatology*. Translated by Gayatri Spivak. Baltimore, Md.: Johns Hopkins University Press, 1974.

————— . *Speech and Phenomena, and Other Essays on Husserl's Theory of Signs*. Translated by David B. Allison. Evanston, Ill.: Northwestern University Press, 1973.

————— . *Writing and Difference*. Chicago: University of Chicago Press, 1978.

Post-Structuralist Essays on Language and Literature

Barthes, Roland. *S/Z*. Translated by Richard Miller. New York: Hill and Wang, 1974. Barthes turns from a structuralist to a post-structuralist approach in this influential work.

Bloom, Harold, *et al. Deconstruction and Criticism*. New York: Seabury Press, 1979. Includes Miller's "The Critic as Host." Also see the essays by Bloom, De Man, Derrida, and Hartman.

De Man, Paul. *Allegories of Reading*. New Haven, Conn.: Yale University Press, 1979. See Part I ("Rhetoric"), especially Chapter 1 ("Semiology and Rhetoric").

————— . *Blindness and Insight*. New York: Oxford University Press, 1971. A new edition of this book, which Vincent Leitch has said marks "the beginning of deconstruction in America," was published in 1983 by the University of Minnesota Press. In it are printed essays not contained in the original.

Johnson, Barbara. *The Critical Difference: Essays in the Contemporary Rhetoric of Reading*. Baltimore, Md.: Johns Hopkins University Press, 1980.

Miller, J. Hillis. "Ariadne's Thread: Repetition of the Narrative Line." *Critical Inquiry* 3 (1967): 57–77.

————— . Introduction to *Bleak House*, by Charles Dickens. Edited by Norman Page. Harmondsworth, Eng.: Penguin, 1971.

————— . *Fiction and Repetition: Seven English Novels*. Cambridge, Mass.: Harvard University Press, 1982.

A Post-Structuralist Approach to Conrad

Bonney, William. *Thorns and Arabesques: Contexts for Conrad's Fiction*. Baltimore, Md.: Johns Hopkins University Press, 1980.

The New Historicism
and
Heart of Darkness

WHAT IS THE NEW HISTORICISM?

A novel written by a man who visited the Congo and witnessed the reactions of tribal peoples to European controls, *Heart of Darkness* cries out for a new historicist analysis. A work of literature, it is at the same time a kind of historical document. It undoubtedly presents as accurate a picture of colonized Africa as many other supposedly non-fictional accounts written during the same period. And it is of anthropological interest as well. It tells us little, perhaps, about Congolese peoples, but a great deal about Europeans of the period: about their behavior, social organization, rituals, prejudices, taboos, and symbols.

In one sense, the paragraph above implicitly defines the new historicism. It is a movement that would destabilize our overly settled conceptions of what literature and history are. It is one, too, that would define history broadly, not as a mere chronicle of facts and events but, rather, as a "thick description" of human reality, one that raises questions of interest to anthropologists and sociologists, as well as those posed by traditional historians.

In another sense, though, the new historicism cannot be adequately defined: not by the paragraph above; not by an introduction several pages in length; not even, implicitly, by a representative essay such as the one by Brook Thomas that follows. No critical approach, of course, can be entirely summed up by an introduction or epitomized by a single essay. But the new historicism, especially, eludes summary description and exemplification. The most recent development in contemporary theory, it is a movement that is still evolving. Enough of its contours have come into focus for us to realize that it exists and deserves a name, but any definition of the new historicism is bound to be somewhat fuzzy, like a partially developed photographic image. Some individual critics we would label as new historicists may also be deconstructors, or feminists, or Marxists. Some would deny that the others are even writing the new kind of historical criticism.

All of them, though, have one thing in common. They share the conviction that, somewhere along the way, something important was lost from literary studies. That something was historical consciousness. Poems and novels came to be seen in isolation, as urnlike objects of precious beauty. The new historicists, whatever their differences and however defined, would have us see that even the most urnlike poems are caught in a web of historical conditions, relationships, and influences. In an essay on "The Historical Necessity for . . . New Historical Analysis in Introductory Literature Courses," Brook Thomas suggests that discussions of John Keats's "Ode on a Grecian Urn" might begin with questions such as the following: Where would Keats have seen such an urn? How did a Grecian urn end up in a museum in England? Some very important historical and political realities, Thomas suggests, lie behind and inform Keats's definitions of art, truth, beauty, the past, and timelessness. They are realities that psychoanalytic and reader-response critics, formalists and feminists and deconstructors, could conceivably overlook.

Although a number of influential critics working between 1920 and 1950 wrote about literature from a psychoanalytic perspective, the majority of critics took what might generally be referred to as the historical approach. With the advent of the New Criticism, or formalism, however, historically oriented critics almost seemed to disappear from the face of the earth. Jerome McGann writes: "A text-only approach has been so vigorously promoted during the last thirty-five years that most historical critics have been driven from the field, and have raised the flag of their surrender by yielding the title 'critic' to the victor, and accepting the title 'scholar' for themselves."[1] Of course, the title "victor" has

---

[1]Jerome J. McGann, *The Beauty of Inflections: Literary Investigations in Historical Method* (Oxford: Clarendon Press of Oxford University Press, 1985), p. 17.

been vied for by a new kind of psychoanalytic critic, by reader-response critics, by so-called deconstructors, and by feminists since the New Critics
of the 1950s lost it during the following decade. But historical scholars
have not been in the field, seriously competing to become a dominant
critical influence.

Or they haven't, anyway, until now. In "Toward a New History in
Literary Study," Herbert Lindenberger writes: "It comes as something
of a surprise to find that history is making a powerful comeback."[2] E. D.
Hirsch, Jr., has also hopefully predicted a comeback. He suggested in
1984 that various avant-garde positions (such as deconstruction) have
been overrated, and that it is time for a turn back to history and to
historical criticism:

> We should not be disconcerted by its imposing claims, or made
> to think that we are being naive when we try to pursue historical
> study. Far from being naive, historically based criticism is the
> newest and most valuable kind . . . for our students (and our
> culture) at the present time.[3]

McGann obviously agrees. In *Historical Studies and Literary Criticism*
(1985), he speaks approvingly of recent attempts to make sociohistorical subjects and methods central to literary studies once again.

As the word "sociohistorical" suggests, the new historicism isn't
the same as the historical criticism practiced forty years ago. For one
thing, it is informed by recent critical theory: by psychoanalytic criticism, reader-response criticism, feminist criticism, and perhaps especially deconstruction. The new historicist critics are less fact- and event-
oriented than historical critics used to be, perhaps because they have
come to wonder whether the truth about what really happened can
ever be purely and objectively known. They are less likely to see history as being linear and progressive, as something developing toward
the present.

As the word "sociohistorical" also suggests, the new historicists
view history as a social science and the social sciences as being properly
historical. Sociology is the social science that McGann most often

---

[2]Herbert Lindenberger, "Toward a New History in Literary Study," in *Profession:
Selected Articles from the Bulletins of the Association of Departments of English and the Association of Departments of Foreign Languages* (New York: Modern Language Association
of America, 1984). See pp. 16–23.

[3]E. D. Hirsch, Jr., "Back to History," in *Criticism in the University*, ed. Gerald Graff
and Reginald Gibbons (Evanston, Ill.: Northwestern University Press, 1985), p. 197.

alludes to when he discusses the future of literary studies. "A socio-logical poetics," he writes, "must be recognized not only as relevant to the analysis of poetry, but in fact as central to the analysis."[4] Linden-berger cites anthropology as being particularly useful in the new his-torical analysis of literature, especially anthropology as practiced by Victor Turner and Clifford Geertz. Geertz, who has related theatrical traditions in nineteenth-century Bali to forms of political organization that developed during the same period, has influenced some of the most important critics writing the new kind of historical criticism. Due in large part to Geertz's influence, new historicists such as Stephen Greenblatt have analyzed literature in such a way as to assert that it is not a sphere apart, something finally distinct from the history that is relevant to it. (That is what historical criticism once tended to do: present history as something you need to know before you can fully appreciate art's separate world.) Thus the new historicists have, while discarding old distinctions between literature, history, and the social sciences, blurred other boundaries as well. They have erased the line dividing historical and literary materials, showing that the production of one of Shakespeare's plays was a political act and that the coronation of Elizabeth I was carried out with the same care for staging and symbol lavished on a work of dramatic art.

In addition to breaking down barriers separating literature and history, history and the social sciences, the new historicists have re-minded us that it is treacherously difficult to reconstruct the past as it really was, rather than as we have been conditioned by our own place and time to believe that it was. And they know that the job is utterly impossible for anyone who is unaware of the difficulty — and of the na-ture of his or her own historical vantage point. "Historical criticism can no longer make any part of [its] sweeping picture unself-consciously, or treat any of its details in an untheorized way,"[5] McGann wrote in 1985. "Unself-consciously" and "untheorized" are key words here; when the new historical critics of literature describe a historical change, they are highly conscious of, and even likely to discuss, the *theory* of historical change that informs their account. They know that the changes they happen to see and describe are the ones that their theory of change allows or helps them to see and describe. And they know, too, that their

[4]McGann, *The Beauty of Inflections*, p. 62. The quoted passage is from the chapter entitled "Keats and the Historical Method," which was first published in *Modern Language Notes* 94 (1979).

[5]Jerome J. McGann, *Historical Studies and Literary Criticism* (Madison: University of Wisconsin Press, 1985), p. 11.

theory of change is historically determined. They seek to minimize the distortion inherent in their perceptions and representations by knowing and admitting that they see through preconceived notions: by learning and revealing, in other words, the color of the lenses in the glasses that they wear.

All three of the critics whose recent writings on the back-to-history movement have been quoted thus far — Hirsch, Lindenberger, and McGann — mention the name of the late Michel Foucault. As much an archaeologist as a historian and as much a philosopher as either, Foucault in his writings brought together incidents and phenomena from areas of inquiry and orders of life we normally think of as being unconnected. And, as much as anyone, he encouraged the new historicist critic of literature to outwardly redefine the boundaries of historical inquiry.

Foucault's views of history are influenced by Nietzsche's concept of a *wirkliche* ("real" or "true") history that is neither melioristic nor metaphysical. That is to say, Foucault, like Nietzsche, doesn't see history as development, as a forward movement toward the present; neither does he view it as an abstraction, totality, idea, or ideal — as something that began "In the beginning" and that will come to THE END, a moment of definite closure, a Day of Judgment. Foucault, in his own words, "abandoned [the old history's] attempts to understand events in terms of . . . some great evolutionary process."[6] He warned new historians to be aware that investigators are themselves "situated." It is difficult, he has reminded them, to see present cultural practices critically from within them, and on account of the same cultural practices, it is almost impossible to enter bygone ages. In *Discipline and Punish: The Birth of the Prison* (1975), Foucault admits that his own interest in the past is fueled by a passion to write the history of the present.

Like Marx, Foucault sees history in terms of power, but his view of power owes perhaps more to Nietzsche than to Marx. Foucault seldom views power as a repressive force. Certainly, he does not view it as a tool of conspiracy by one specific individual or institution against another. Power, rather, is a whole complex of forces; it is that which produces what happens. Thus, even a tyrannical aristocrat does not simply wield power, for he is formed and empowered by discourses

---

[6]Michel Foucault, *L'ordre du discours* (Paris: Gallimard, 1971), p. 58. The passage has been translated by Alan Sheridan in *Michel Foucault: The Will to Truth* (London: Tavistock Publications, 1980), p. 129.

and practices which amount to power. And so power, as viewed by Foucault, is "positive and productive," not "repressive" and "prohibitive."[7]

Those two concepts — that power is not essentially conspiratorial and that power is positive and productive — are difficult to grasp, but a brief sketch of several of Foucault's major works may help to clarify them. A survey of a few of these books will also show just how intricately Foucault connects any single historical event or institution with a web of other economic, social, and political factors. No one of these causes the others; indeed, the existence of each is bound up with the others and is as much a response as a catalyst.

Foucault begins *Discipline and Punish* with a shocking but accurate description of the public drawing and quartering of a Frenchman who had botched his attempt to assassinate King Louis XV. Then he describes rules governing the daily life of modern Parisian felons. What happened to torture, to punishment as public spectacle? he asks. What complex network of forces made it disappear? In working toward a picture of this "power," Foucault turns up many interesting puzzle pieces. One of them is the fact that, in the early revolutionary years of the nineteenth century, crowds would sometimes identify with the prisoner and treat the executioner as if *he* were the guilty party. But Foucault sets forth another, related reason for keeping prisoners alive, for moving punishment indoors, and for changing discipline from physical torture into mental rehabilitation: colonization. In this period, people were needed to establish colonies and trade (this we know from reading *Heart of Darkness,* set at the end of the century of colonization), and prisoners could be used for that purpose. Also, because the times were politically unsettled, governments needed infiltrators and informers. Who better to fill those roles than prisoners pardoned or released early for showing a willingness to be rehabilitated? As for rehabilitation itself, Foucault compares it to the old form of punishment, which began with a torturer extracting a confession. In more modern, "reasonable" times, psychologists probe the minds of prisoners with a scientific rigor that Foucault sees as a different kind of torture (a kind that our modern perspective does not allow us to see as such).

Thus, a change took place, but perhaps not so great a change as we generally assume. It may have been for the better or for the worse;

[7]Barry Smart, *Michel Foucault* (London: Ellis Horwood and Tavistock Publications, 1985), p. 63.

the point is that agents of power didn't make the change because humanity is evolving and, therefore, more prone to do goodhearted deeds. Rather, different objectives arose, including those of a new class of doctors and scientists bent on studying aberrant examples of the human mind.

In the first volume of his *History of Sexuality* (1976), Foucault once again describes a change in human understanding and behavior without identifying any single primary cause for that change. To the commonly stated claim that sexuality in the West has recently reattained its status as something natural after centuries of repression by the Church, Foucault responds with the counterclaim that we have *not* liberated sexuality. (If we had, we wouldn't need to proclaim that we have; thus, the powers that supposedly thwart sexuality also produce the rhetoric of liberation.) As for Christianity, Foucault provocatively suggests that there is a way in which the Church *increased* sexuality, turning desires of the flesh into something to dwell upon, talk about, confess. Discipline didn't disappear with rack and chopping block; rather, it took on a number of new and subtle psychological forms. Similarly, sexuality wasn't eradicated by ecclesiastical repression (the existence of which Foucault doesn't deny). Rather, it became the subject of study and categorization and thereby proliferated into new forms. It even, Foucault suggests, became something people could do in a variety of new and unacceptable ways in order to outwardly flout or secretly mock authority.

Furthermore, the powers behind the history of sexuality are too multiple and various to be simply associated with Christianity. Governments have long been interested in controlling sex (discouraging it, encouraging it, changing the way it is practiced). Sexuality has, for centuries, been as tangled up with the discourses devoted to population, labor, and resources as it has been with theological discourse. And, certainly, the history of sexuality is intricately intertwined with the history of medicine. Nor can the history of medicine, the history of something like population management, and the history of sexuality be unwound from one another, since institutions such as medicine focus their interest on something like sexuality not because it is a good thing to do but, rather, because a particular problem (such as one affecting populations) has arisen. It then may turn out to be in the *interest* of the institution to investigate and advise.

Foucault's type of analysis has recently been practiced by a number of literary critics at the vanguard of the back-to-history movement.

One of these critics, Stephen Greenblatt, has written on Renaissance changes in the development both of literary characters and of real people. Like Foucault, he is careful to point out that any single change is connected with a host of others, no one of which may simply be identified as the cause or the effect. Greenblatt, like Foucault, insists on seeing literary devices as if they were continuous with other representational devices in a culture; he turns, therefore, to scholars in other fields to better understand the workings of literature. "We wall off literary symbolism from the symbolic structures operative elsewhere," he writes, "as if art alone were a human creation, as if humans themselves were not, in Clifford Geertz's phrase, cultural artifacts." Following Geertz, Greenblatt sets out to practice what he calls "anthropological or cultural criticism." Anthropological literary criticism, he goes on to say, addresses itself "to the interpretive constructions the members of a society apply to their experience," since a work of literature is itself an interpretive construction, "part of the system of signs that constitutes a given culture." He suggests that criticism must never interpret the past without at least being "conscious of its own status as interpretation."[8]

Not all of the critics trying to lead students of literature back to history are as "Foucauldian" as Greenblatt. E. D. Hirsch lumps Foucault with a reader-response critic (Stanley Fish) and a deconstructor (the late Paul de Man), attacking all three for the relativism of their approach. Hirsch simply does not believe we need to emphasize, as much as Foucault does, the degree to which we are imprisoned in our own cultural situation and prevented by our historical and cognitive *a priori* — the history that precedes us and defines the bias of our thought — from entering the past with confidence. Hirsch implies that Foucault is as guilty as de Man and Fish of overstating the problem, "to which common sense gives the reply of Karl Popper: the doctrine of the cognitive *a priori* simply exaggerates a difficulty into an impossibility."[9] Jerome McGann, like Hirsch, seems to follow a path other than Foucault's. In *The Beauty of Inflections* he takes the lead of the Soviet critic M. M. Bakhtin, who long ago began attacking schools of criticism that wall literature off from social realities. And Brook Thomas claims to have been more influenced by Walter Benjamin, best known for essays such as "Theses on the

[8]Stephen Greenblatt, *Renaissance Self-Fashioning: From More to Shakespeare* (Chicago: University of Chicago Press, 1980), p. 4.
[9]Hirsch, "Back to History," p. 194.

Philosophy of History" and "The Work of Art in the Age of Mechanical Reproduction."

There are other reasons, moreover, for stopping short of declaring that Foucault has been the central influence on the new historicism. For one thing, his commitment to radically remapping relations of power and influence, cause and effect, has caused him, in the view of some new historicists, to adopt a cavalier attitude toward chronology and facts. For another, it goes against the very spirit of the new historicism to identify and label a single or master or central influence. Practitioners of the new historicism have sought to de-center the study of literature: to move toward the point where literary studies overlap with anthropological and sociological studies. They have also struggled to see history from a decentered perspective, both by recognizing that their own cultural and historical position may not afford the very best understanding of other cultures and times and by realizing that events seldom have any single or central cause. It is thus appropriate to pause and suggest, at this point, that Foucault shouldn't be seen as *the* cause of, the central force behind, the new historicism, but rather as one of several powerful, interactive influences.

It is equally appropriate, though, to suggest that the implicit debate over the roots or sources of the movement, differences of opinion about Foucault, and even my own need to assert his importance cautiously may be historically contingent; that is to say, they may all be a function of the very *newness* of the new historicism itself. New intellectual movements often cannot be summed up or represented by a key figure, any more than they can easily be summed up or represented by a single introduction or essay. They respond to disparate influences, and they almost inevitably include thinkers who represent a wide range of backgrounds. Like movements that are disintegrating, new movements are bound to include a broad spectrum of opinions and positions.

But just as differences within a new school of criticism cannot be overlooked, neither should they be exaggerated, since it is the similarity between a number of different approaches that makes us conscious of the fact that a new movement is underway. Greenblatt, Hirsch, McGann, and Thomas all start with the assumption that works of literature are simultaneously influenced by and influencing reality, broadly defined. Thus, whatever their disagreements, they share a belief in referentiality — a belief that literature refers to and is referred to by things outside itself — that is fainter in the works of formalist, post-structuralist, and even reader-response critics. They believe, as

Greenblatt says, that the central concerns of criticism "should prevent it from permanently sealing off one type of discourse from another or decisively separating works of art from the minds and lives of their creators and their audiences."[10]

McGann, in his introduction to *Historical Studies and Literary Criticism*, makes referentiality into a rallying cry:

> What will not be found in these essays . . . is the assumption, so common in text-centered studies of every type, that literary works are self-enclosed verbal constructs, or looped intertextual fields of autonomous signifiers and signifieds. In these essays, the question of referentiality is once again brought to the fore.[11]

In "Keats and the Historical Method in Literary Criticism," he outlines a program for those who have rallied to the cry. These procedures, which he says are "practical derivatives of the Bakhtin school," assume that historical critics, who must be interested both in a work's point of origin and in its point of reception, will understand the former by studying biography and bibliography. (When was *Heart of Darkness* printed? How much time elapsed between Conrad's return from the Congo and his completion of a manuscript draft?) After learning these details, the critic must consider the expressed intentions of the author, for, if printed, they have modified the developing history of the work. Next, the new historicist should know the history of the work's reception, for that body of opinion has become part of the platform on which we are situated when we study the book. Finally, McGann urges the new historicist critic to point toward the future, toward his or her *own* audience, defining for its members the aims and limits of the critical project and injecting the analysis with a degree of self-consciousness that alone can give it credibility.[12]

In the essay that follows, Brook Thomas begins by claiming that if we are to catch a glimpse of the hazy truths that *Heart of Darkness* has to offer, we are going to have to approach Conrad's work with a renewed willingness to read historically. After all, the epigraph to his essay shows Conrad thought of fiction as history. Thomas begins his

---

[10]Greenblatt, *Renaissance Self-Fashioning*, p. 5.
[11]McGann, *Historical Studies and Literary Criticism*, p. 3.
[12]McGann, "Keats and the Historical Method," in McGann, *The Beauty of Inflections*, p. 62.

approach by providing a kind of history *of* history, by reminding us that, during the nineteenth century, history tended to be seen as an organic development toward the present. Consequently, the discontinuities of history were overlooked or, at least, glossed over by historians who all the while believed that they were describing the past as it really was.

Thomas critiques the old history not only to avoid its pitfalls but also because he sees Conrad as a kind of prototype of the new historicist, as a writer who, though in some ways biased in the ways of his culture, was nonetheless effective at debunking the melioristic historicism of his own age. Thomas uses "counter-memory," a phrase of Foucault's, to describe Conrad's picture of Kurtz, a man who gives the lie to meliorism by showing how the most "civilized" of Europeans can also be subhuman in savagery. In Thomas's view, Conrad anticipated the new historicism, too, by not choosing to try to tell how it was in the Congo via an objective-sounding, third-person, omniscient narrative. Even though Conrad had himself been there, he chose to tell his story indirectly, through an idiosyncratic, first-person narrator, Marlow, whose narrative is in turn relayed by another narrator who presumably has not even been to Africa. This elaborate structure makes us aware of structure *as* structure; thus, the novel doesn't pretend to offer us a perfectly clear, uncluttered, unbiased, perfectly natural view of the facts of the past.

Thomas, of course, is a newer historicist than Conrad; we can see this by the characteristics of his own text. The text praises Nietzsche, who helped decenter Western historical narrative, which had tended to assume that Western, idealist values were central and definitive and to judge the past of other cultures accordingly. Thomas also makes use of biographical and bibliographical information and, especially, of Conrad's own writings about his works. Those nonfiction writings, because they have shaped the critical reception of the fiction, must be attended to by the new historicist, in whose view the history of a work includes the work's point of origin, its point of reception, and even its future relationship with its audience. Finally, Thomas is not only familiar with but also adept at using the insights of avant-garde schools of criticism that have flourished since the demise of the old history. And yet, even as he uses them, he distances himself from them by situating them historically.

But Thomas can ill afford to historically situate and critically account for everyone and everything — from Conrad to psychoanalytic criticism to J. Hillis Miller — except himself. Were he to do so he would fall into the old trap in which the historical critic fails because he fails to admit his own historical limitations and consequent capacity for failure. Thomas implicitly does the former and explicitly admits the latter. "There is no guarantee that we will penetrate to the . . . heart of *Heart of Darkness*," Thomas writes. There is, in its place, only the conviction that the heart of Conrad's novel can only be approached by the critic who practices sociohistorical criticism.

A NEW HISTORICAL CRITIC AT WORK

BROOK THOMAS

Preserving and Keeping Order
by Killing Time in *Heart of Darkness*

Fiction is history, human history, or it is nothing. But it is also more than that; it stands on firmer ground, being based on the reality of forms and the observation of social phenomena, whereas history is based on documents, and the reading of print and handwriting — on second-hand impression. Thus fiction is nearer truth. But let that pass. A historian may be an artist too, and a novelist is a historian, the preserver, the keeper, the expounder, of human experience.

—JOSEPH CONRAD, *Notes on Life and Letters*

We can start, contrary to current critical practices, with some old-fashioned generalizations about the history of ideas. And, when we journey, as we must, to more specificity about Conrad's story there is no guarantee that we will penetrate to the essential Truth — or non-Truth — lying at the heart of *Heart of Darkness;* certainly not in a story informing us that for Marlow "the meaning of an episode was not inside like a kernel but outside, enveloping the tale which brought it out only as a glow brings out a haze, in the likeness of one of these misty halos that sometimes are made visible by the spectral illumination of moonshine" (pp. 19–20). But we may be able to come closer to a truth that we can glimpse only if we read historically the narrative that Conrad weaves in his role as a historian of human experience.

1

The century that preceded the 1899 publication of *Heart of Darkness* was the great century of historiography; that is to say, the one in which history sought to become a science. The eighteenth century's emphasis on natural, universal laws that governed human society did not suddenly vanish, but it was superseded by an emphasis on the organic development of peoples and nations, developments that became the object of study for the new science of history. In medieval times events in history had been seen as *exempla:* as illustrations of moral laws or truths. Relying on the sense of time that allowed anticipations of Christianity to be read into the ancient world and the Old Testament, historians in the Middle Ages had placed an event in the past on the same temporal plane as the present. Past and present events were interchangeable, capable of being interpreted to exhibit a moral truth to guide behavior. With the advent of a self-consciously modern age in the Renaissance, this sense of time began to alter.

Defining itself as a distinct epoch that had broken with that which came before, the Renaissance produced thinkers who, increasingly, considered events in the present to be different in kind from events in the past. Events were unique to the epochs in which they occurred. History no longer merely took place *in* time, it also took place *through* time; that is, history became temporalized. As a result, the passage of time gave each generation a novel perspective on the past. Past events were no longer so easily interpreted to be timeless *exempla.* Instead, they needed to be continually reinterpreted from the standpoint of a new present. To enter the Renaissance, Reinhart Koselleck has written in his recent book entitled *Futures Past,* is to enter the *Neuzeit,* the age of "new time."[1]

By the eighteenth century this sense of history's temporality was widely held. Goethe, for instance, felt that it was self-evident that each generation had to rewrite world history. Nonetheless, eighteenth-century histories still stressed the universality of history. This stress on universal history continued to link history to moral philosophy, since history was often used to illustrate natural laws and the natural rights of man. The rise of the science of history was an attempt to break even this connection with moral philosophy. As the great spokesman of nineteenth-century historiography Leopold von Ranke wrote, his task was not to judge the past or to instruct the present for the profit of future ages, but "to show only what actually happened (*wie es eigentlich gewesen*)."[2] To accomplish this goal, Ranke emphasized the difference

---

[1] See Reinhart Koselleck, *Futures Past,* trans. Keith Tribe (Cambridge, Mass.: MIT Press, 1985).

[2] Quoted in Stephen Bann, *The Clothing of Clio* (Cambridge: Cambridge University Press, 1984), p. 10.

between primary and secondary sources. A history that wanted accurately to relate the past needed to rely on primary sources — documents actually produced in the period — not secondary ones — documents recording another period's interpretation of the past.

From our twentieth-century perspective Ranke's goal to tell only what actually happened sometimes seems naive. For instance, the attempt to reconstruct the past on the basis of primary source material seems to neglect the very real difficulties that arise in giving the past representation. As we are continually reminded by literary critics today, no history can possibly relate the past as it really was because our histories will always be influenced by our present perspective. Furthermore, histories are written in language; the rhetoric the historian adopts shapes and determines his representation of the past. This critical commonplace of today is in turn indebted to the insights of people like Conrad who, in the passage I quote at the start of this essay, reminds us that the documents that Ranke called "primary" sources merely give the historian a "second-hand impression" of an age. One of the concerns of this essay is to understand historically why Conrad felt that "the reality of forms and observation of social phenomenon" in his fiction produce more truthful histories than those of most historians.

At least part of the reason is the crisis in historicism that occurred in the late nineteenth and early twentieth centuries. If historicism rested on the belief that the historian could objectively reconstruct the past, the ultimate truth it delivered seemed to be the impossibility of discovering the truth. Feeling that their task was to relive an era as sympathetically as possible by blotting out everything they knew about the latter course of history, historians came to see that all beliefs were historically contingent, including the belief in scientific objectivity. If this awareness came dangerously close to what Friedrich Meinecke called "the bottomless pit of relativism,"[3] it was tolerated because historicism retained a faith in progress. Nineteenth-century histories might demonstrate that beliefs were historically contingent, but many adopted a teleological narrative structure: in other words, one that assumed that history had a design or purpose and that whatever was becoming was right. Values changed, but they were always appropriate to their age, and they progressed and developed over time. Even this faith, however, was undermined by the way historicism linked its histories to the emergence of individual nations. As each nation's history emerged, it became clear that not all

[3]Quoted in George G. Iggers, *The German Conception of History* (Middletown, Conn.: Wesleyan University Press, 1968), p. 175.

narratives of progress could be right. If academic dispute did not bring this point home, World War I did.

But even before the destruction of the war, many Europeans had lost faith in the values that gave coherence to the historicist project. Increasingly, the attempt to give an objective description of the past gave way to modern subjectivist philosophies. As J. Hillis Miller summarizes, "Historicism does not mean merely an awareness of the contradictory diversity of cultures and attitudes. The ancient world had that. The modern historical sense means rather the loss of faith in the possibility of ever discovering the right and true culture, the right and true philosophy or religion."[4]

2

Miller's passage is an excellent one to place Conrad's fiction in the context of the history of ideas. By having Kurtz, who embodies Europe's most noble ideals, recognize the horror at the heart of darkness, Conrad brings us face to face with the disillusionment that many twentieth-century thinkers continue to confront, although much of the culture operates by trying to forget it. Marlow embodies this double perspective. On the one hand, back in Europe Marlow tries to forget Kurtz, "to surrender personally all that remained of him with me to that oblivion which is the last word of our common fate" (p. 89). On the other, Marlow cannot will Kurtz's memory away. For him and the reader it serves as what the French historian Michel Foucault has called a "counter-memory," a memory that disrupts the narrative of enlightened progress that official European culture tried to tell about its history. Unable completely to repress this counter-memory when he visits Kurtz's Intended, whose forehead, as the room grows darker, "remained illumined by the unextinguishable light of belief and love" (p. 91), Marlow refuses to destroy her illusions and tells her that the last word Kurtz had uttered was her name, thus linking this woman and all she stands for with "the horror." Official memory of light and counter-memory of darkness are in Conrad's narrative inextricably connected, even though the official memory's ascendancy depends upon the lies that repress the counter-memory.

In a world in which the truth that Marlow tells about civilized Europe is expressed through a lie, it is no wonder that Conrad claimed

---

[4]J. Hillis Miller, *The Disappearance of God* (Cambridge, Mass.: Harvard University Press, 1963), p. 10.

that fiction is nearer to truth than history. The way Conrad's art approaches the truth is not by stating it but by reminding us of the lie that accompanies every effort to name the truth. Art is closer to truth only in so far as it carries within it the counter-memory that its efforts to express the truth repress, just as the ivory keys of the grand piano that Marlow sees as he waits to greet the Intended become an emblem for the exploitation that Europe's high culture tried to cover up. Embodying the structural relationship between what is said and what is left unsaid, Conrad's story proves to be truer than history, not in its explicit statements, but in its forms.

For instance, Conrad does not offer an omniscient narrative perspective that knows and states how it really was. Instead, he constructs a story in which his perspective gives way to a narrator's, that gives way to Marlow's, that gives way to Kurtz's. If this perspective does not tell us the truth, there is a certain truth in the formal techniques that illustrate the impossibility of directly stating the truth. Similarly, the linear narrative of nineteenth-century historicism, in which we move progressively towards a fuller understanding, is replaced by a narrative that concludes with a lie. Even so, there is a certain truth in the way the story unfolds, moving forward and backward in time, its narrative flow interrupted by Marlow's addresses to his audience and his own psychological avoidance of the actual encounter with Kurtz, who is mentioned early in the story but is not met until pages later.

To enter the world of *Heart of Darkness* is, in other words, to enter the world of modern fiction, a world in which authors' technical innovations responded to the loss of faith described by Miller as the "modern historical sense." But if the crisis in historicism helps place *Heart of Darkness* in context, the story also places the context in context. For Conrad's narrative about a European's journey to the heart of Africa helps us see the extent to which the crisis in late nineteenth-century European thought was related to Europe's contact with what some recent critics, following Jacques Lacan's revision of Hegel, have come to call "the Other." It is probably no accident that the most important British modernist novelists are situated in positions on the borders of mainstream British culture that force them to encounter "the Other." Perhaps no other writer in the twentieth century achieved a mastery over the English language to match James Joyce. But Joyce was in an important sense a colonial writer, an Irish Catholic who spent his life in self-imposed exile on the Continent and who considered English an acquired tongue. An exiled Pole, Conrad quite literally wrote in an acquired language. D. H. Lawrence meanwhile came from a working-class family in the Midlands, carrying an accent that marked his difference from those producing "proper" English arts and letters. Only Virginia Woolf and E. M. Forster could be considered insiders. And Woolf, as a woman, occupied her own border country, while Forster's greatest work, *A Passage to India*, is about the encounter between East and West. Indeed, Europe's encounter with the non-European, so poignantly portrayed by Conrad in *Heart of Darkness*, played a part in one of the most important aspects of modern thought: Europe's discovery of "the Other" within itself.

As early as the late eighteenth century, Europeans had been forced to alter their view of a universal history centered in Europe. Paradoxically, this alteration resulted from the very imperialistic, overseas expansion that drew its ideological justification from the belief that reason, progress, and enlightenment emanated from the West. Brought into contact with such various cultures, Europeans found it impossible to retain belief in one universal culture. Instead, there were many cultures, each with its own history. Recognition of non-European cultures did not mean the abandonment of a Eurocentric perspective. Quite the contrary. Nineteenth-century historicism was adept at absorbing all cultures into a Eurocentric history. Nonetheless, the very presence of "the Other" within those histories heightened the possibility that their narratives would be "decentered." The crisis in historicism can be linked to this decentering, a decentering made possible, ironically, by the success of the West's imperialism.

One of the most important expressions of the decentering of Western narratives of progress and rationality is found in the work of the German philosopher Friedrich Nietzsche, who died the year after Conrad's story appeared. Nietzsche has had a strong influence on recent post-structuralist thought. It is, I think, no accident that two essays cited as starting points for post-structuralism contain explicit critiques of Eurocentrism. One is Paul de Man's "Crisis in Criticism" (1967), which emphasizes the blindness of the philosopher Edmund Husserl to non-Western cultures. The other is Jacques Derrida's "Structure, Sign, and Play in the Discourse of the Human Sciences" (1966), which points out that even the noble efforts to understand non-European cultures by the structuralist anthropologist Claude Lévi-Strauss inevitably adopt a Western perspective. Offering a theory that assures us that the desire for the presence of the truth is inevitably an unfulfilled desire, poststructuralism can productively analyze the world Conrad presents in *Heart of Darkness*. It can also serve as a sort of new faith, albeit a negative one, for critics like Miller trying to cope with the loss of confidence in the Eurocentric view that is dramatized by Conrad's narrative. In turn, Conrad's narrative helps locate the historical situation that created the conditions for the formation of post-structuralist thought.

This reciprocal relation between *Heart of Darkness* and post-structuralism also holds for another approach that proves so fruitful in reading Conrad's story: psychoanalysis. Albert J. Guerard's use of Sigmund Freud to describe *Heart of Darkness* as "A Journey Within" remains one of the most important pieces of Conrad criticism. Certainly, a powerful aspect of Conrad's story is the economy by which his tale about a physical journey into the darkness of Africa becomes a story about a psychological journey into the darkness of the human unconscious. But it is not only the case that psychoanalysis can be used to illuminate Conrad's narrative. Freud's narrative about the human psyche is also illuminated *by* narratives like Conrad's about what happens when a rational Westerner journeys into Africa. While it is commonplace to consider psychoanalysis a new scientific theory, one that provides a universal account of the structure of the human mind, an examination of Freud's metaphors suggests that we might consider psychoanalysis a historical event as well, one partly enabled by Western narratives about encounters with "the Other."

There are numerous similarities between Freud's narrative about the unconscious and Conrad's narrative about the European encounter with the non-European. Trying to describe the "wild and gorgeous apparition" (p. 76) of the African woman trying to protect Kurtz, Marlow tells his audience, "She stood looking at us without a stir, and like the wilderness itself, with an air of brooding over an inscrutable purpose" (p. 77). Freud, in a famous passage, compares female sexuality to the dark continent of Africa. For both of these Western males the otherness of female sexuality is described in terms of the otherness of the African continent. Just as in Freud's theory the unconscious eludes representation and rational understanding, so in Conrad's narrative Africa eludes all attempts of the Western mind — especially a male mind — to understand it. In this context we can better appreciate Marlow's description of himself as a young boy staring, as did Conrad, at the "many blank spaces" on the map of the world. Vowing some day to visit those unexplored regions, he finds, by the time he sets out on his journey, that what had once been "a blank space of delightful mystery — a white patch for a boy to dream gloriously over" — had become "a place of darkness" (p. 22). Finally recognized by the West, those unexplored, blank spots on the

globe known as Africa were represented as darkness, the same metaphor psychoanalysis uses to represent the unexplored areas of the
mind.

The way *Heart of Darkness* helps us analyze some of the critical
approaches we use to analyze it proves very satisfying for our classical
sense of balance. Having arrived at this symmetrical formulation, however, we should not rest too comfortably, because it raises a problem.
To merge critical approaches and text is to risk the disappearance of
the encounter with "the Other," which seemed of such historical significance. Just as in Conrad's story what seems to be an encounter
with another turns out to be an encounter with the self — so that
Marlow's encounter with Kurtz really becomes an encounter with himself and readers' encounters with Marlow transform into encounters
with themselves — so in some critical schools today even the otherness of the story we are reading is denied. Although we can hold a
material object in our hand with *Heart of Darkness* written on the
title page and the words Conrad wrote printed on the pages to follow, we are told that what we call the text is in fact the product of
our interpretations.

Ironically, then, a project that seems intent on decentering a Eurocentric point of view turns out to be the most Eurocentric of all. For
just as Conrad's story can be read, not as a story about Africa, but
actually as a story about Europe, so the decentering set in motion by
Europe's encounter with "the Other" can be read as a statement about
European thought, not about that which is foreign to it. Thinking we
are encountering something outside of ourselves or Western culture,
we end up merely discovering "the Other" within ourselves, a discovery that could be described as the most imperialistic of all, since what
was once thought to be truly different is now absorbed into a system
that accounts for its own decentering. In the meantime, "the Other"
seems to be of interest only in so far as it can help the West in its task
of self-definition.

3

If Conrad's narrative is one of the most effective expressions of
the encounter between self and "Other," between the European and
non-European, our task is not to affirm the truth of his narrative but to
interrogate it. And what needs interrogation is Conrad's representation
of the non-European. Why, we need to ask, in this narrative about
Europe's encounter with Africa are Africans reduced to the mere function of providing us a spectral illumination about Europe? To answer

that question we can turn to a passage in which Marlow describes the Africans:

> The earth seemed unearthly. We are accustomed to look upon the shackled form of a conquered monster, but there — there you could look at a thing monstrous and free. It was unearthly, and the men were — No, they were not inhuman. Well, you know, that was the worst of it — this suspicion of their not being inhuman. It would come slowly to one. They howled and leaped, and spun, and made horrid faces; but what thrilled you was just the thought of their humanity — like yours — the thought of your remote kinship with this wild and passionate uproar. Ugly. Yes, it was ugly enough; but if you were man enough you would admit to yourself that there was in you just the faintest trace of a response to the terrible frankness of that noise, a dim suspicion of there being a meaning in it which you — you so remote from the night of first ages — could comprehend. And why not? The mind of man is capable of anything — because everything is in it, all the past as well as all the future. What was there after all? Joy, fear, sorrow, devotion, valour, rage — who can tell? — but truth — truth stripped of its cloak of time. (p. 51)

Starting the paragraph with the paradox that the earth seemed unearthly, Marlow sets up the expectation that the human beings inhabiting that unearthly earth will be inhuman, an expectation easy to arouse because it would confirm his listeners' racial prejudices. But Conrad's narrative disrupts such commonplace prejudices. The horror of the story is not that the Africans are a deviant form of humanity, but that the monster is also within the Europeans who consider themselves superior. Thus, the passage suggests a number of ironic reversals. On the one hand, the African continent is a shackled and conquered monster. On the other, it is the European conquerors who are conquered, as their ruthless and violent imperialism unleashes their latent savagery, making them more monstrous than those they profess to civilize. Whereas the West has a tradition of believing that to make the unknown known it has to be brought under control, Marlow suggests that what allows Westerners to understand Africans is loss of control. Released from the constraints of civilization, Europeans can feel a kinship with those people who on the surface seem so different. Understanding of the non-Western can occur, therefore, only when the West is conquered by the very people it feels it is conquering. True courage, a courage in Marlow's world reserved for men (". . . but if you were man enough . . ."), comes in admitting the possibility of being conquered by "the Other," an "Other" that exists all along within the European.

One of the most obvious reasons why Westerners do not immediately recognize "the African" within themselves is the physical difference between races. But for Marlow physical differences, such as skin color, are a surface deception. The real otherness is not physical but temporal. When Westerners travel to Africa, they make a temporal journey as well as a physical one. As Marlow tells his listeners, "Going up that river was like travelling back to the earliest beginnings of the world, when vegetation rioted on the earth and the big trees were kings" (p. 48). The incomprehensibility of the landscape and the people inhabiting it is caused because to travel to Africa is to travel to prehistoric times.

> We were wanderers on a prehistoric earth, on an earth that wore the aspect of an unknown planet. We could have fancied ourselves the first of men taking possession of an accursed inheritance, to be subdued at the cost of profound anguish and of excessive toil. But suddenly, as we struggled round a bend, there would be a glimpse of rush walls, of peaked grass-roofs, a burst of yells, a whirl of black limbs, a mass of hands clapping, of feet stamping, of bodies swaying, of eyes rolling, under the droop of heavy and motionless foliage. The steamer toiled along slowly on the edge of a black and incomprehensible frenzy. The prehistoric man was cursing us, praying to us, welcoming us — who could tell? We were cut off from the comprehension of our surroundings; we glided past like phantoms, wondering and secretly appalled, as sane men would be before an enthusiastic outbreak in a madhouse. We could not understand because we were too far and could not remember, because we were travelling in the night of first ages, of those ages that are gone, leaving hardly a sign — and no memories. (p. 50)

But Marlow eventually does comprehend these people. He can because, as different as they seem from civilized human beings, they constitute the prehistory of the West. If the veneer of civilization has made Westerners forget the truth of their prehistory, the function of Conrad's art is to make them remember what they have forgotten. As he writes in the preface to *The Nigger of the "Narcissus,"* his task is, "by the power of the written word," to present "that glimpse of truth for which you have forgotten to ask." The way he stimulates his readers' memories, however, is at odds with the way nineteenth-century historians tried to do so. As we saw, for the historians time constituted reality. The truth of an event had to do with the time in which it took place. To discover a truth we had forgotten was to reconstruct it historically. But Conrad has a different notion of temporality. For him truth has to be discovered by stripping it of "its cloak of time." The passage of history does not lead to continually new truths. Instead, it places a barrier between us and the memory of our prehistory. Truth is not to be found by remembering history but by forgetting it.

The belief that truth is located in a realm of a prehistory that is still present but disguised by modern life is typical of modernist writers. T. S. Eliot, for instance, praised the work of Wyndham Lewis for "sinking to the most primitive and forgotten, returning to the origin and bringing something back, seeking the beginning and the end."[5] Whereas for nineteenth-century historians the past and present existed on different temporal planes, for many modernists past and present occupied the same plane. Flattening history in *The Waste Land,* Eliot continually juxtaposes past and present, just as in *Heart of Darkness* Marlow links the past of England with the present of Africa by comparing the Thames to the Congo: "And this also . . . has been one of the dark places of the earth" (p. 19).

Europeans like Conrad, then, possessed not only a progressive, Eurocentric vision of world history but also the temporal sense of the synchronicity of the nonsynchronic. It seemed to them, in other words, that by studying other, primitive-seeming cultures existing simultaneously (or synchronically) with their own, they could study something chronologically disparate, namely, their own deep, prehistoric past. Each culture, it seemed, had its own temporal logic. Whereas the West followed a fairly steady line of progress (despite a backward slide in the "Dark Ages"), other cultures plotted different curves. Thus, at any moment, the world's cultures were at different stages of development. To employ a widely used metaphor, some countries were developed, others underdeveloped. Since the standard of development remained European, cultures different from Europe were, almost by definition, underdeveloped, and the most underdeveloped land of all was Africa, which still existed in a prehistoric state. Drawing on this notion of the synchronicity of the nonsynchronic, Conrad is able to turn a story about a present journey to Africa into a journey to Europe's past, as well as one into each human being's primitive psyche.

[5]T. S. Eliot, quoted in F. O. Matthiessen, *American Renaissance* (New York: Oxford University Press, 1941), p. 466.

Conrad's reliance on the temporal notion that allowed the West to absorb non-Western cultures into its view of history indicates how complicated his portrayal of Western imperialism is. On the one hand, he undercuts the West's self-righteousness by inverting its narrative about "the Other." Africa does not embody a lesser truth because it exists in an earlier stage of history. Instead, it embodies a more profound truth because it has not travelled as far from its prehistoric origins. Thus, like Freud and Nietzsche, Conrad subverts prevailing European values, offering a "counter-memory" to the belief in rationality and progress. On the other hand, by merely inverting the narrative Conrad remains within a Eurocentric logic. The "Other" is of interest for what it reveals about Europe. Indeed, Conrad's subversion of prevailing values yields a conservative, not a radical, social vision.

The political message of Conrad's encounter with the non-European may well be anti-imperialistic, but not because Conrad espouses liberation of the people he associates with a dark truth about human nature. Instead, for Conrad, European control of non-European cultures is a symptom of its inability to control "the Other" within itself. Conrad's political theory, like that of Hobbes, remains one of control and restraint. There is, it seems, a counter-memory to this narrative that reveals the counter-memory of Western notions of progress and enlightenment. We can try to evoke it by examining Conrad's fictional forms.

4

For Conrad narrative has a function similar to that of history. Inevitably taking place within time, narrative, like history, disguises a truth that he feels exists prior to time. Just as the nature of European humanity is to be discovered in an encounter with Africans who exist in a state prior to history, so the meaning of Conrad's tale seems to exist in a realm prior to narrative time. Nonetheless, just as we have to travel through history to encounter our prehistory, so we have to travel through narrative to encounter a meaning that lies deeper than the tale's narrative surface.

To recognize the impossibility of bringing an atemporal truth into narrative representation is to start to understand the importance of one of the most noticeable formal characteristics of Conrad's narrative: its breaks and gaps. Disrupting the narrative flow, they suggest something that resists narrativization; that is, the glimpse of the truth we have forgotten to ask. For instance, the first interruption of Marlow's story occurs when Marlow cries out about his inability to adequately represent Kurtz in words.

> He was just a word for me. I did not see the man in the name any more than you do. Do you see him? Do you see the story? Do you see anything? It seems to me I am trying to tell you a dream — making a vain attempt, because no relation of a dream can convey the dream-sensation, that commingling of absurdity, surprise, and bewilderment in a tremor of struggling revolt, that notion of being captured by the incredible which is the very essence of dreams. . . . (p. 42)

Marlow's outcry is an obvious reminder to the reader of Conrad's own task as a novelist, for he must make his audience see not only Kurtz but also Marlow. And Conrad's task is even more difficult than Marlow's. Marlow's listeners have access to the voice of someone who has seen Kurtz. Conrad's audience confronts nothing but silent, black words on a white page. But Marlow's outcry does more than comment on the difficulty of representation in words.

To remain within narrative is to remain within the realm of consciousness that veils truth. By interrupting the flow of Marlow's narrative Conrad establishes contact with his readers, momentarily freeing them from the shackles of a linear narrative and throwing them back on their own imaginations. In their imaginations, which contain "all the past as well as the future," not in conscious attention to the story's surface, readers will be able to evoke the memory of their prehistory necessary to comprehend the story's meaning. It was, for instance, in a dreamlike state that Marlow was able to remember his kinship with prehistoric humanity. "There were moments when one's past came back to one, as it will sometimes when you have not a moment to spare to yourself; but it came in the shape of an unrestful and noisy dream, remembered with wonder amongst the overwhelming realities of this strange world of plants, and water, and silence" (pp. 48–49). To relate a dream is to distort the dream-sensation. In *Heart of Darkness* Conrad's disruption of narrative forms works to recreate a dream-sensation in the reader.

But it is not quite so simple. If words seem to block us from a deeper truth accessible only through the imagination, it is words that provoke the imagination. It is, for instance, the mention of Kurtz's name that provokes Marlow's outcry over his inability to use words to make us see Kurtz. Since the very narrative that must be disrupted in

order for us to have a glimpse of a forgotten truth is our only means
to approach that truth, the gaps in Marlow's narrative can be said to
serve a different function from the one we have examined. If, on the
one hand, they suggest a truth that resists narrativization, on the other, they reveal Marlow's reluctance to continue his narrative journey
toward the glimpse of truth he experienced at the heart of darkness.
For Marlow to mention Kurtz is to recall all that Kurtz came to embody for him. Not yet capable of facing that horror, Marlow interrupts
the story that inevitably leads to Kurtz. The very breaks and gaps that
seem to be the only way to suggest the truth also indicate an avoidance of it.

If these two functions seem at odds, they ultimately converge,
because for Conrad "the horror" is associated with the inability fully
to represent the truth and what that inability implies about the human
condition. So long as truth cannot fully be represented, lies become part
of the truth of the world. Indeed, immediately preceding the first interruption of the story Marlow announces his hatred of lies. This hatred
does not, however, stem from Marlow's love of truth over falsehood,
for what he hates about lies is that they remind him of the inevitable
truth of mortality. "There is a taint of death, a flavour of mortality in
lies — which is exactly what I hate and detest in the world — what I
want to forget" (p. 41). Marlow wants to forget the truth of human
finitude that lies remind him of: the truth of our existence in a fallen
state in which we cannot have full access to truth, a state making lies
inevitable. The lie Marlow tells Kurtz's Intended at the end of the
story signals Marlow's ability to overcome his hatred of lies and his
acceptance of a world of finitude. At odds with the Enlightenment's
faith in humankind's ability through time to liberate itself by expanding its sphere of influence in the world in order to gain a fuller access
to truth, Marlow's vision has affinities with a medieval view that a fallen
humankind will never have full knowledge of God's truth. For Conrad,
as for many contemporary theorists, humanity's finitude is intricately
related to humanity's existence within language. Language, our only
access to truth, by its very nature offers only a trace of what it seeks
to represent. To be within language is to be in a perpetual state of lost
presence.

Politically for Conrad this necessitates the acceptance of a world
in which lies and repression are inevitable, a political vision that is intricately linked to the seemingly contradictory functions of a narrative
that, on the one hand, helps reveal the horror at the heart of darkness
and, on the other, serves to cover it up and hold it at bay. Humanity,

or the male part of it at least, must confront the horror Kurtz had the courage to face. Survival of the species, however, demands that unlike Kurtz it must not succumb to it, but instead, like Marlow, learn to cover it up. The work of civilization is a lie, but since the alternative is so terrifying it must go on.

In a world in which all other values seem to be relativized, restraint, therefore, becomes an important value for Conrad. In *Heart of Darkness* restraint is by no means the sole property of Westerners. For Marlow the Africans who accompany him on the journey up the river display more restraint than any European when they resist "the devilry of lingering starvation" (p. 57) by not killing and eating the whites. Marlow, however, cannot explain this restraint, which he finds a mystery greater than the inexplicable sounds of savagery emanating from the primeval forest. He cannot explain it, because for Marlow restraint is associated with work, the work of civilization that separates the West from the savage forest. How much Marlow values work is made clear in another break in his narrative.

Interrupted by a skeptical grunt from one of his listeners, Marlow responds.

> You wonder I didn't go ashore for a howl and a dance? Well, no — I didn't. Fine sentiments, you say? Fine sentiments be hanged! I had no time. I had to mess about with white-lead and strips of woollen blanket helping to put bandages on those leaky steam-pipes — I tell you. I had to watch the steering, and circumvent those snags, and get the tin-pot along by hook or by crook. There was surface-truth enough in these things to save a wiser man. (p. 51)

The necessity to work, just to keep the ship moving, not some idealistic values, keeps Marlow from participating in "unspeakable rites" (p. 65). And, as the reference to "surface-truth" reminds us, Conrad self-consciously compares Marlow's journey up the river to the act of narrating that journey. As a comment directly before another break in Marlow's tale makes even clearer, Conrad's narrative also offers a surface truth that hides a profounder truth. "When you have to attend to things of that sort, to the mere incidents of the surface, the reality — the reality, I tell you — fades. The inner truth is hidden — luckily, luckily" (p. 49).

Within the logic set up by the implied analogy between Marlow's journey and his narrative, the leaky steam-pipes that threaten to sink the ship invite comparison with the gaps and breaks in Marlow's narrative. Just as covering the holes in the steam-pipes allows the ship to continue its journey on the surface of the river, so filling the gaps in Marlow's narrative allows the surface narrative to continue, thus protecting us from the groundless horror they suggest. Told by an agent at the station about "the necessity for every man to get on," Marlow responds, "Did I see it? I saw it. What more did I want? What I really wanted was rivets, by Heaven! Rivets. To get on with the work — to stop the hole. Rivets I wanted" (pp. 42–43). But rivets, although in abundance at a station closer to shore, are not available. Thus, Marlow, like Conrad, must improvise techniques that will allow him to stop the holes so dangerously exposed and difficult to repair in this outpost of progress.

5

In the preface to *The Nigger of the "Narcissus,"* Conrad explicitly compares his work as an artist to the work of civilization by referring to "the workman of art." But there is an important difference. Workers' hands are kept so busy that they never take a moment to glimpse "the truth." Thus, the hand of a writer must produce a work that arrests,

> for the space of a breath, the hands busy about the work of the earth, and compel men entranced by the sight of distant goals to glance for a moment at the surrounding vision of form and colour, of sunshine and shadows; to make them pause for a look, for a sigh, for a smile — such is the aim, difficult and evanescent, and reserved only for a very few to achieve. But sometimes, by the deserving and the fortunate, even that task is accomplished. And when it is accomplished — behold! — all the truth of life is there: a moment of vision, a sigh, a smile — and the return to an eternal rest.

What interests me most about this passage is the effect that the work of art has, according to Conrad, on the workers of the earth. The initial image is one of labor — hands busy at toil. The final image is one of tranquility — an eternal rest. That final image is clearly an image of death, but, as J. Hillis Miller points out, it also suggests a return "to the forgetful sleep of everyday life."[6] The implication is, therefore, that after people have had a glimpse of the truth of life provided by the workman of art their lives of everyday labor can be considered ones of rest. Arrested for the space of a breath, the hands busy about the work

[6]J. Hillis Miller, *Poets of Reality* (Cambridge, Mass.: Harvard University Press, 1965), p. 39.

of the earth are set in motion again, returning to the world of time that, because it protects them from the truth at the heart of darkness, is actually one of repose. Serving to protect humanity from the horror it discovers when truth is stripped from the cloak of time, work not only takes place within history but also produces history. It is work, then, that constructs the lie of civilization that hides humanity, necessarily, from the prehistoric truth about itself.

But what if Conrad's location of truth in an atemporal realm is itself a lie? What if the horror of human existence is not to be found in a realm of savagery that we discover by escaping history, but instead lies within history itself — not a Eurocentric construction of a universal History, but one that refuses to indulge in Conrad's mystification that turns Africa into the mere site of Europe's prehistory? If this is the case, work might serve a very different function from the one Conrad attributes to it.

Just as the narrative Conrad uses to hold the horror at bay produces gaps and breaks that bring us face to face with it, so the very work that is supposed to cover up the horror might also produce it. Rather than protecting humanity from an unnameable horror, work might be part of the unnamed horror of Conrad's story. Whereas Conrad sees work providing Europeans with the restraint and discipline necessary to control the horror of "the Other" within themselves, European history records the horror of the enforced labor of others — European and non-European — to maintain structures of domination. Work does indeed restrain. Perhaps, however, the reason why people with hands busy about the work of the earth are restrained from seeing a glimpse of the truth is not because they repress an unconscious world of the imagination that contains an ahistorical truth about the reality of forms, but because they are given no time to become conscious of the history of how the time of their lives has been wasted. Or to put this another way, the unconsciousness of narratives about the unconscious might turn out to be the history of human labor.

As we have seen, Conrad's tale easily lends itself to psychoanalytical and post-structuralist analyses at the same time that it helps us place in a historical context both psychoanalysis' narrative about the journey to the unconscious and post-structuralism's narrative about the decentering of the West's logocentrism. Conrad's representation of work indicates the need to introduce another form of narrative explanation in our attempt to analyze *Heart of Darkness:* Karl Marx's insistence that historians tell the history of work. Whereas the affinities of Conrad's narrative with Freudian and Nietzschean narratives help explain how it serves as a counter-memory to prevailing Eurocentric narratives, its differences from the Marxist narrative help expose the counter-memory of such counter-narratives. To say this is not to argue that the Marxist narrative is the master narrative that explains all others. But so long as there are those who offer narratives of human history that neglect the role human labor has played in shaping history — or even more, who, like Conrad, offer a narrative in which human labor hides us from the "truth" of human experience — so long as such narratives influence our sense of history, Marx's narrative will serve as a reminder of acts of repression.

Like Conrad, Marx constructs a narrative in which human beings quite literally make history through their labor. But, unlike Conrad, Marx would consider any escape from that history to be an escape from the truth of human experience. People are prone to escape from the truth *within* human history because it is not a pleasant one. Human beings might make history, but they do not, Marx reminds us, make it under conditions of their own choosing. Humanity's lack of control over the conditions under which it labors makes history, as it is for Joyce's Stephen Dedalus, a nightmare from which we are trying to awake. The role the historian plays in helping us awaken from the nightmare of history is quite different for Conrad and Marx. In expounding human experience Conrad's novelist as historian becomes its "preserver" and "keeper." He does so by revealing a prehistorical, unchanging truth about humanity. In expounding human experience, Marx's philosopher as historian tries to help change it. He does so by providing explanations of the historical forces that keep humanity from laboring under conditions of its own choosing with the hope that consciousness of those conditions can help liberate humanity from them. Any new historical criticism worthy of its name will share in this goal of using historical analysis as a way to help those in the present work towards the construction of a new future, a future in which work is no longer used as a means to control "the Other" within, but instead directed toward liberating ourselves to help improve the lives of others truly different from us. In terms of Conrad's *Heart of Darkness* this means recognizing that, whereas Conrad's attempt to separate truth and history serves the important function of demystifying nineteenth-century notions of progress and European superiority, it generates a mystification of its own by absorbing the encounter with "the Other" into a narrative about European identity. Precisely because Conrad's narrative tells us more about Europe than the Africa it supposedly represents, it compels us, not to strip truth from the cloak of time, but to imagine a radically different form of temporal narrative that allows "the Other" to be represented.

THE NEW HISTORICISM: A SELECTED BIBLIOGRAPHY

The New Historicism: Further Reading

Dollimore, Jonathan, and Alan Sinfield, eds. *Political Shakespeare: New Essays in Cultural Materialism*. Manchester, Eng.: Manchester University Press, 1985. See especially the essays by Dollimore, Greenlatt, and Tennenhouse.

————. *Radical Tragedy: Religion, Ideology and Power in the Drama of Shakespeare and His Contemporaries*. Brighton, Eng.: Harvester Press, 1984.

Graff, Gerald, and Gerald Gibbons, eds. *Criticism in the University*. Evanston, Ill.: Northwestern University Press, 1985. This volume, which contains Hirsch's essay, "Back to History," in the section entitled "Pedagogy and Polemics," also includes sections devoted to the historical backgrounds of academic criticism; the influence of Marxism, feminism, and critical theory in general on the new historicism; and varieties of "cultural criticism."

Greenblatt, Stephen. Introduction to *The Forms of Power and the Power of Forms in the Renaissance*. *Genre* 15 (1982): 1–4.

————. Chapter 1 of *Renaissance Self-Fashioning from More to Shakespeare*. Chicago: University of Chicago Press, 1980.

Goldberg, Jonathan. *James I and the Politics of Literature*. Baltimore, Md.: Johns Hopkins University Press, 1983.

Lindenberger, Herbert. "Toward a New History in Literature Studies." *Profession: Selected Articles from the Bulletins of the Association of Departments of English and the Association of Departments of Foreign Languages*. New York: Modern Language Association of America, 1984. See pages 16–23.

McGann, Jerome. *The Beauty of Inflections: Literary Investigations in Historical Method and Theory*. Oxford: Clarendon Press of Oxford University Press, 1985. See especially the Introduction and Chapter 1, "Keats and the Historical Method in Literary Criticism."

————. *Historical Studies and Literary Criticism*. Madison: University of Wisconsin Press, 1985. See especially the Introduction and essays in the following sections: "Historical Methods and Literary Interpretations" and "Biographical Contexts and the Critical Object."

————. "The Text, the Poem, and the Problem of Historical Method." *New Literary History* 13 (1981): 269–88.

Morris, Wesley. *Toward a New Historicism*. Princeton, N.J.: Princeton University Press, 1972.

Thomas, Brook. "The Historical Necessity for — and Difficulties with — New Historical Analysis in Introductory Literature Courses." *College English* 49 (1987): 509–22.

Foucault and His Influence

As I point out in the introduction to the new historicism, some new historicists would question the "privileging" of Foucault implicit in this section heading ("Foucault and His Influence") and the following one ("Other Writers and Works"). They might cite the greater importance of one of these other writers or point out that to cite a central influence or a definitive cause runs against the very spirit of the movement.

Foucault, Michel. *Discipline and Punish*. Translated by Alan Sheridan. New York: Pantheon, 1978.

————. *The History of Sexuality*, vol. 1. Translated by Robert Hurley. New York: Pantheon, 1978.

————. *Language, Counter-Memory, Practice* (selected essays and interviews), edited by Donald F. Bouchard. Translated by Bouchard and Sherry Simon. Ithaca, N.Y.: Cornell University Press, 1977.

Dreyfus, Hubert L., and Paul Rabinow. *Michel Foucault: Beyond Structuralism and Hermeneutics*. Chicago: University of Chicago Press, 1983.

Smart, Barry. *Michel Foucault*. New York: Ellis Horwood and Tavistock Publications, 1985.

Sheridan, Alan. *Michel Foucault: The Will to Truth*. New York: Tavistock Publications, 1980.

Other Writers and Works of Interest to New Historicist Critics

Bakhtin, M. M. *The Dialogic Imagination: Four Essays*, edited by Michael Holquist. Translated by Carly Emerson. Austin: University of Texas Press, 1981. Bakhtin is author of a number of influential studies of subjects as various as Dostoevsky, Rabelais, and formalist criticism. But this book, in part because of Holquist's helpful introduction, is probably the best place to begin learning about Bakhtin.

Benjamin, Walter. "The Work of Art in the Age of Mechanical Repro-
    duction." [1936] *Illuminations*. Translated by Harry Zohn. New
    York: Schocken, 1969.

Fried, Michael. *Absorption and Theatricality: Painting and Beholder in the
    Works of Diderot*. Berkeley: University of California Press, 1980.

Geertz, Clifford. *The Interpretation of Cultures*. New York: Basic Books,
    1973.

—————. *Negara: The Theatre State in Nineteenth-Century Bali*. Prince-
    ton, N.J.: Princeton University Press, 1980.

Goffman, Erving. *Frame Analysis*. New York: Harper, 1974.

Jameson, Fredric. *The Political Unconscious*. Ithaca, N.Y.: Cornell Uni-
    versity Press, 1981.

Koselleck, Reinhart. *Futures Past*. Translated by Keith Tribe. Cam-
    bridge, Mass.: MIT Press, 1985.

Mannoni, O. *Prospero and Caliban: The Psychology of Colonization*. New
    York: Praeger, 1956.

Representations. This quarterly journal, printed by the University of
    California Press, regularly publishes new historical studies and
    cultural criticism.

Said, Edward. *Orientalism*. New York: Columbia University Press,
    1978.

Recent Anthropological and Historical Studies of Colonialism

Brantlinger, Patrick. "Victorians and Africans: The Genealogy of
    the Myth of the Dark Continent." *Critical Inquiry* 12 (1985):
    166–203.

Fabian, Johannes. *Time and the Other*. New York: Columbia University
    Press, 1983.

Jan Mohamed, Abdul R. "The Economy of the Manichean Allegory:
    The Function of Racial Difference in Colonist Literature." *Critical
    Inquiry* 12 (1985): 59–87.

Mahood, M. M. *The Colonial Encounter*. London: Rex Collings, 1977.

Recent Historical Studies of Conrad

Achebe, Chinua. "An Image of Africa," *Massachusetts Review* 18 (1977):
    782–94.

Brantlinger, Patrick. "*Heart of Darkness:* Anti-Imperialism, Racism,
    or Impressionism?" *Criticism* 27 (1985): 363–85.

Hawkins, Hunt. "Conrad and the Psychology of Colonialism." *Conrad Revisited: Essays for the Eighties,* edited by Ross C Murfin. University: University of Alabama Press, 1985.

Jameson, Fredric. "Romance and Reification: Plot Construction and Ideological Closure." Chapter 5 of Jameson, *The Political Unconscious,* cited above.

Nazareth, Peter. "Out of Darkness: Conrad and Other Third World Writers." *Conradiana* 14 (1982): 173–97.

Parry, Benita. *Conrad and Imperialism.* London: Macmillan, 1983.

Glossary of Critical
and Theoretical Terms

Most terms have been glossed parenthetically where they first appear in the text. The glossary mainly lists terms that were too complex to define in a phrase or a sentence or two. A few of the terms listed are discussed at greater length elsewhere ("deconstruction," for instance); these terms are defined succinctly and a page reference to the longer discussion is provided.

AFFECTIVE FALLACY   First used by William K. Wimsatt and Monroe C. Beardsley to refer to the practice of interpreting texts according to the psychological responses of readers, a practice they saw as erroneous. "The Affective Fallacy," they wrote in a 1946 essay later republished in *The Verbal Icon* (1954), "is a confusion between the poem and its *results* (what it *is* and what it *does*). . . . It begins by trying to derive the standards of criticism from the psychological effects of a poem and ends in impressionism and relativism." The affective fallacy, like the intentional fallacy (confusing the meaning of a work with the author's expressly intended meaning), was one of the main tenets of the "new criticism," or "formalism." The affective fallacy has recently been contested by reader-response critics, who have dedicated their efforts to describing the way individual readers and "interpretive communities" go about "making sense" of texts.

See also Authorial Intention, Formalism, Reader-Response Criticism.

AUTHORIAL INTENTION   Defined narrowly, an author's intention in writing a work, as expressed in letters, diaries, interviews, and conversations. Defined more broadly, "intentionality" involves unexpressed motivations, designs, and purposes, some of which may have remained unconscious.

The debate over whether critics should try to discern an author's intentions (conscious or otherwise) is an old one. William K. Wimsatt and Monroe C.

Beardsley, in an essay published in the 1940s, coined the term "intentional fallacy" to refer to the practice of basing interpretations on the expressed or implied intentions of authors, a practice they saw as erroneous. As proponents of the "new criticism," or "formalism," they argued that a work of literature is an object in itself and should be studied as one. They believed that it is sometimes helpful to learn what an author intended, but the critic's real purpose is to show what is in the text — not what an author intended to put there.

See also Affective Fallacy, Formalism.

BINARY OPPOSITIONS See Oppositions.

BLANKS See Gaps.

DECONSTRUCTION A post-structuralist approach to literature strongly influenced by the writings of the philosopher Jacques Derrida. Deconstruction, partly in response to structuralism and formalism, posits the undecidability of meaning for all texts. In fact, as the deconstructive critic J. Hillis Miller points out, "deconstruction is not a dismantling of the structure of a text but a demonstration that it has already dismantled itself." See "What Is Deconstruction?" page 199.

DISCOURSE Used specifically, this term can refer to (1) spoken or written discussion of a subject or area of knowledge; (2) the words in, or text of, a narrative, as opposed to its story line; or (3) a "strand" within a given narrative that argues a certain point or defends a certain value system.

More generally, "discourse" refers to the language in which a subject or area of knowledge is discussed or a certain kind of business is transacted. Human knowledge is collected and structured in discourses. Theology and medicine are defined by their discourses, as are politics, sexuality, and literary criticism.

A society is made up of a number of different discourses or "discourse communities," one or more of which may be dominant or serve the dominant ideology. Each discourse has its own vocabulary, concepts, and rules, knowledge of which constitutes power. Feminist and new historicist critics tend to see literary works in terms of discourses that inform or compete with their discourses. The psychoanalyst and psychoanalytic critic Jacques Lacan has treated the unconscious as a form of discourse, the patterns of which are repeated in literature.

See also Feminist Criticism, Ideology, Narrative, New Historicism, Psychoanalytic Criticism.

FEMINIST CRITICISM An aspect of the feminist movement whose primary goals include critiquing masculine-dominated language and literature by showing how they reflect a masculine ideology; writing the history of unknown or undervalued women writers, thereby earning them their rightful place in the literary canon; and helping create a climate in which women's creativity may be fully realized and appreciated. See "What Is Feminist Criticism?" page 172.

FORMALISM Also referred to as "the new criticism," formalism reached its height during the 1940s and 1950s but is still in practice today. Formalists treat a work of literary art as if it were a self-contained, self-referential object. Rather than basing their interpretations of a text on the reader's response, the author's stated intentions, or parallels between the text and historical contexts (such as the author's life), formalists concentrate on the relationships *within* the text that give it its own distinctive character or form. Special attention is paid to repetition, particularly of images or symbols, but also of sound effects and rhythms in poetry.

Because of the importance placed on close analysis and the stress on the text as a carefully crafted, orderly object containing observable formal patterns, formalism has often been seen as an attack on romanticism and impressionism, particularly impressionistic criticism. It has sometimes even been called an "objective" approach to literature. It would be more accurate to say that formalists are more likely than certain other critics to believe and say that the meaning of a text can be known objectively. (Reader-response critics, for instance, see meaning as a function either of each reader's experience or of the norms that govern a particular "interpretive community," and deconstructors would argue that texts mean opposite things at the same time.)

Formalism was originally based on essays written during the 1920s and 1930s by T. S. Eliot, I. A. Richards, and William Empson. It was significantly developed later by a group of American poets and critics, including R. P. Blackmur, Cleanth Brooks, John Crowe Ransom, Allen Tate, Robert Penn Warren, and William K. Wimsatt. Although formalism is associated with certain principles and terms (such as the "affective fallacy" and the "intentional fallacy" as defined by Wimsatt and Monroe C. Beardsley), formalists were trying more to make a cultural statement than to establish a critical dogma. Generally southern, religious, and culturally conservative, they advocated the inherent value of literary works (particularly of literary works regarded as beautiful art objects) because they were sick of the growing ugliness of modern life and contemporary events. Some recent theorists have even suggested that the rising popularity of formalism after World War II was a feature of American isolationism, the formalist tendency to isolate literature from biography and history being a manifestation of the American fatigue with wider involvements.

See also Affective Fallacy, Authorial Intention, Deconstruction, Reader-Response Criticism, Symbol.

GAPS   This term, used mainly by reader-response critics familiar with the theories of Wolfgang Iser, refers to "blanks" in texts that must be filled in by readers. A gap may be said to exist whenever a reader perceives something to be missing between words, sentences, paragraphs, stanzas, or chapters. Readers respond to gaps actively and creatively, explaining apparent inconsistencies in point of view, accounting for jumps in chronology, speculatively supplying information missing from plots, and resolving problems or issues left ambiguous or "indeterminate" in the text.

Critics sometimes speak as if a gap exists in a text; it is, of course, to some extent a product of the readers' perceptions. Different readers may find gaps in different texts and different gaps in the same text. Furthermore, they may fill these gaps in different ways — which is why, a reader-response critic might argue, works are interpreted in different ways.

Although the concept of the gap has been used mainly by reader-response critics to explain what makes reading an active, interactive process, it has also been used by critics who, though taking other theoretical approaches, are conversant with the vocabulary and practices of reader-response criticism. A deconstructor might use "gap" when speaking of the radical self-contradictoriness of a text. Johanna M. Smith, in her feminist essay in this volume, uses the term to refer to the places in which we suddenly see through the ideology of Conrad's times and text: the patriarchal ideology of masculine domination. And Brook Thomas, in his new-historicist approach to the novel, uses "gaps" to refer to those disruptions in the narrative flow that sometimes suggest truths that cannot be put into words — and that sometimes amount to significant evasions.

See also Deconstruction, Feminist Criticism, Ideology, Narrative, New Historicism, Reader-Response Criticism.

FIGURE See Metaphor, Metonymy, Symbol.

GENRE A French word referring to a kind or type of literature. Individual works within a genre may exhibit a distinctive form, be governed by certain conventions, and/or represent characteristic subjects. Tragedy, the epic, and romance are all genres.

Perhaps inevitably, the term "genre" is used loosely. Lyric poetry is a genre, but so are characteristic *types* of the lyric, such as the sonnet, the ode, and elegy. Fiction is a genre, as are detective fiction and science fiction. The list of genres constantly grows as critics establish new lines of connection between individual works and discern new categories of works with common characteristics.

Some writers form hybrid genres by combining the characteristics of several in a single work. (According to Kenneth Bruffee, Conrad wrote several "elegiac romances.") Frederick Karl finds in *Heart of Darkness* an epic descent into the underworld, whereas J. Hillis Miller sees in it aspects of the "apocalypse" or book of revelation.

Knowledge of genres helps critics see what is conventional and unconventional, borrowed and original, in a work.

IDEOLOGY A system of beliefs underlying a set of customs, habits, or practices common to a given social group. To members of that group, the beliefs will seem obviously true, natural, and even universally applicable. They may seem just as obviously arbitrary, idiosyncratic, and even false to members of another group who adhere to another ideology. Within a society, there may be several ideologies, one or more of which may be dominant.

Ideologies may be forcefully imposed or willingly accepted. Their component beliefs may be consciously or unconsciously held. In either case, they come to form what Johanna M. Smith has called "the unexamined ground of our experience." Ideology governs our perceptions, judgments, and prejudices, our sense of what is acceptable, normal — and deviant. It is ideology that causes men to receive preferential treatment in Western societies; it is ideology that allows imperialistic exploitation such as the kind described by Conrad in *Heart of Darkness*.

Ideologies are of special interest to sociologically-oriented critics of literature because of the way authors reflect or resist ideologies in their texts. Feminist critics, for instance, have sought to expose (and thereby call into question) the "patriarchal" ideology mirrored or "inscribed" in works written by men — even men who, by and large, have sought to counter sexism and break down sexual stereotypes. New historicists have been interested in demonstrating the ideological underpinnings not only of literary representations but also of our interpretations of them.

See also Feminist Criticism, New Historicism.

INTENTIONAL FALLACY See Authorial Intention.

INTENTIONALITY *See* Authorial Intention.

INTERTEXTUALITY The condition of interconnectedness among texts. Every author has been influenced by others, and every work contains explicit and implicit references to other works. Writers may consciously or unconsciously echo a predecessor or "precursor"; they may also consciously or unconsciously disguise their indebtedness, making intertextual relationships difficult for the critic to trace.

Reacting against the formalist tendency to view each work as a free-standing object, some post-structuralist critics have suggested that the meaning of a work only emerges intertextually; i.e., within the context provided by other works. But there has been a reaction, too, against this type of intertextual criticism. Some new historicists have suggested that literary history is itself too narrow a context and that works should be interpreted in light of a larger set of cultural contexts.

There is, however, a broader definition of intertextuality, one that refers to the relationship between works of literature and a wide range of other "narratives" or "discourses" that we don't usually think of as being literary. Thus defined, intertextuality could be used by a new historicist to refer to the significant interconnectedness between *Heart of Darkness* and contemporary "discourses" about imperialism. Or it could be used by a post-structuralist to suggest that a work can only be recognized and read within a vast field of signs and tropes that is *like* a text — and that makes any single text self-contradictory and "undecidable."

See also Discourse, Formalism, Narrative, New Historicism, Post-Structuralism, Trope.

METAPHOR The representation of one thing by some other related or similar thing. The image (or activity or concept) used to represent or "figure" something else is known as the "vehicle" of the metaphor; the thing represented is called the "tenor." In other words, the vehicle is something we substitute for the tenor. Additional meaning can be gained by the relationship between the two terms. Thus, instead of saying, "Last night I read a book," we may say, "Last night I plowed through a book." "Plowed through" (or the activity of plowing) is the vehicle of the metaphor; "read" (or the act of reading) is the tenor, the thing being figured. The increment in meaning attributable to metaphor is obvious. Our audience knows not only *that* we read but also *how* we read, for to read a book in the way that a plow rips through earth is surely to read in a relentless, unreflective way. (Note that in the sentence above a new metaphor — "rips through" — has been used to explain an old one. This serves [a metaphor] as an example of just how thick [a metaphor] language is with metaphors!)

Metaphor is a kind of *trope* (literally, a "turning," i.e., a figure that alters or "turns" the meaning of a word or phrase). Other tropes include allegory, conceit, metonymy, personification, simile, symbol, and synecdoche. Traditionally, metaphor and symbol have been viewed as the principal tropes; the other, minor tropes have been seen as *types* of these two major ones. Similes, for instance, have been defined as simple metaphors that usually employ "like" or "as" and state the tenor outright, as in "My love is like a red, red rose." Synecdoche involves a vehicle that is a *part* of the tenor, as in "I see a sail" to mean "I see a boat." And metonymy has been viewed as metaphor involving two terms commonly if arbitrarily associated with (but not fundamentally or intrinsically related to) one another. Recently, however, deconstructors such as Paul de Man and J. Hillis Miller have questioned the "privilege" granted to metaphor and the metaphor/metonymy distinction or "opposition." They have suggested that all metaphors are really metonyms, and that all figuration is arbitrary.

See also Deconstruction, Metonymy, Opposition, Symbol.

METONYMY The representation of one thing by another that is commonly (often physically) associated with it. To refer to Conrad's handwriting as "Conrad's hand" is to use a metonymic "figure" or "trope." The image or thing used to represent something else is known as the "vehicle" of the metonym; the thing represented is called the "tenor."

Like other tropes (such as metaphor), metonymy involves the replacement of one word or phrase by another. Liquor may be referred to as "the bottle," a monarch as "the crown." Narrowly defined, the vehicle of a metonym is arbitrarily, not intrinsically, associated with the tenor. (The bottle just happens to be what liquor is stored in and poured from in our culture. The hand may be involved in the production of handwriting, but so are the brain and the pen. There is no special, intrinsic likeness between a crown and a monarch; it's just that crowns traditionally sit on monarchs' heads and not on the heads of university professors.) More broadly, "metonym" and "metonymy" have been used by some recent critics to refer to a wide range of figures and tropes. Deconstructors have questioned the distinction between metaphor and metonymy.

See also Deconstruction, Metaphor, Trope.

NARRATIVE A story or telling of a story; an account of a situation or of events. *Heart of Darkness* and Frederick Karl's biography of Conrad are narratives, as are Freud's case histories.

Some critics use the word "narrative" even more generally; Brook Thomas writes of "psychoanalysis' narrative about the journey to the unconscious" and of "narratives of human history that neglect the role human labor has played."

NEW CRITICISM *See* Formalism.

NEW HISTORICISM The most recent development in contemporary critical theory. Its practitioners share certain convictions, the major ones being that literary critics need to develop a high degree of historical consciousness and that literature should not be viewed apart from other human creations, artistic or otherwise. See "What Is the New Historicism?" page 226.

OPPOSITIONS A concept highly relevant to linguistics, since linguists maintain that words (such as "black" and "death") have meaning not in themselves but, rather, in relation to others ("white" and "life"). Jacques Derrida, a post-structuralist philosopher of language, has suggested that in the West we think in terms of these "binary oppositions" or dichotomies, which upon examination turn out to be evaluative hierarchies. In other words, each opposition — whether it is beginning/end, presence/absence, or consciousness/unconsciousness — contains one term that our culture views as being superior and one term we view as negative or inferior.

Derrida has "deconstructed" a number of these binary oppositions, including two — speech/writing and signifier/signified — that he believes to be central to linguistics in particular and Western culture in general. He has concurrently critiqued the "law" of noncontradiction, which is fundamental to Western logic. He and other deconstructors have argued that a text can contain opposed strands of a "discourse" and, therefore, mean opposite things: reason *and* passion, life *and* death, hope *and* despair, black *and* white. Traditionally, criticism has involved choosing between opposed or contradictory meanings and arguing that one is present in the text and the other absent.

French feminists have adopted the ideas of Derrida and other deconstructors, showing that we not only think in terms of binary oppositions such as male/female, reason/emotion, and active/passive, but also associate reason and activity with masculinity, emotion and passivity with femininity. Because of this, they have concluded, language is "phallocentric," or masculine-dominated.

See also Deconstruction, Discourse, Feminist Criticism, Post-Structuralism.

POST-STRUCTURALISM The general attempt to contest and subvert structuralism made by deconstructors and certain other critics associated with psychoanalytic, Marxist, and feminist theory. Whereas structuralists, using linguistics as a model and employing semiotic (sign) theory, posit the possibility of systematically knowing a text and revealing the "grammar" behind its form and meaning, post-structuralists argue against the possibility of such knowledge and description. They counter that texts can be shown to contradict not only structuralist accounts of them but also themselves. In making their adversarial claims, they rely on close readings of texts and the work of theorists such as Jacques Derrida and Jacques Lacan.

Post-structuralists have suggested that structuralism rests on distinctions between "signifier" and "signified" (signs and the things they point toward), "self" and "language" (or "text"), texts and other texts, and text and world that are overly simplistic, if not patently inaccurate. Post-structuralists have shown how all signifieds are also signifiers, and they have treated texts as "intertexts." They have viewed the world as if it *were* a text (we desire a certain car because it *symbolizes* achievement), and the self as if it were the subject — as well as the user — of language. (We may shape and speak through language, but it also shapes and speaks through us.)

See also Deconstruction, Feminist Criticism, Intertextuality, Psychoanalytic Criticism, Semiotics, Structuralism.

PSYCHOANALYTIC CRITICISM Grounded in the psychoanalytic theories of Sigmund Freud, this is one of the oldest critical methodologies still in use. Freud's view that works of literature, like dreams, express secret, unconscious desires led to criticism that interpreted literary works as manifestations of the author's neuroses. More recently, psychoanalytic critics have come to see literary works as skillfully crafted artifacts that may appeal to *our* neuroses by tapping into our repressed wishes and fantasies. Other forms of psychological criticism that diverge from Freud, though they ultimately derive from his insights, include those based on the theories of Carl Jung and Jacques Lacan. See "What Is Psychoanalytic Criticism?" page 113.

READER-RESPONSE CRITICISM An approach to literature that, as its name implies, considers the way readers respond to texts as they read. Stanley Fish describes the method by saying that it substitutes for one question — "what does this sentence mean?" — another, more operational question — "what does this sentence do?" Reader-response criticism shares with deconstruction a strong textual orientation and a reluctance to define *the* meaning of a work; with psychoanalytic criticism it shares an interest in the dynamics of mental response to textual cues. See "What Is Reader-Response Criticism?" page 139.

SEMIOLOGY, SEMIOTIC   *See* Semiotics.

SEMIOTICS   The study of signs, sign systems, and the way meaning is derived from them. Structuralist anthropologists, psychoanalysts, and literary critics developed semiotics during the decades following 1950, but much of the pioneering work had been done at the turn of the century by the founder of modern linguistics, Ferdinand de Saussure, and the American philosopher, Charles Pierce.

Semiotics is based on several important distinctions, including the distinction between "signifier" and "signified" (the sign and what it points toward), and the distinction between *langue* and *parole*. *Langue* refers to the entire system within which individual utterances or usages of language have meaning, *parole* to particular utterances or usages. A principal tenet of semiotics is that signs, like words, are not significant in themselves but, rather, have meaning only in relationship to other signs and the entire system of signs, or *langue*.

The affinity between semiotics and structuralist literary criticism derives from this emphasis on *langue*, or system. Structuralist critics, after all, were reacting against formalists and their procedure of focusing on individual works as if meanings didn't depend on anything external to the text.

Post-structuralists have used semiotics but questioned some of its underlying assumptions, including the "opposition" between signifier and signified. The feminist post-structuralist Julia Kristeva has used the word "semiotic" to describe feminine language, a highly figurative, fluid form of discourse she opposes to rigid, symbolic, masculine language.

See also Deconstruction, Feminist Criticism, Formalism, Post-Structuralism, Oppositions, Structuralism, Symbol.

SIMILE   *See* Metaphor.

SOCIOHISTORICAL CRITICISM   *See* New Historicism.

STRUCTURALISM   A science of humankind whose proponents attempted to show that all elements of human culture, including literature, may be understood as parts of a system of signs. Structuralism, according to Robert Scholes, was a reaction to "'modernist' alienation and despair."

Using Ferdinand de Saussure's linguistic theory, European structuralists such as Roman Jakobson, Claude Lévi-Strauss, and Roland Barthes (before his shift toward post-structuralism) attempted to develop a "semiology" or "semiotics" (science of signs). Barthes, among others, sought to recover literature and even language from the isolation in which they had been studied and to show that the laws that govern them govern all signs, from road signs to articles of clothing.

Particularly useful to structuralists were two of Saussure's concepts: the idea of the *phoneme* in language and the idea that phonemes exist in two kinds of relationships: *synchronic* and *diachronic*. A phoneme is the smallest consistently significant unit in language; thus, both "a" and "an" are phonemes, but "n" is not one. A diachronic relationship is the relationship a phoneme has with those that have preceded it in time and those that will follow it. These "horizontal" relationships produce what we might call discourse or narrative — what Saussure called *parole*. The synchronic relationship is the "vertical" one a word has in a given instant with the entire system of language (*langue*) in which it may generate meaning. "An" means what it means in English because those of us who speak the language are using it in the same way at a given time.

Following Saussure, Lévi-Strauss studied hundreds of myths, breaking them into their smallest meaningful units, which he called "mythemes." Removing each from its diachronic relations with other mythemes in a single myth (such as the myth of Oedipus and his mother), he vertically aligned those mythemes that he found to be homologous (structurally correspondent). He then studied the relationships within as well as between vertically aligned columns, in an attempt to scientifically understand, through ratios and proportions, those thoughts and processes that humankind has shared, both at one particular time and across time. One could say, then, that structuralists followed Saussure in preferring to think about the overriding *langue* or language of myth, in which each mytheme and mytheme-constituted myth fits meaningfully, rather than about isolated individual *paroles* or narratives. Structuralists followed Saussure's lead in believing what the post-structuralist Jacques Derrida later decided he could not subscribe to — that sign systems must be understood in terms of binary oppositions. In analyzing myths and texts to find basic structures, structuralists tended to find that opposite terms modulate until they are finally resolved or reconciled by some intermediary, third term. (Thus, a structuralist reading of *Paradise Lost* would show that the war between God and the bad angels becomes a rift between God and sinful, fallen man, the rift then being healed by the Son of God, the mediating third term.)

See also Deconstruction, Discourse, Narrative, Post-Structuralism, Semiotics.

SYMBOL   A thing, image, or action that, though it is of interest in its own right, stands for or suggests something larger and more complex — often an idea or a whole range of interrelated ideas, attitudes, and practices.

Some things are understood, within a given culture, to be symbols: the flag of the United States is an obvious example. Other, perhaps more subtle, cultural symbols would be the river as a symbol of time and the journey as a symbol of life and its manifold experiences. (Conrad obviously makes use of both of these in *Heart of Darkness,* as Mark Twain had earlier made use of them in *The Adventures of Huckleberry Finn.*)

Instead of appropriating symbols generally used and understood within their culture, writers often create symbols by setting up, in their works, a complex but identifiable web of associations. As a result, one object, image, or action suggests others, and often, ultimately, a whole range of ideas. The skulls used to ornament fence posts in *Heart of Darkness,* like the color white in Herman Melville's *Moby Dick,* serve as symbols of what Conrad calls "the horror." But what, exactly, *is* the horror? In *Heart of Darkness* it is at once death, cruelty, imperialism, meaninglessness, and unconscious desire. It includes Kurtz and the practice of ornamenting one person, place, or thing at a terrible cost to many others. (The skulls on fence posts subtly suggest tusks, ivory, and all the animals and people that suffer and die for the decoration of a few.)

A symbol, then, might be defined as a metaphor in which the "vehicle" — the thing, image, or action used to represent something else — represents many related things (or "tenors"). In comparison with symbols, metaphors are relatively easy to define or interpret. Like similes, they often involve a simple substitution made by a narrator. ("The yarns of seamen" are said in *Heart of Darkness* to "have a direct simplicity, the whole meaning of which lies within the shell of a cracked nut.") An object, image, or action used *symbolically* — whether it is the river in *Heart of Darkness* or the urn in Keats's "Ode on a Grecian

Urn" — is more intrinsically involved in the story or poem and at the same time more broadly suggestive. Keats's urn suggests a whole range of interrelated concepts, including art, truth, beauty, and timelessness.

Symbols have been of particular interest to formalists, who study how meanings emerge from the complex, patterned relationships between images in a work, and psychoanalytic critics, who are interested in how individual authors and the larger culture both disguise and reveal unconscious fears and desires through symbols. French feminists have also focused recently on the symbolic. They have suggested that, as wide-ranging as it seems, symbolic language is ultimately rigid and restrictive. They favor "semiotic" language and writing, which, they contend, is at once more rhythmic, unifying, and feminine.

See also Feminist Criticism, Psychoanalytic Criticism, Metaphor, Trope.

SYNECDOCHE   *See* Metaphor, Metonymy.

TENOR   *See* Metaphor, Metonymy, Symbol.

TROPE   A figure, as in "figure of speech." Literally a "turning"; i.e., a turning or twisting of a word or phrase to make it mean something else. The principal tropes include metaphor, metonymy, simile, personification, and synecdoche.

See also Metaphor, Metonymy.

VEHICLE   *See* Metaphor, Metonymy, Symbol.

About the Contributors

THE EDITOR

Ross C Murfin is professor of English and associate dean of the College of Arts and Sciences at the University of Miami. He has also taught at Yale and the University of Virginia, published books on Thomas Hardy and D. H. Lawrence, and is the editor of *Conrad Revisited: Essays for the Eighties* (1985).

THE CONTRIBUTORS

Frederick R. Karl, professor of English at New York University, is the author of a standard biography, *Joseph Conrad: The Three Lives* (1979), and coeditor of the multivolume collection of Conrad's letters.

J. Hillis Miller, now at the University of California, Irvine, has been professor of English and chair of the English Department at Yale. His important studies of nineteenth- and twentieth-century literature include *The Disappearance of God* (1963), *The Form of Victorian Fiction* (1968), *Thomas Hardy: Distance and Desire* (1971), *Fiction and Repetition* (1982), and *The Linguistic Mind* (1985).

Adena Rosmarin is professor of English at the University of Texas at Austin, where she teaches courses in critical theory. Her publications include many scholarly articles and a book on critical theory, *The Power of Genre* (1985).

Johanna M. Smith is assistant professor of English at the University of Texas at Arlington. The author of articles on Jane Austen and Harriet Beecher Stowe, she is currently completing a book on *Sister-Brother Incest in the Nineteenth-Century Novel*.

Brook Thomas is professor of English at the University of California at Irvine, where he teaches courses in literary criticism and critical theory. He is the author of numerous scholarly articles and two books: *James Joyce's* Ulysses: *A Book of Many Happy Returns* (1982), and *Cross-examinations of Law and Literature: Cooper, Hawthorne, Stowe, and Melville* (forthcoming).